D.J. ENRIGHT

Signs and Wonders

Selected Essays

CARCANET

This collection first published in Great Britain in 2001 by
Carcanet Press Limited
4th Floor, Conavon Court
12–16 Blackfriars Street
Manchester M3 5BQ

A CIP catalogue record for this book
is available from the British Library

ISBN 1 85754 548 6

The publisher acknowledges financial assistance
from the Arts Council of England.

Set in Monotype Garamond by XL Publishing Services, Tiverton
Printed and bound in England by SRP Ltd, Exeter

Contents

Author's Note   vii

I

Aimez-vous Goethe?: an Enquiry into English Attitudes
    of Non-liking towards German Literature   3
Wilhelm Meister and the Ambiguousness of Goethe   11
The Story of Two Souls: Goethe and the Manns   27
The Anti-diabolic Faith: Thomas Mann's *Doctor Faustus*   37
The Stupendous Cannot be Easy: on Robert Musil   55
Hesse *versus* Hesse   71
Svevo's Progress: or, The Apotheosis of the Poor Fish   79
The Ghosts of Apes: Franz Werfel's *The Forty Days*
    of Musa Dagh   86

II

Democracy of Gods: Life and Works of Heine   105
Cavafy: Poet-Historian   125
Echt Brecht   130
The Lord's Song: on Paul Celan   142
'My Muse, Mnemosyne': Czeslaw Milosz   148
Did Nobody Teach You?: on Stevie Smith   153

III

The Tale of Genji; and Japanese Women Diarists   165
Chinese Fictions – At Home and Abroad   179
Flaubert: His Letters and Ladies   193

IV

What Happened to the Devil?   207
Hell's Angels: Stefan Heym's *The Wandering Jew*   221
Master of Horror: Karl Kraus   227
The Executioner Himself: Elias Canetti   239
A Doomsday Book: Günter Grass   248
Signs and Wonders: Robertson Davies   254

More than Mere Biology: Josef Skvorecky   259
Last Words: on Anthony Burgess   264

Index of Names   271

Author's Note

While some of these essays[1] have not been previously collected, for the most part they are drawn largely unchanged from earlier books: *The Apothecary's Shop* (1957), *Conspirators and Poets* (1966), *Man is an Onion* (1972), *A Mania for Sentences* (1983), *Fields of Vision* (1988).

I imagine they belong to the species of literary criticism described (or stigmatized) as 'humanist', if only to distinguish it from what, with a nice mixture of grandeur and vagueness, is called 'Theory'. The latter seemingly promises to fulfil the longing some people have felt ever since the inception of English as an academic subject to see their 'discipline' established on an equally respectable footing with scientific investigation or philosophical enquiry. Fortunately literature tends to *mean* too much and too irresistibly to yield to the charms of meaninglessness, however ingenious. And what other term than humanist can be used of those who stand detached from any sovereign church? Lawrence's non-definition, simple and practical, is worth recalling: 'Literary criticism can be no more than a reasoned account of the feeling produced upon the critic by the book he is criticizing. Criticism can never be a science; it is, in the first place, much too personal, and in the second, it is concerned with values that science ignores.' Hence, 'all this pseudo-scientific classifying and analysing of books in an imitation-botanical fashion is mere impertinence and mostly dull jargon'.

As for 'chatter about Shelley', or research into the more sensational aspects of a writer's life, supposing that such a pursuit be deemed in some sense humanistic, this is now the prerogative of literary biography. Should any animus against the art of biography reveal itself here, I can only repeat what I have said elsewhere. If biography is a sin, it is advisable to heed that ancient counsel and hate the sin but love the sinner. Otherwise one will have no friends left.

Many of the essays here bear on work in English translation. What gets found in translation can far exceed what gets lost: for all but a

---

1 Editorial note: the dates listed at the ends of essays refer to the first publication of each section of the essay.

handful of genuine bilinguals, what we read in our mother tongue, regardless of the work's provenance, affects us more powerfully and inwardly than what we read in another language. And literary translation, it seems to me, is one of the few arts to have made incontestable strides over recent decades.

My thanks go to Jacqueline Simms and Madeleine Enright for help in selecting material, and to Janet Montefiore for championing one particular inclusion. Also to Michael Schmidt of Carcanet Press, clearly a humanist among publishers.

2001

I

Aimez-vous Goethe?: an Enquiry into English Attitudes of Non-liking towards German Literature

'Naturellement, you think I have in mind your ferocious discipline, and que vous enchaînez votre art dans un système de règles inexorables et néo-classiques, forcing it to move in these iron bands – if not with grace, yet with boldness and esprit. But if it is that that I mean, I mean at the same time more than that when I speak of your qualité d'Allemand; I mean – how shall I put it? – a certain four-squareness, rhythmical heaviness, immobility, grossièreté, which are old-German – en effet, entre nous, one finds them in Bach too. Will you take offence at my criticism? Non, j'en suis sûr – you are too great. Your themes – they consist almost throughout of even note values, minims, crotchets, quavers; true enough, they are syncopated and tied but for all that they remain clumsy and unwieldy, often with a hammering, machine-like effect. C'est "boche" dans un degré fascinant. Don't think I am finding fault, it is simply énormément caractéristique, and in the series of concerts of international music which I am arranging, this note is quite indispensable…'

(Fitelberg, the impresario, Doctor Faustus)

Introduction: Not all English non-likers of German literature non-like it for all of the reasons about to be cited, of course. Nor should it be assumed that these various reasons are all equally reasonable, or unreasonable. They are all real reasons in that they exist, at least.

(1) Since the essence of scholarship lies in its exhaustiveness, its refusal to leave anything unsaid, no matter how obvious it might seem to the layman, we must commence with the following proposal: many English people do not like literature of any sort, not even English literature. Further, among those who like English literature – indeed, among those who must like English literature a lot, since they make their living out of it – there are many who don't like foreign literature of any sort: on the grounds that it is foreign to them, they are innocents abroad, they might be horribly hoodwinked by a false rhythm or a corrupt metaphor.

(2) Research indicates that the commonest or most commonly-voiced English objection to German literature has it that this literature is wordy, philosophical, humourless, highly abstract and crammed with details. In brief, heavy-handed. The objection comes equally from those who have read some German literature and from those

who haven't read any because they know it is wordy, highly abstract, crammed with details, etc. Largely it derives from atavistic memories of Goethe and a nervous perusal of the opening pages of *Buddenbrooks*. If this is not altogether an idle prejudice, it is (especially as regards the two writers referred to) an unfortunate one. The German mind appears to be naturally more ruminative than the English – and more pedagogic. We like our novelists to arrive; the Germans are content to watch their novelists travelling hopefully, slowly and instructively. Thus all the landscape gardening in Goethe's *Die Wahlverwandtschaften* (*Elective Affinities*) – though it must be granted that this particular item might carry the implication that human relationships cannot be as neatly planned as an estate. (A piece of symbolism too gross by far for our sensitive British stomachs.) Thus all the discursuses and excursuses of *Faust*, or of Thomas Mann's novels. (The greatest European novelist of the twentieth century? Thomas Mann, alas!) Thus *Wilhelm Meister*, that cultural hitch-hiker, of which work Goethe is reported to have said, 'I should think a rich manifold life, brought close to our eyes, would be enough without any express tendency, which, after all, is only for the intellect.' (But then, Goethe was an old fox by anybody's standards, and often contrived to eat his cake and moralize over it.) How one longs to edit Mann's *Doctor Faustus* and *The Magic Mountain*, to render them digestible to our dainty and civilized appetites! (And yet how much of them would we dare – or even want – to throw out when we came to it, when we had actually read the books with the care required of an editor?)

The English reader of novels tends to have a high opinion of himself (fair enough, he *reads*!): he reckons he can do without the trimmings, the writer can leave a whole lot to his imagination: he has grown up into a 60,000-words man. It has been said that the distinctively German contribution to the Novel is the *Bildungsroman*, detailed, digressive, with no clearly defined terms of reference, and a long time in the building. *Doctor Faustus* was described by its English translator (a translator whose like, whatever complaints we might make of her work, we may well not see again) as a 'cathedral of a book' – an apt metaphor, if we allow that a cathedral can house the Devil as well. (A lot of little dogs have lifted their legs against *this* cathedral, too.) The British reader prefers a neat and tidy chapel of a book.

(3) The charge of humourlessness calls for closer inspection. 'What the German thinks exquisitely ludicrous, is to a Frenchman, or an Englishman, generally of mediocre mirthfulness,' wrote G.H. Lewes in 1855. 'Wit requires delicate handling; the Germans generally touch it with gloved hands. Sarcasm is with them too often a sabre

not a rapier, hacking the victims where a thrust would suffice.' True, humour with the German tends to run to extremes, either boorish slapstick or else high rarefaction. As with the Japanese, a whole middle range of comedy seems inaccessible to them. This is indeed a sad deficiency, both in literature – if only Rilke could have laughed at himself, if only one of Rilke's ladies could have laughed at him! – and also in life, many of whose frictions are most tactfully palliated by the lubricant of an easy, natural, middle-register sort of humour.

What is also sad is that the English reader, missing the sort of sense of humour to which he is accustomed and which he traditionally prizes, assumes the absence of humour of any species. Mann's stateliness, the deliberation and meticulousness with which he builds up his world, seem only pomposity to us, a laboriousness which we quickly characterize as 'Teutonic'.[1] (*Il est bête – oui, si l'on veut, mais comme l'Himalaya.*) Having made up our minds on this point with characteristic firmness, then, despite our characteristic sense of humour, we fail to sense Mann's own characteristic brand of humour, an irony too complex to attempt to analyse here, the very presence of Mann himself in his work. (Or we assume Dr Thomas Mann's presence in Dr Serenus Zeitblom, a sheep in sheep's clothing, and grow peevish when at last we are forced to admit that the two doctors don't quite agree.) We fancy we have taken *Doctor Faustus* by storm, we have simply failed to note that (in Professor Erich Heller's words) '*Doctor Faustus* is… its own critique, and that in the most thorough-going manner imaginable. There is no critical thought which the book does not think *about itself.*'

(4) Arising out of the previous point: it would seem that in German fiction the author tends to be rather obtrusive; he orders the material around in parade-ground fashion, he deafens us with his stentorian comments on his characters and incidents. Eckermann reports Goethe as having said, 'Germans are strange people. By their profound thoughts and ideas, which they look for everywhere and which they insert into everything, they burden their lives more than

---

1   Hans Magnus Enzensberger's essay, 'In Search of the Lost Language' (*Encounter*, September 1963), seeks to define the English use of the word 'Teutonic': 'The wealth of associations attached to this word is considerable. They range from the primaeval forest to the study of Dr Faustus, from bearskins to Hegel's *Phenomenology of Spirit*. Castles and fortresses are Teutonic, but so are abstract terminologies. Wagner's operas and long complex sentences are Teutonic. Leather shorts, bull necks, and exaggerated studiousness are Teutonic. The Teutons are boring, have sweaty feet, and moreover are most unfairly "daemonic".' This definition is far from complete.

is proper.' Yet this remark ought to alert us to something in Goethe at any rate – whom *primus inter pares* we think of as inserting profundities into everything and making the reader's life a burden to him – which doesn't quite chime with our conception of him. That he is 'Godlike' we know, but there is also something oddly Mephistophelean about his interventions in his own work. Alas, we expect our rebels, our outsiders, to proclaim their dispositions unequivocally, whether by dissipation and despair, drugs and divorce, or syntactical eccentricities and misuse of commas. When Goethe misbehaves we don't notice it: we just can't believe that he isn't continuously Godlike, sublime, prudent, four-square and a bore. Our notion of German literature is certainly not baseless, but it is based on a set of lowest common factors.

(5) The German novelist does not scruple to be 'symbolic' in a way that strikes us as grossly naïve and naïvely gross.[2] An associated complaint will be that German writers are heavily aphoristic, self-appointed sages of some small provincial Weimar or other, each having an eye to the school textbook market. The English reader resents and distrusts this habit: a moral tendency should be implicit, not explicit, enacted, not announced: never trust the artist, trust the tale – and alas the artist seems to be everywhere in the tale! To make matters worse, in some of the authors more celebrated though still unread, the aphorisms appear to contradict one another and thus to cancel out. It is infuriating to have to complain, for example of *Faust*, that the work is at the same time insistently symbolic and not symbolic enough, that the poor reader is forever being got at and finally is left in the lurch. For all the heaviness and earnestness of German writers, some of them permit themselves an elusiveness and an irony which arouse grave misgivings in us. We expect the monumental to stand still. There is a real difficulty here for English readers, whether of Goethe, of Thomas Mann or of Günter Grass, and unhappily no easy solution proposes itself: the only proof of these large puddings is in the eating, and sampling won't work, you may have to eat the whole thing.

(6) Another aspect of this difficulty is the frequent mingling in German literature of fantasy and realism, of the elephantine tread and the fairy footstep. German scholars seem more addicted to categorization than their British colleagues – yet German writers are readier

2 Cf. the verdict of the *New Yorker* in 1947 on the English translation of Elias Canetti's *Die Blendung (Auto da Fè)*: 'Overstuffed, highly complex novel, rigid with symbolism in the best German tradition.'

to mix categories, less embarrassed by the allegorical, than are we, with our stronger sense of humour (or more nervous one) and our greater sophistication (or more potent philistinism). Similarly disconcerting is the element of piety, reverence – 'Seid nur fromm...' – seen most obviously (blatantly?) in the 'Confessions of a Beautiful Soul', which comprise Book VI of the otherwise morally ambiguous *Wilhelm Meister*, and seen in the disquisition on funeral monuments in the rather scandalous context of *Elective Affinities*, in the poet of the *Roman Elegies* tapping out hexameters on the naked back of his Roman mistress, pervasively and despite his irony, in Mann's references to great men and great works – and perhaps, for all I can tell, in Canetti's dealings with classical Chinese culture in *Auto da Fé*. This *Frömmigkeit*, especially in association with *Gemütlichkeit*, can strike the English reader as hypocrisy (*Frömmelei* in German, incidentally), as in some contexts the very nastiest brand of sentimentality – like the commandant of a concentration camp having solemn thoughts about the sunset.[3]

The German novel has been less securely removed from poetry than the English novel. H.M. Waidson sums up the *Elective Affinities* as 'a novel by a great poet; it contains questioning and acceptance, defiance and resignation, sophistication and innocence, irony and reverence'. For a novel, we may be inclined to feel, it contains far too much. But our great poets don't usually write novels. Günter Grass on his present showing could conceivably be an English poet, but hardly an English novelist (unless perhaps a painter writing a novel). Canetti couldn't possibly be an English novelist. Kafka couldn't even be an Englishman.

Again, there is no simple test of failure or success, legitimacy or otherwise, no portable touchstone. As we know, the adjective 'poetic', applied to a novel, can as easily be a term of abuse as of praise.

(7) Scholarship is not a bed of footnotes, and what could be more painful than to be compelled by scholarly honour to complain of scholars? I allude to the paucity of stimulating criticism or commentary on the part of British Germanists. With a few honourable exceptions, our Germanists are thoroughly academic, I mean uninformative. The standard acceptable in them seems to be well below

---

3 I now read in H.M. Enzensberger (*op. cit.*): 'The S.S. officer who carried Hölderlin in his knapsack and the concentration-camp commandant who played Schubert sonatas *"nach Feierabend"* (when "off duty") were by no means legends; these were the consequences of a "life of the mind" for which the "higher values", for which *Bildung* has always been a fig leaf to cover betrayal to those in power.'

the minimum level of discourse expected from specialists in English literature (even) – as if the ability to read German literature is already so remarkable that little more is to be asked from those who have gained it. British Germanists appear to have picked up from German *Anglisten* a deep horror of literary experience and a distaste for literary judgment. The situation is exacerbated by a shortage of criticism from the German side. Where are the great German critics? Judge not – is that what *Frömmigkeit* demands? – that ye be not judged. From my own brief experience of working in a German university – it may have been quite unrepresentative – I came to understand that the literary critic was a form of life only surpassed in vulgarity and frivolity by the creative writer. Learning is *Wissenschaft* is science: which means that the only true learning is philology, and perhaps (because it can be refined upon but hardly refuted) literary categorizing. Mann didn't have to go far to find his early idea of the writer as criminal – the degenerate who commits unscientific mayhem on sweet innocent words!

(8) Granted, a few of our Germanists have written feelingly about their subject, and some have made available to us timely and inexpensive editions of German writers. But those who have done most for German literature in our time have been chiefly amateurs, chiefly translators. Rilke and Hölderlin were especially fortunate in their translators, one of them an *Anglist*, another a Germanist (but also by some administrative error a poet). C.F. MacIntyre and Louis MacNeice did more for Goethe in England and America than all the Bi-Centennial papers of 1949 put together. True, Goethe's lyrics remain an unsolved problem – the simpler they are, the more difficult to translate – and those translators of *Faust* who are at home with the humorous, sophisticated, Mephistophelean passages will be foxed by the 'nobility' of other parts, while those who succeed with the reflective sections – has anyone really succeeded? – may be defeated by the colloquial and mischievous note. Here, as elsewhere, Goethe's diversity of tone is the great stumbling block.

But clearly we cannot blame 'translation' in this general matter. It would be base cowardice to impute the relative neglect of Thomas Mann to his translators, and ridiculous to so ascribe the absolute neglect of Franz Werfel's *The Forty Days of Musa Dagh*. And among recent efforts – I mention only those which have reached me even in far-flung Singapore, where some twenty languages and dialects are spoken, but not German – we have Grass, Uwe Johnson's *Speculations about Jakob*, Hans Hellmut Kirst's *Officer Factory* (a German *Catch-22* which gets bogged down in pious thoughts about the Good German Soldier), Goethe's *Italian Journey* in a version by W.H. Auden and

Elizabeth Mayer, the poetry and plays of Hugo von Hofmannsthal and (particularly the poetry) of Brecht, and the bilingual anthology, *Modern German Poetry 1910–1960*, by Michael Hamburger and Christopher Middleton.[4]

(9) We are forced to take cognizance of another distasteful possibility: that in some cases non-admiration of German literature arises out of – or *is* – non-admiration of Germans. The factors operative in this latter phenomenon do not require to be aired. In the nineteenth century things were very different. German literature was eminently respectable, French wasn't.[5] Goethe's first biographer (or almost first) was an Englishman, and the consort of George Eliot. No doubt the associations evoked by the phrase 'French novel' still vary from circle to circle, but they will always be potent: the phrase 'German novel' draws forth either a groan or nothing.

An extra factor is often at work in our reading of a foreign literature. We tend to keep an eye open for racial characteristics; we read, if we are unfavourably disposed towards the country of origin, censoriously. We do not think of Quilp or Mr B. as typical Englishmen – but in reading foreign novels we incline to attribute the villain to the race, and more readily than we attribute the hero. In a similar spirit we read our own literature 'historically', that is tolerantly – witches are being burned, but it all happened long ago, and times have changed – whereas we admit the historical element into our consideration of a foreign literature only for damnatory purposes. 'A certain gay and noisy type of life is needed to make monkeys, parrots and coloured people tolerable around us,' we read in *Elective Affinities* (H.M. Waidson's translation, *Kindred by Choice*). Monkeys, parrots and coloured people! Shades of the *Herrenvolk* indeed!

But in fact the speaker – a schoolmaster as reported in Ottilie's diary – is merely proposing, fairly harmlessly, that forms of life cannot with impunity be torn from their natural context, that a zoo is disquieting because it is not nature. And Ottilie supplies the corollary: 'No one can walk unpunished among palm-trees, and one's opinions must surely change in a country where elephants and tigers are at home.' Ah yes, the Englishman running to seed under a tropical sun! Ottilie

4 '…two poets who are also excellent linguists, two poets who know German – can they be found again in this part of the world?' (H.M. Enzensberger, *op. cit.*).

5 With reservations, e.g. Matthew Arnold on Edmond Scherer ('A French Critic on Goethe'): '…his point of view is in many respects that of an Englishman. We mean that he has the same instinctive sense rebelling against what is verbose, ponderous, roundabout, inane – in one word, *niais* or silly – in German literature, just as a plain Englishman has.'

continues, 'Only the scientific investigator of nature is worthy of respect, the man who is able to describe and depict what is most strange and exotic in its own element, its locality and its surroundings. How glad I should be if I could only once hear Humboldt relating his findings!' Well said, young (1808) lady!

(10) Finally it might be noted, in extenuation of our English unresponsiveness in this matter, that a number of Germans have failed to admire German literature, or have admired it temperately. Even Herr Enzensberger admits that 'there is no denying that German literature has very often gone a long way to meet the stupidity, presumption, and arrogance of its British critics' – if this sounds a shade discourteous, remember what the man said: '*Im Deutschen lügt man, wenn man höflich ist*' – and though he speaks severely of 'the limits of Anglo-Saxon taste', Herr Enzensberger doesn't himself seem to care much for German poetry written before 1950.[6] Thomas Mann remarked in *The Genesis of a Novel*, apropos of his ignorance of *Der grüne Heinrich*, that 'my youth had been shaped far more by European literature, Russian, French, Scandinavian, and English, rather than German'. And Professor Roy Pascal (*The German Novel*) tells us that 'even for Germans, to read the great German novels is mostly a "cultural task" – infinitely rewarding, I believe, but never likely to become a dangerous passion in the reader'.

Conclusion: 'Interdum vulgus rectum videt, est ubi peccat.' It would appear from our investigations, then, that the English are right not to like certain parts of German literature and wrong not to like other parts. Further than that it would be unsafe to go. In its carefulness, impartiality, fearlessness and self-effacement, this conclusion might seem a modest exemplification of true scholarship, and *énormément caractéristique* of *Wissenschaft*, perhaps.

(1964)

---

6 '…Rilke, Stefan George, and von Hofmannsthal (all of whom have a place in the *bürgerliche* literary pantheon though not among the German moderns) …' (*op. cit.*).

Wilhelm Meister *and the Ambiguousness of Goethe*

'Snow is a false cleanliness'

I

In the past, before interest in Goethe was confined to Germanists and centenaries, even more time and energy went to the elucidation of *Wilhelm Meisters Lehrjahre* than to the Second Part of *Faust*. The conclusions arrived at were as diverse as may be. Where one commentator tells us that the novel is a philosophical document crammed full of deep and consistent thinking, another says outright, 'The Idea of *Wilhelm Meister* is precisely this – that is has no Idea.' Both views are right, to some extent, and both are wrong. With Goethe's famous aphorism on *Hamlet* in mind, we might feel tempted to say that the book is full of ideas but the author is without an idea. But that, too, would be less than accurate.

Wilhelm Meister's Apprenticeship is a long way from being a perfect work of art; in some ways, indeed, it is incredibly bad. It lacks any certain unity of plot or theme; the characters are mostly silly or boring or even unpleasant; the action, already contorted, is frequently interrupted by long and irrelevant set speeches. The work gives the immediate impression of falling into two pieces, as cleanly as if its binding were broken. The first five books constitute a *Theaterroman*: Wilhelm has ambitions to be actor-manager-poet and to redeem the German stage, and so we move in the company of actors and actresses, paint, footlights and manuscripts. The sixth book, a pietistic history called 'The Confessions of a Beautiful Soul', lies uneasily between the two sections like a buffer. And the seventh and eighth books are sheer *Lebensroman*: Wilhelm deserts the stage and his old friends, and embraces the company of a set of intellectual aristocrats, a species of Freemasons' Society, with the aim of helping others to reach a working agreement between their talents and their way of life.

It would seem that Goethe's original idea was to allow Wilhelm to develop into a successful man-of-the-theatre, and thus provide himself with an opportunity to expound his own ideas about plays and play production. The plan, simple and straightforward, corresponds to the First Part of *Faust*. But then Goethe changed his mind. Wilhelm's apprenticeship was to be an apprenticeship in life itself: he was to develop into a successful human being and thus provide his author with an opportunity to expound his ideas on that more ambitious and vaguer subject. Readers were to be warned against the dangers of yielding to a false tendency – 'we should guard against a talent which we cannot hope to practise in perfection'[1] – and Wilhelm's long traffic with the stage (all five books of it) came in useful as an admonitory case in point. The greater issues of the last three books, sometimes presented directly and sometimes only to be reached by a twisting and roundabout path, may be said to correspond to those of the Second Part of *Faust*.

This is obviously not the way to write a popular novel; nor is it the way to write a great one. *Wilhelm Meister* breaks all the rules of criticism, even the most sensible rules; yet the fact remains that it is a memorable anomaly. (And one finds oneself remembering it again and again, in all sorts of contexts.) It is a work which calls for an immense amount of perseverance on the part of the reader. But, given that perseverance, a certain kind of unity can be detected in the end, and it is realized that the two parts of the work share the same bloodstream after all. It is true that this unity is as precarious as that of the complete *Faust*. In spite of the injunctions which he addressed to both the human being and the artist – 'You have to limit yourself. To "have to" is hard but it is the only way a man can show what is in him' – Goethe refused in each of these inimitable works to limit himself. He erred, perhaps, in the opposite direction from the aesthete: life interested him so much, he led his own with such energy and unbookish zest, that he attempted to bring art a little closer to real life than was safe for it. The 'figure in the carpet' of an individual life rarely emerges with much clarity of definition, and it is the same with *Wilhelm Meister* and *Faust*. Eckermann reports Goethe as having said, apropos of the former, 'I should think a rich manifold life, brought close to our eyes, would be enough without any express tendency, which, after all, is only for the intellect.' But many of Goethe's sayings originated in a desire to correct views which had been carried to extremes, and possibly this remark was intended for the ears of his excessively profound commentators. There is plenty of evidence in Goethe's work – without mentioning his other explicit pronouncements – to dissociate him from the realist or documentary school.

Yet I think we are near to the root of the difficulty. Goethe appears to be doing two different things at the same time: he is describing 'a rich manifold life' in a style so free from moral comment that pious readers have accused him of immorality, while simultaneously his

1 The English quotations throughout are taken from Carlyle's translation.

writing is thickly interspersed with moral apophthegms and – more than that – informed with a kind of moral passion which, spasmodic though it may be, is yet too intense to be disregarded. He is both romantic and classical, and often he is one when you would expect him to be the other; he is both philosopher and artist; he is a warm moralist and yet a dispassionate reporter. His Faust, with the blood of Gretchen and of Baucis and Philemon on his soul, is received into a highly organized and even ritualistic Heaven. After falling into almost every sort of muddle possible to a young man, Wilhelm is clapped on the back and assured that he is indeed a 'Meister'.

It stands to reason that Goethe will not enjoy much popularity today, when criticism has become so self-conscious and the cultivated public is tolerant enough to accept both romantic and classical so long as the item fits into one category or the other. Ours is the age of 'taking sides', and the man who does not take a clearly recognizable side will be buffeted from all directions. What is rarely perceived is that Goethe does take a side, that he does commit himself, and with a loving whole-heartedness that has become increasingly uncommon among writers. He accepts, above all other considerations, the prime value of being alive: from this acceptance follows the conclusion that, however wrongly a man is living his life, it can only be taken away from him for the strongest and most practical of reasons. It is the sin against life that is dreadful, not the sin against ideas: the scaffold might be necessary in Goethe's world, but the concentration camp would not exist.

The precarious 'unity' of the work – if indeed one accepts its existence – is the last surprise in a sequence of surprises. For the work is an interesting study in ambiguousness – the unexpected juxtaposition of the exquisite and the coarse, of sensibility and cynicism, of tragedy and farce, in which a romantic apparatus, in all its full-blown glory, is suddenly put to a cold, rational and realistic use. The continual changing of tone cannot be attributed to the author's change of intention: it is not merely consequent on the fact that those personages who must have a great significance for Wilhelm as student of the theatre may mean nothing at all for Wilhelm as student of life – or may, indeed, have an altogether different kind of significance. The irony is there in the very first pages; it dominates the creation of the book's first character, Mariana, who is dead long before Wilhelm forsakes the stage. And this ambiguousness of tone is almost the only truly consistent element in the novel.

2

The plot of *Wilhelm Meister* is so unmemorable that a summary of its chief events may not be out of place here. Although the book served Goethe as a kind of rag-bag for aphorisms, points of view, anecdotes and pieces of literary criticism entirely unconnected with the plot, nevertheless the main incidents deserve as close attention as the chief characters and speeches. If the reader dismisses the events of the story as so much trash (and one is tempted in this direction), he will naturally devote himself to the characters and, more particularly, their set speeches. In that case his conception of *Wilhelm Meister* will be quite inaccurate. For on the whole the characters, as revealed in their appearance, situation and ways of feeling, are what we call 'romantic' – having in mind *Werther*, *Pamela* and the later novels of sensibility. Mariana seems to be the glamorous free-living actress who brings sunshine into the young burgher's dull life; Aurelia appears in the traditional role of the sensitive, faithful, though abandoned mistress; the Countess displays all the characteristics of the beautiful and refined noblewoman faced with a problem of honour – and so on.

But then the author intervenes. For the events of the story and Goethe's own comments are frequently at odds with the characters as originally announced and with our own expectations. They are *terre-à-terre*, humiliating, ridiculous or even cynical. Mariana is neither as fine as Wilhelm believes nor as light of morals as we are led to believe: she is a rather ordinary girl who falls victim to Wilhelm's adolescent conception of romantic love. The man who has betrayed Aurelia turns up as the leading spirit of the high-minded intellectuals of the second part of the book and is presented as its noblest character. The Countess, with her problem of honour brushed casually aside in the rush of events, retires apathetically to a Herrnhuter community together with her husband, an unfortunate gentleman with ambitions to be a saint. That is to say, character – however solemnly Goethe appears to have created it – is at odds with the action: the novel is full of dead-ends, halts, turnings back, changes of direction.

In some of its manifestations, this device of Goethe's is a triumph of irony. And irony of this kind, after all, is to be looked for in a work which sets out to depict the delusions under which its characters are living, and which announces through its most authoritative speakers that Error alone can teach us to avoid Error:

> To guard from error, is not the instructor's duty; but to lead the erring pupil; nay, to let him quaff his error in deep satiating

draughts, this is the instructor's wisdom. He who only tastes his error, will long dwell with it, will take delight in it as in a singular felicity: while he who drains it to the dregs will, if he be not crazy, find it out.

Goethe's quest was for a means of avoiding chaos without the imposition of any categorical law – the reconciliation of a reasonably unified society with the diverse demands of the individual being. The compromise in which such a problem can only be resolved is reflected in the structure of *Wilhelm Meister*. Goethe cannot abstain from teaching, but he must refrain from dogma: the result often takes the form of an ironical dénouement to an impossible situation. One man's poison is another man's meat – Friedrich, the gay young aristocrat, sets up house with the attractive but wanton Philina (on the grounds that paternity depends upon persuasion), and the serious Jarno marries the romantic young Lydia, another of Lothario's cast-off lovers. To consider a different kind of situation: Natalia and the Abbé, both respected personages, are both educationists, yet their methods are opposed. Natalia believes in the helping hand before the fall, while the Abbé places his faith in the helping hand after the fall. Goethe presents their methods, says as much for each as any fairly ardent supporter could, and leaves the matter at that. It should be noticed, however, that when Natalia speaks of her difference of opinion with the Abbé, she remarks that it is a measure of the latter's tolerance that he has never attempted to interfere in her projects. This tolerance of Goethe's is apt to confound the modern reader: either it passes unrecognized, in which case neither *Wilhelm Meister* nor *Faust* will make sense, or else it is misinterpreted in such a way that Goethe must be rejected as a callous and complacent old man whose hypocritical aphorisms do not hide his fundamental *jem'enfichisme*.

The 'Prologue in Heaven', that invaluable preface to *Faust*, is also the best preparation for *Wilhelm Meister*:

> Though as yet his service is confused,
> Soon shall I lead him into clarity.
> The gardener knows, when the sapling's green,
> That blossom and fruit will grace the future years....
>
> As long as he strives, man must err ...
> A good man, in his dim urgency,
> Is conscious of the right way still.

The novel begins with a sentimental love-story. Wilhelm, the son

of a business family, falls in love with an actress, Mariana. His other
passion, for the theatre, goes back to childhood; he is the 'young
genius', inspired to write dramas and revive the German stage, and it
is an obvious trick to introduce by way of contrast his friend Werner,
the hard-headed young business man whose only passion is the system
of book-keeping by double entry. It is indeed a scene from the
Bohemian Life that lies before us, if we look at it through Wilhelm's
eyes. Our hero's ecstasies are unconfined – not so our author's, who
remarks on the dirty state of Mariana's room and even of her person.
'Love,' he tells us, 'is so strong a spice, that tasteless, or even nauseous
soups are by it rendered palatable.'

Circumstances cause Wilhelm to believe that Mariana has deceived
him, and he renounces her. Wilhelm Scherer in his *History of German
Literature* tells us that Wilhelm is 'too hasty in entering into binding
relations'; we note though that he is quite nimble in getting out of
them again. There is a fair amount of Wertherism, but no suicide. He
burns his manuscripts and turns to the family business. While on a
business trip, however, he falls in with a group of actors and his old
ambitions revive and overcome him. The players and their mode of
life – their jealousies, intrigues, adventures and misfortunes – are
excellently depicted, and this part of the work is by far the liveliest.
The novel appears to be firmly set upon its picaresque path: the
company moves from theatre to theatre (instead of from inn to inn),
it meets with success and failures, new people join it from time to time
and we are regaled with their biographies, and the actors are even
attacked by highwaymen and robbed of their clothes, like Joseph
Andrews. All the ingredients of the once popular novel are there: even
those characters of mysterious origin and gloomy past who are to
struggle under a load of obscure guilt and painful eccentricity right up
to the last chapter. For Wilhelm adopts two strange waifs, Mignon the
dancing girl and the old Harper. The first encounter with Mignon is
suitably enigmatic: here we have an element not to be found in the
English picaresque epic of Fielding and Smollett –

'What is thy name?' he asked. 'They call me Mignon.' 'How old art
thou?' 'No one has counted.' 'Who was thy father?' 'The Great
Devil is dead.'

The modern reader will find Mignon – in spite of her songs – rather
trying. Her Cassandra-like antics soon pall. But for the romantic
reader of an earlier day she was the *raison d'être* of the work; and, like
Gretchen in *Faust*, she is still apt to distract our attention from matters
which, though less sensational, are of greater import. It is Wilhelm,

'milksop' as he may be, and Faust, that disgraceful rejuvenated don, who are the heroes of their stories, and we should not surrender our loyalties to those insidiously pathetic maidens who fall by the way. The way is long and hard, and Goethe is considerably less sentimental than his readers. The Harper – a bearded old gentleman who twangs his instrument into accents of despair on the slightest provocation and vacillates uneasily between suicide, child-murder and arson – is plainly a stock figure from the Tale of Terror. Yet in the end he is taken to pieces, explained, allowed to kill himself as an appropriate way out of his spiritual impasse, and in short serves to point a moral plainer and more practical than any psychoanalyst could deduce. This is the author's habit here: the use and deliberate abuse of the conventions of his time, in the service of disabusing. We shall return to the Harper later: an understanding of Goethe's treatment of this figure – some will find it callous, others will consider it healthy – is the beginning of an understanding of the novel.

The troupe is engaged by a Count to perform at his castle. Wilhelm has been enamoured of Philina, a light-minded but amusing actress; now, with that facility of emotion which oppresses both him and the reader, he falls in love with the Countess. And the Countess (like most of the female characters, she never really takes shape: we are simply informed of her 'beauty and youth, her graceful dignity and refined manner') is very taken with Wilhelm. The guests decide to play a trick on the Countess: while the Count is out, Wilhelm will put on his cloak and sit in his dimly lighted room; the Baroness will inform the Countess that her husband has returned in a bad temper; the Countess will come to soothe him… Wilhelm is instructed 'to play the cross husband as long and as well as possible; and when obliged to disclose himself, he must behave politely, handsomely and gallantly'. To do him justice, Wilhelm is not too happy about this aristocratic sport: 'the fear of displeasing the Countess, and that of pleasing her too well, were equally busy in his mind' – but he is unable to refuse anything to a woman as pretty as the Baroness.

It is a situation worthy of the most arrant novelette, and we can foresee what will happen. The Count will return unexpectedly, he will find Wilhelm in his place (and in his clothes), he will jump to unpleasant conclusions, and he will challenge our poor milksop to a duel. But, as always, the conventional situation is resolved in an unconventional way. The Count does return unexpectedly, he does see Wilhelm occupying his chair. But then he turns and leaves the room without a word. Can it be that he is biding his time, that he is meditating a peculiarly sinister revenge? Not at all. It transpires that the poor man believes that he has seen his own ghost – a warning of his approaching end. He therefore withdraws from social life, gives himself up to devotional literature and prepares for sainthood. His noble friends refrain from disillusioning him; they even attempt to frighten him further. Nor does his wife, who is told the truth, take any action. The tragi-comedy is given an extra twist: there is an impulsive love-passage between Wilhelm and the Countess just before the latter's departure. The two fall into each other's arms – suddenly, with a shriek, the Countess tears herself away: 'Fly, if you love me!' As the chapter closes, Goethe remarks, 'Unhappy creatures! What singular warning of chance or of destiny tore them asunder?' And we are reminded of the end of some lurid serial instalment.

Towards the end of the book we meet the Count and Countess again. The Count has renounced his estates and is about to enter a Herrnhuter community together with his wife; she too is possessed by a secret sorrow. It seems that during the embrace Wilhelm pressed against her breast a jewelled portrait of her husband – this would account for the shriek which one had attributed to a lacerated conscience – and the lady is firmly though wrongly convinced that she has incurred cancer. The confirmed novel reader of Goethe's time must have found it hard to know exactly what his feelings were, as he said goodbye to this miserably maltreated couple. They have done no particular harm to anyone, and the Countess at least has been shown in an attractive light. But they are the weak, the defeated, they cannot be helped for they have sinned against life: we must just leave them to their years of remorse and piety. There is perhaps something a little Nietzschean here, but there is nothing of the Superman about our hero, a very middling sort of person who survives and is well rewarded. Goethe was never an idealist of Nietzsche's intensity.

Their engagement at the castle having ended, the company moves on – reluctantly because there are bandits in the neighbourhood. But Wilhelm, for once the man of action, insists, with the result that they are set upon and Wilhelm is seriously wounded while the others lose their belongings. They blame the young man for this mishap and, though weak from loss of blood, he makes a lengthy, formal and pompous speech in his own defence. This is only one example among many of the unnovelistic aspects of the work: here, the holding up of action and the defiance of common probability in order to make room for a set speech and some weighty aphorisms. And the only possible excuse is the chance it gives Goethe to remark, apropos of Wilhelm's feeling of responsibility, that 'this was but another folly for which he had to blame himself, the folly of presuming to take upon his single shoulders a misfortune that was spread over many'. True, Wilhelm has many lessons to learn; but it is hard that so often he should learn them at the reader's expense.

At this point Serlo, a more authentic theatrical manager, enters the story, and the novel turns more decidedly towards *Theaterroman*. While the discussions on *Hamlet* seem to constitute one of the few tangible grudges against Goethe today, there is not time to examine them in detail here. What we should bear in mind is that Wilhelm says many things about the play, some of them mutually contradictory, and that Goethe does not necessarily agree with them all. The conclusion of the affair is that Wilhelm undertakes to re-fashion the play – he will not tamper with the poetry, but intends to 'rationalize' the plot-mechanism. The last we hear is that 'satisfied as he was with his own conception, it still appeared to him as if in executing it he were but spoiling the original'. After all Wilhelm proves more modest than many of his colleagues in Shakespearean commentary. Goethe's private attitude is ambiguous. He advances several theories, clearly he is interested in them – he would hardly set down some thousand words of nonsense solely to demonstrate Wilhelm's immaturity as a literary critic – but clearly he does not consider them more than interesting theories which still remain to be proved or disproved. There is no sign of dogma. And T.S. Eliot's comment that Goethe 'made of Hamlet a Werther' is based on a misconception of Goethe's attitude towards both Hamlet and Werther, and more attention needs to be paid to the context of the *Hamlet* passages. The best footnote to this interlude is provided by the authoritative Abbé in the speech on art which he makes towards the end of the novel:

> Most men are wont to treat a work of art, though fixed and done, as if it were a piece of soft clay. The hard and polished marble is again to mould itself, the firm-walled edifice is to contract or to expand itself, according as their inclinations, sentiments and whims may dictate; the picture is to be instructive, the play to make us better, everything is to do all. The reason is, that most men are themselves unformed, they cannot give themselves and their being any certain shape: and thus they strive to take from other things their proper shape, that all they have to do with may be loose and wavering like themselves.

The climax of the *Theaterroman* is reached with the first performance of *Hamlet*. With Wilhelm in the title-role it is a great success, and the company celebrates afterwards in lively style. The same night Wilhelm has a female visitor, but his dazed condition prevents him from recognizing her (though he proves adequate to the situation otherwise). Both the sentimental and the serious-minded reader may have been able to shut an eye to the book's general ambiguousness of tone, but incidents such as this have always baffled them; they have had uneasy recourse to the manners of the time, when, G.H. Lewes said, 'on the subject of the sexes the whole tone of feeling was low'. *Wilhelm Meister* is, as it were, a synthesis of Richardson and Fielding – with something of *Rasselas* added. Not so much a balanced synthesis as a disquieting mixture, for Richardson's sensibility is continually being affronted by Fielding's cynicism: a sentimental love-scene, pastoral or polite, is succeeded by a Molly Seagrim rough and tumble among the ladies of the troupe – or a woman dies of disappointed love and the gentleman in the case (who is also the beau ideal of the novel) remarks coolly, 'Alas! she was not lovely when she loved; the greatest misery that can befall a woman.'

This woman, Aurelia, sister of the manager Serlo, is a miserable bore. Deserted by her noble lover, her only consolation is their (apparent) son, a young child called Felix. Everything serves to remind her afresh of her unhappiness; especially, of course, the role of Ophelia. The gallant Wilhelm becomes her confidant – the reader too, though less willingly. Eventually she dies, her last days having been edified by the reading of an autobiographical manuscript, 'Confessions of a Beautiful Soul'. This constitutes Book VI and is the story of 'the woman who had valued God above her bridegroom', a Woman of Sensibility who became a woman of religion. It is an unequivocally pious piece of work in which we are not aware of Goethe's personal attitude –unless perhaps it is one of approval – and indeed a friend of his solemnly burnt the whole of *Wilhelm Meister* with the exception of this one section.

The one point in the 'Confessions' at which the author may be felt to intervene is probably the most interesting: the 'Beautiful Soul' is drawn towards the doctrines of the Herrnhuter Brethren, tolerating the bad taste and even ugliness in which their piety manifests itself. While visiting her uncle's castle, however, she is shown his collection of paintings, and is impressed by this revelation of a different kind of spiritual cultivation. Her uncle tells her,

> those do not act well, who, in a solitary exclusive manner, follow moral cultivation by itself. On the contrary, it will be found that he whose spirit strives for a development of that kind, has likewise every reason, at the same time, to improve his finer sentient powers; that so he may not run the risk of sinking from his moral height, by giving way to the enticements of a lawless fancy, and degrading

his moral nature by allowing it to take delight in tasteless baubles, if not in something worse.

Moral cultivation must go hand in hand with the cultivation of the senses, if the former is not to risk destroying itself – in perhaps the crude paraphernalia of a sect. This pleas for the arts is backed up by the 'Beautiful Soul's' joy on hearing her uncle's trained choir for the first time: 'without pretending to edify, they elevated me and made me happy in the most spiritual manner'. She compares it with the pious mode of praising God to which she is accustomed. None the less she continues on her own path: if Goethe does not wholly approve of it, at least he refrains from the savagery with which he treated the unfortunate Count. The 'Beautiful Soul' is a civilized devotee and undeluded.

The novel now gives up all pretence of being a *Theaterroman*. Wilhelm leaves the company in order to convey Aurelia's last letter to her delinquent lover, Lothario, and add his own reproaches. On the way he meets a stranger to whom he complains of the time he has wasted among the actors; the other replies,

Here you are mistaken; everything that happens to us leaves some trace behind it, everything contributes imperceptibly to form us.

Experience must never be despised, but – the stranger continues (for everyone is ready to help our hero) – nor should we brood too deeply over our experiences, for that can make us either arrogant because of our successes or morbid because of our failures. 'The safe plan is, always simply to do the task that lies nearest us.' Here we are as near as we can be to an explicit definition of the novel's 'meaning', or at least one of its meanings.

On reaching the Baron Lothario's castle, Wilhelm is shocked to find what little effect his news has on the dead Aurelia's late lover. (The latter is admittedly rather preoccupied with a duel resulting from some other affair of the heart.) Wilhelm rehearses the stern and pathetic speech with which he is to scorch Lothario's conscience. Luckily one of the Baron's friends, Jarno, overhears this and intimates to our hero that the Countess is Lothario's sister and that Lothario knows the whole story:

'O let me fly!' cried Wilhelm: 'How shall I appear before him? What can he say to me?'
'That no man should cast a stone at his brother; that when one composes long speeches, with a view to shame his neighbours, he should speak them to a looking-glass.'

It transpires, to baffle further the conventionally-minded reader, that Lothario is meant to be the finest male character of the work: noble, generous, active, cultivated, and the beloved of all women. We may boggle at the abundance and casualness of his love affairs and we may fail to perceive the moral grandeur of his nature. But we simply have to accept it – we have the word of Goethe and the unanimous opinion of all the best people in the novel. And Scherer's too: 'in Lothario we are introduced to the noblest type of an aristocrat and German gentleman, a character bearing an indubitable resemblance to Karl August.' Certainly he is an eminently active person: while convalescing from the wound received during the duel he is engaged on the details of a scheme whereby the labourers on his estates will profit directly from their efforts. This is obviously a parallel to the final adventure of Faust, that which more than anything else enables him to escape Mephistopheles – his reclamation of the inundated land and the prosperous hard-working colony which he founds thereon.

Far though he is from being a fascinating character (or even a character at all in the usual literary sense), Jarno too is worth a little attention; his behaviour on one point helps to clarify the ambiguousness of the novel. On his first appearance he remarks to Wilhelm,

> I have often thought with vexation and spleen, how, in order to gain a paltry living, you must fix your heart on a wandering ballad-monger, and a silly mongrel, neither male nor female.

This harsh description of Mignon and the Harper upsets Wilhelm, who (together with the generality of readers) repudiates Jarno as a 'dead-hearted worldling'. But now we discover him to be the trusted friend of the great Lothario. Mignon and the Harper are touching figures – on the other hand, Jarno is above suspicion. The crux is eased when the history of the two eccentrics emerges in the last book. The Harper was a monk of noble Italian family who fell in love with the supposed daughter of a neighbour: it was discovered, too late, that the girl was his own sister. The young monk then ran mad and escaped from the monastery, grew a beard and sang mournful ballads. The girl succumbed to a kind of religious mania; and Mignon, the child of this relationship, was stolen by a strolling party of rope-dancers and took to wearing boy's clothes and singing nostalgic songs. Eventually she dies from an excess of various emotions, including her longing for 'das Land wo die Zitronen blühn' and a precocious love for Wilhelm, while shortly afterwards the Harper cuts his throat under the compulsion of his morbid sense of guilt.

The casual way in which the old man is pushed out of the story is calculated to offend softer-hearted readers. Goethe's point, as implied in Jarno's callous remark, is that he who consorts with weakness will himself become weak – obey the demands of the day, by all means, but do not involve yourself in the irretrievable sorrows of other people. Mignon and the Harper are moral lepers, in spite of all the romantic mystery and lyric poetry which surrounds them; and Jarno (though we may not like his choice of words) has good reason to warn his impressionable young acquaintance against too close an association with them. (Similarly, Settembrini is right in warning his young protégé, in old-womanish rather than brutal accents, against the morbid charms which surround him on *The Magic Mountain*.) The reader's pity for Gretchen may lead him to find Faust's speedy recovery from her death more than a little shocking. Victorian taste often looked for nemesis in the form of damnation, or at least a lifelong remorse: morality demanded it. Modern taste, equally reluctant to accept the reappearance of a buoyant and energetic Faust, looks for a similar nemesis – though now it is 'art' that demands it. Yet Goethe's attitude is at least feasible: if Faust surrenders to remorse, then he will never build the great colony along the seashore –

> When phantoms haunt him, let him go his way,
> And find in onward-striding both happiness and pain,
> He, uncontented very moment!

It is ironical that Mignon's songs, the extreme expression of that morbid longing for the past which *Wilhelm Meister* denounces, should be precisely that small part of Goethe's huge output which is still universally known and applauded.

To return to the story: Wilhelm discovers that the child Felix, whom he had adopted on the death of Aurelia, is actually his own son by Mariana, and that Mariana, faithful to him despite appearances, has died of grief at his desertion. Naturally Wilhelm is upset, but he recovers quite as expeditiously as Faust. He is now conducted to a secret part of the castle (over which a mildly Radcliffean atmosphere has hung), and here a mysterious voice resembling that of his dead father tells him:

> Thou art saved, thou art on the way to the goal. None of thy follies wilt thou repent; none wilt thou wish to repeat; no luckier destiny can be allotted to a man.

He is forthwith initiated into a kind of benevolent secret society and the Abbé presents him with his Indenture: 'Thy Apprenticeship is done; Nature has pronounced thee free.'

So ends Book VII, but in the following book our poor hero complains that ever since he was pronounced a true 'Meister' life has seemed more confusing than before. This is a good touch: in spite of everything, Wilhelm – like Mann's Castorp – retains something of his ingenuousness: he is not educated out of existence. And he compares favourably with his old friend Werner who shows up again at this point. The romantic reader will have considered Werner (the Spirit of Commerce) an unattractive figure by the side of Wilhelm (the Spirit of Art), whereas the more realistic reader has probably been anticipating his eventual glorious vindication. For after all Werner has been actively employed in useful business ventures while the shiftless Wilhelm was flirting ineffectively with the stage. This time, however, the more cautious reader is in the wrong: Werner has been busy enough, but he has fallen into the sin of specialization. He has gained money, but he has lost his figure, his hair and his joy in living: he has become 'a diligent hypochondriac'. A comment passed by Wilhelm in a different connection is relevant to Werner, and to much else in the novel:

> Woe to every sort of culture which destroys the most effectual means of all true culture, and directs us to an end, instead of rendering us happy on the way!

Love among the nobility is more polished than among the players but, alas, it is also more complicated. Lothario has long been in love with a very practical lady called Theresa, but their union is forbidden by the fact that Lothario in his youth had been too intimately connected with her mother. (One feels it would have been fitting had the first edition of *Wilhelm Meister*, like that of *Les Liaisons dangereuses*, been on sale 'à la Sagesse, rue Galande'.) Wilhelm proposes to this Theresa and is accepted. Whereupon – which is hardly what we expect from a 'Meister' – he realizes that he is in love with Natalia, Lothario's second sister.[2] It seems a situation more proper to the beginning of a novel than to its end. But the problem is shelved while Wilhelm visits the Hall of the Past where he sees the sarcophagus of Natalia's uncle

---

2 We share D.H. Lawrence's indignation: 'I think *Wilhelm Meister* is amazing as a book of peculiar immorality, the perversity of intellectualized sex, and the utter incapacity for any *development* of contact with any other human being, which is peculiarly bourgeois and Goethian.' But then we have to laugh: it is, after all, a comic novel, about the adventures of an over-read young intellectual, half in league with and half at war with the *Zeitgeist*. And Wilhelm is ready to discard his literary conceptions of life and to admit his mistakes; especially ready, as we note in the case of Theresa, when he can do it gracefully.

(who was also the cultivated uncle of the 'Confessions'), upon which are inscribed the words 'Gedenke zu leben'. Here is an explicit repudiation of the morbid romanticism of Mignon and the Harper: they had thought of death all through their lives whereas the uncle, at the moment of his death, had thought of living. The Hall of the Past, incidentally, is built in 'Egyptian style'.

It is now revealed that Theresa is not the daughter of her reputed mother and can therefore safely accept Lothario. A welcome respite from this comedy of errors is provided by the death of Mignon. The funeral is Grand Opera at its most florid: the assembled characters stand about in attitudes of grief or dismay, the voices of two hidden choirs are heard, and a visiting Italian marquis recognizes the dead child from a crucifix pricked on her arm: 'O God. Poor child! Unhappy niece!' Nevertheless the fantastic melodrama echoes the book's preoccupation – even in so unpropitious a context – as it ends on a strengthening sentiment: 'Travel, travel, back into life! Take along with you this holy Earnestness; – for Earnestness alone makes life eternity.'

Goethe's own irony displays itself in a little incident which occurs at this juncture. The Harper, still hovering on the edge of suicide, has left a glass of milk mixed with laudanum next to a bottle of pure milk, and it is feared that the child Felix has drunk from the glass. It transpires that in fact he drank from the bottle, a bad habit of his, and claimed to have drunk from the glass lest his father should punish him. His disobedience has saved his life: Goethe could never have given his novel the subtitle 'Virtue Rewarded'. Moreover, the Harper has cut his throat in an access of guilt and *Weltschmerz* before the truth of the matter comes to light.

The novel ends on a conventional note, with a series of marriages. Lothario takes his Theresa and Wilhelm is thus released to unite himself with Natalia. Then they all combine to form a philanthropic association which shall help others to find their true path through life. Wilhelm shows embarrassment when his theatrical past is referred to, and he is told,

> The times were very good times: only I cannot but laugh to look at thee: to my mind, thou resemblest Saul the son of Kish, who went out to seek his father's asses, and found a kingdom.

3

The chief objection to the work has been that it falls apart into two largely irreconcilable halves; that is, in Croce's words, 'a book guided by a thought superadded to it and entirely different from it'. The critics have let off their heavy artillery: the first part is *Theaterroman*, the second is *Lebensroman*. But a cannon ball equally ponderous can be fired back at them: the novel, even so, is continuously *Bildungsroman*. Any insignificant little piece of fiction can have unity of a sort – a machine-made beginning-middle-end. But the unity of *Wilhelm Meister*, like that of *Faust*, needs to be searched for; and perhaps one can never be sure that one has found it. But in the search one will have found – besides much cause for complaint – many good things which no other writer has to offer.

There is a passage in Wilhelm's 'Indenture' which helps to explain the work's unwieldiness:

> Whoever works with symbols alone, is a pedant, a hypocrite, or a bungler... The instruction which the true artist gives us, opens the mind; for where words fail him, deeds speak.

Goethe is out to teach in this work: he refuses to use symbols only – indeed he very nearly repudiates altogether the principle of synecdoche – and consequently he introduces an uncomfortably large number of characters engaged in an uncomfortably large number of diverse activities. The 'direct method' of teaching is not an economical way of going to work in literature, even though it strikes a refreshing note in an age tyrannized over by the 'symbolic'. *Wilhelm Meister's Apprenticeship*, in spite of being a most inadvisable model, compels our respect. In it Goethe has tried to apply to the novel-form the very principle which this particular novel sets out to convey: that it is life itself, rich in action, not free from error, but uncluttered by the symbols of introspection or abstract thought, that counts. And Goethe himself has said the best word on the 'meaning' of his book. Its origins, he wrote in his old age, in the *Tag- und Jahreshefte*,

> sprang from a dim presentiment of the great truth that man often seeks that for which Nature has denied him a talent, and desires to undertake and practise that in which he can never excel... Yet it is possible that every false step should lead to an inestimable good, and some intimation of this unfolds itself ever more clearly and certainly in *Wilhelm Meister*, and indeed at last reveals itself in the unambiguous words, 'to my mind, thou resemblest Saul the son of Kish, who went out to seek his father's asses, and found a kingdom'.

(1953)

The Story of Two Souls:
Goethe and the Manns

By Way of Goethe

As the eighty-two-year-old poet was dying, those present saw him tracing on his blanket a large W. Was it for his middle name, Wolfgang? Or was it, as others have surmised, for *Welt*, World? It could well have been for both, since Goethe was himself a world.

During his long and unceasingly working life he produced lyrics, philosophical poems, plays, satires, travel books, novels, auto-biographies, criticism and scientific treatises. He was not so much a man of letters as a literature; and later generations of German writers must have felt there was little for them to add beyond footnotes. More than that, it was he who by an unparalleled one-man effort dragged Germany into the intellectual forefront of the nine-teenth century.

In our century and in this country his reputation has fallen sadly into abeyance – possibly because we prefer our authors to confine themselves to provinces or parishes, so that we know what to expect from them. It is true that Goethe was fond of the sound of his own mind, and he didn't always distinguish (nor did his Boswells) between the perceptive and the pedantic, for he was interested in everything and had something to say about most of it. I think that what is often missed, especially in translations, is the tone of his voice, the humorous or ironic inflections that modify the utterances of the Sage of Weimar including Greater Germany (and for some time the Rest of the World). The reader is aware of his wisdom, but takes insuffi-cient account of the élan, the intensities and the comedy that go with it. Hence we tend to find stodgy or platitudinous (granted, Goethe had no objection to an occasional solid platitude) what may be mischievous or ambiguous. Much the same is true of Thomas Mann: the question is which of them is the better introduction to the other. Both were public figures, not a good thing for a writer to be when the romantic idea of him as a slightly higher species of drop-out still persists: Mann as the representative of the 'good Germany', Goethe as the representative of Germany. And Goethe was the more diverse of the two, for where Mann researched, he pioneered – in botany, biology, zoology, optics, mineralogy – besides taking a lively interest in history, law and the arts, and an active part in the administration of the grand (though fortunately small) duchy of Weimar, where he lived from 1775 till his death. (Like Mann, he was himself in some degree the 'Establishment' which he satirized.) It was the large view of the world that he took, the largest possible one at the time, looking for connections or inventing them, rejoicing in the spirit of life in himself and, in the terms of Wordsworth's definition of the poet, 'delighting to contemplate similar volitions and passions as manifested in the goings-on of the Universe'. It is impossible to name an English writer or thinker with whom he can be compared. The nearest thing would be a cross between Dr Johnson and Shakespeare with traces of the nineteenth-century Romantics thrown in.

How disconcerting that could (and can) be is not hard to imagine! Disconcerting even for Goethe himself…Having presented *The Sorrows of Young Werther* as a possible state of affairs, he found that it was being taken as a desirable state of affairs and the young men of Europe were copying not only the hero's dress but also his suicide. As for *Wilhelm Meister's Apprenticeship*: studded with aphorisms and emblems, the book seems to throb with 'meaning', yet the author said of it, 'I should think a rich manifold life, brought close to our eyes, would be enough without any express tendency, which, after all, is only for the intellect.' *Only* for the intellect! Johnson declared 'Great thoughts are always general.' But characters and events in plays and novels need to be particular. And therein lies the weakness of Goethe's other novel, *Elective Affinities*: its events are signs and portents or (as we say with a grimace) symbols, while its characters too obviously stand for general types of humanity or states of mind and heart.

Elective Affinities is bound to strike us as artificial, programmatic and deliberately manipulated. When the married couple, Eduard and Charlotte, have a baby, it resembles the two other people they were thinking of at the time, and the good old parson dies of some symbolic shock to the religious system while baptizing it. Despite which, the novel is a work of considerable power and originality. In the process referred to in its title chemical elements can separate and remarry in differing combinations with ease; but not so men and women. The story ends neither in old-fashioned renunciation nor in modern divorce, but in a stalemate resolved only in death, if then. Ottilie, the other woman, accidentally drowns the beloved baby and starves herself to death, re-emerging as a kind of saint with healing powers (not unlike Gretchen in *Faust*), while Eduard dies soon after and is buried by his wife beside Ottilie. The moral is thus 'open-ended', and the conclusion neither happy nor exactly tragic. Goethe said that his nature was too conciliating for tragedy, but here he found no way of reconciling passion and conscience – or, more accurately, love and love.

Even more unsatisfactory to those who don't like theology but prefer it straight will be the ending of *Faust*, whose protagonist evades hell through the combination of a legal technicality and the intercession of a good (and dead) woman's love. But the ambiguity sets in much earlier, and persists through the play's transitions – from an ageing don's discontent with his studies and his bank balance alike, by way of a rather shabby affair with a lower-class innocent, to financial shenanigans at the Imperial Court, a protracted idyll with Helen in Sparta (judging by the resulting offspring, both parties were thinking of Byron at the time), and a final career in German real estate. Such is a possible summary of the story: it mentions neither the passages of sublime poetry nor the shrewd hits and humour that occur *en route*. It also leaves out Mephistopheles, the one totally translatable element here, relatively immune (it would seem) to change in times and manners. Nor of course does it throw light on the fact that, impossible though *Faust* is, it is impossible to imagine European culture without it.

A notable stumbling-block for many readers is the episode towards the end when Faust, busy reclaiming land from the sea and 'opening space for millions', is responsible for the death of the old couple whose cottage is a thorn in his side. In this civic project he has needed the assistance of Mephistopheles – who, as the Lord remarked at the outset, 'excites and works and must, though devil, create' – and the devil will have his due, always striving to turn good into evil. Neither Goethe nor Faust (though he behaves like Henry II in the matter of Becket) condones the fate of the old couple, and it is not their fault that more recent events give the incident a darker dimension. When Goethe is sentimental, we turn away in disgust; when he is realistic (allowing the world what the world will take anyway), we grow indignant. He seeks unity within diversity, an ambition which affronts us somewhat; but then, and with his connivance, the diversity looms larger than the unity, and this in turn confuses us.

A more modest example of the author's versatility, or his shapelessness, is the *Roman Elegies*, a sequence of poems in classical distichs, in which a cultivated and vigorous German tourist, lightly disguised as Propertius, experiences several kinds of awakening. The *Elegies* used to be thought shocking, and two of them were long suppressed. While nowadays they will be found sexually innocuous, if a trifle male-chauvinistic, they still ought to shake the British myth of Goethe as the serene or pompous Olympian. In subject and tone they comprehend tenderness, sensuality, humour, the joys of classical art, ambience and history at the fingertips (followed by further exploration in bed with a mistress, called Faustina by the way), the all-too-human antics of the gods, the ferocity of Amor attached to his prey, the smug domesticity of a settled liaison (how pleasant to have a girl you can trust!). And also a discourse (unanticipated but not incongruous) on the treacherous worm in the grass of venereal disease; in David Luke's translation,

> Secretly there in the bushes he squirms, befouling the waters,
>   Slavering poison and death into Love's life-giving dew.

It is alarming or at the very least discomposing to find oneself plunged into such a rich mixture of matter and modes. And in this respect the *Roman Elegies* are characteristic. It appears that many-sidedness on the Goethean scale is no longer possible, and these days we are required to possess specialist qualifications. What the great German lacked was discretion: he failed to conceal his belief that the world was his oyster. As indeed it practically was.

The Brothers Mann

In this dual biography Nigel Hamilton has undertaken to do something so intimidating as to be virtually impossible; it is not surprising that he has not been entirely successful. When their subject has led a life long in years and rich in achievement, biographers (at any rate biographers of the more reputable kind) often end by losing the life-line under a mass of creases and folds. There is so much to tell, and it gets told whether or not it adds to our sense of the man: but if it doesn't add, it subtracts. Mr Hamilton has taken on two long parallel lives, and he deserves a medal for outstanding bravery in the face of heavy material odds.

Thomas Mann's life is pretty well covered, in English too: there are the monumental *Letters*, the early *Sketch of My Life* and the late *Genesis of a Novel*, the memoirs by Erika Mann and Katia Mann. But Heinrich's life, like his work, is practically unknown here, and Hamilton has done much to rectify this imbalance.

Rivalry between the two brothers evinced itself at an early stage: there is a trivial but bitter tale here about Heinrich's broken toy violin. The elder by four years, Heinrich soon rebelled against the pompous materialism of mercantile Lübeck, and in the obvious way: he began to write, publishing his first poem at the age of nineteen in a 'radically modern' magazine dedicated to Zola and the new realism. This was in the very year, 1890, when the firm of J.S. Mann celebrated its centenary. Thomas started to write poetry too, and later published his first poem in the same magazine. In 1891 their father the Senator died, plagued by business worries and two unsuitable sons, these latter left to the care of their suitably artistic, partly Portuguese-Creole mother (who paid for the publication of Heinrich's first novel). In 1904 Heinrich remarked, with his brother's first (and acclaimed) novel, *Buddenbrooks*, in mind: 'After having been Hanseatic merchants for two thick volumes, with the help of Latin blood we finally got to Art – according to Nietzsche this always produces nervous disorders and artists.'

Describing the brothers' different reactions to their sister Julia's marriage to a Munich banker, Heinrich opposing and Thomas accepting, Hamilton comments, 'In the isolated, unyielding pride of Heinrich and the ironic, compromising nature of Thomas one can already trace the pattern of their latent conflicts.' Mutual sniping apropos of their literary productions there had already been, as if each brother defined himself – Thomas more obviously – by reaction against the other. In a letter of 1904 Thomas questioned Heinrich's liberalism: 'I understand little about so-called freedom… The great works of Russian literature were written under enormous oppression, weren't they? Would they have been produced without this oppression?' (One of those abiding hard questions.) By now Heinrich was resolutely democratic, socialist, European. Thomas was none of these, yet neither was he exactly the opposite. While his fiction often invoked extreme situations – how could *Doctor Faustus* be exceeded in that respect? – the author himself never runs to extremes. A few months later he was writing thus to Katia Pringsheim in courtship: 'I am quite conscious of not being the sort of man to arouse plain and uncomplicated feelings… To prompt mixed emotions, perplexity, is after all, if you will forgive me, a sign of personality.'

The rift between the brothers reached its widest with the Great War, which Heinrich abhorred and Thomas supported. Indeed, Heinrich with his essay on Zola, attacking nationalism, and Thomas with his *Reflections of a Non-Political Man*, a defence of irony, demurring pessimism, privacy against *bien-pensant* politics, appeared to be fighting a civil war of their own, progressive idealist versus conservative sceptic. The *Reflections* is a document of large and lasting pertinence, and a much subtler account of it is given by Erich Heller in his study, *The Ironic German*: the feud at the heart of the work is not so much a quarrel between brothers, barely concealed though this is, as 'an interior dialogue between the Germanically traditional two souls in the one breast'. Thomas had said much the same in a letter of 1919 written to someone who praised the *Reflections* at his brother's expense: 'As a critic you have the right to do so, but this is neither the intention nor the meaning of the book, and the antithesis itself strikes me as too important and symbolic for me really to welcome the intrusion of this question of rank and worth.' We can hardly not think of the symbolic antithesis of Naphta and Settembrini in *The Magic Mountain*. That it was the Heinrich-like Settembrini who survived suggests that if extremes were to be run to – as is often the case with antitheses and symbols – then Thomas considered Settembrini's extremes at least preferable to Naphta's.

Postwar developments brought the brothers together. Thomas soon saw where nationalism was leading, while Heinrich was forced to witness the failure of the Republic. Both of them went into exile within three weeks of Hitler's appointment as Chancellor of Germany, Heinrich (who was in more immediate danger) as 'national vermin', Thomas as guilty of 'pacifistic excesses' and 'intellectual high treason' – for instance, by proposing that while Wagner's art was national, its nationalism was soaked in the currents of European art. Thomas had become the '*Zivilisationsliterat*' he had once attacked in the person of his brother.

No one would presume to pity Thomas Mann, but Heinrich's is a saddening story. His greatest worldly success derived from the filming of his satirical novel, *Professor Unrat* (first published in 1905), as 'a dazzlingly perverse celluloid love-story' called *The Blue Angel*. The film was released in April 1930, shortly after Thomas had received the Nobel Prize. There was some irony in that too, for the prize was for *Buddenbrooks* (1901) rather than the more recent and (from the Swedish Academy's point of view) somewhat 'perverse' novel, *The Magic Mountain*. Moreover, while Thomas, the expert in mixed emotions, had married an apparently spoilt rich girl and made one of the most successful matches on record, the straightforward Heinrich's first marriage foundered and friends saw in his second a painful resemblance to the relationship portrayed in *The Blue Angel* by Emil Jannings and Marlene Dietrich. His second wife committed suicide on her fifth attempt. When the English translation of *Professor Unrat* came out in 1931 it was of course called *The Blue Angel*; and when the original was reissued in 1947 Heinrich had to agree to the title, *Der blaue Engel*.

The rest of the story is mainly Thomas's and reasonably well known: although in exile he met with private distresses and public tribulations, he achieved literary and financial success. Heinrich failed in both spheres. He died in 1950, in Los Angeles, while preparing to move to Berlin as President of the East German Academy of Arts – Thomas had recently visited East Germany and felt that the respect Heinrich would be accorded there was preferable to his American obscurity. Himself accused of pro-Communist sympathies and alarmed by the seeming collapse of democracy in the United States, Thomas left California for a second exile in Switzerland, and died there in 1955. His final summing-up of the fraternal situation was not merely pious: 'The stupid Germans are always squabbling over which one of us is really the greater; but the "really" great one would be the one nature would have made had she taken from us both.'

Erich Heller has doubted the possibility of writing Thomas Mann's 'Life' except by writing about his writings, since for him living and writing were virtually identical activities. What little discussion of the brothers' literary work is found in the present book, otherwise minutely documented, is superficial or lame. It is possible that the spirit of fraternity communicated itself to the biographer, inhibiting him from any sharp indication of Thomas's superiority as a writer, in both lucidity and complexity, over Heinrich. The opposite of the self-flaunting practitioner, Nigel Hamilton comes rather too close to complete invisibility.

Thomas Mann: The Making of an Artist, 1875–1911

The difficulty that any biographer of Thomas Mann faces is that the subject has already supplied an autobiography, in the form of the memoirs mentioned earlier and pre-eminently in his fiction – and in language more powerful, complex and telling than anyone else is likely to bring to bear. Little is left for biographers to do except stitch together the pieces, most genuinely self-revealing when seemingly self-concealing.

In an Afterword to her husband's book Clara Winston speaks of the 'startling discovery' he made when working on his introduction to their admirable English translation of the selected *Letters*. A new Thomas Mann emerged. Readers and critics had taken Aschenbach of *Death in Venice* and Leverkühn of *Doctor Faustus* and their coldness, their aloofness from the human condition, as self-portraits. Instead, it was now seen that Mann's personal history 'had all the elements of a great novel'. I am loath to quarrel with the Winstons, but who supposed that Mann was really a cold fish? To begin with, who can believe that Aschenbach and Leverkühn, despite the drain their art has imposed on 'ordinary life', are frigid, unfeeling, contentedly detached? Only somebody constitutionally incapable of reading could miss the pain that suffuses Leverkühn. We do not assume that a writer who is forever throwing himself or his words into orgasmic spasms is truly in touch with cosmic vitality. Conversely, we should not assume that ordered waters cannot run deep. As for the 'great novel' – in the first place that would need to *be* a novel, and Mann, who wrote several great novels, would hardly be gratified to find his life passed off as a rival to them.

But reason not the need for a biography. It may attract new readers to what matters about Mann, and it is a compliment to observe that in reading this partial biography (whose author died in 1979) one cannot always tell where *Buddenbrooks*, say, ends and Richard Winston's commentary begins: he quotes so well, orders the material firmly and writes lucidly. It is not that Mann had no life, as that term is generally understood, but that his was a writer's life, a life not to be separated out from the work, and impoverished to the point of insignificance if it were.

Quite properly, much is said here about the family background (Hanseatic merchant-princes leavened or tainted by a taste for the arts) and, again, Thomas's relationship with Heinrich. Heinrich emerges with credit – a younger brother is more susceptible to envy and the wish to go one better, or one different – and was the greatest single stimulus for Thomas in these early years. At school Thomas did poorly, managing to scrape a school-leaving certificate with 'barely satisfactory' in all subjects excepting Conduct, in which his one grade of 'good' was crossed out in favour of 'on the whole good'.

The family having moved from Lübeck to Munich, Thomas went to work as an unpaid apprentice in the South German Insurance Bank for six months; a year, says Mann in *A Sketch of My Life*, when describing the snuff-taking clerks and the sloping desk at which he secretly wrote his first story. Thereafter he registered as an auditor at the University: he could thus be a student without the nuisance of examinations. At an early stage the ability showed itself to work up a subject for literary purposes (musical techniques, syphilis, in *Doctor Faustus*: 'concrete reality, exactitude, were needed') through research or the soliciting of advice – and the ability, too, to forget it all, once used. Likewise his habit, often to get him into hot water despite his insistence that he 'exposed' himself far more than he exposed others, of introducing bits and pieces of real people and actual happenings into his fiction. Identity lists were drawn up in Lübeck after the appearance of *Buddenbrooks*, and Mann's conception of the artist as swindler (*Tonio Kröger*, *Felix Krull*) is amusingly linked with his detention as a suspected con man while visiting his native city in 1899.

In connection with his Jewish schoolmates Winston comments at length on Mann's attitude towards the Jews. Mixed they were: after all, not all Jews are one Jew. Some of his most savage critics were Jewish, so were his publisher and some of his most ardent admirers. The predilection was there early on, for what he later called 'an adventurous and hedonistic note…a picturesque fact calculated to increase the colourfulness of the world', and in particular lighten the greyness of bourgeois Lübeck and his own strain of melancholy. Jewishness was 'romance' – to the extent that he married into a Jewish family (there is a charming account of the courtship of Katia Pringsheim here), and promptly fell into embarrassment over his new and 'anti-Semitic' story, 'The Blood of the Walsungs'. In short, 'though not otherwise richly blessed with wholly unequivocal convictions', he rightly considered himself 'a convinced and unequivocal "philo-Semite"', fearing only that a Zionist exodus would enfeeble Europe.

And so the story, though not a 'great novel', moves busily through the hero's connection with the magazine *Simplicissimus*; the composition and reception of *Buddenbrooks* (the publisher wanted it cut by half but finally capitulated, offering a royalty of twenty per cent without an advance); friendships with Jakob Wassermann (later to write *Caspar Hauser*), the novelist Kurt Martens ('he belonged to the few people – I could count them on the fingers of one hand – whom I ever addressed as "*du*"'), and his publisher Samuel Fischer; in 1905 a 'fairy-tale' marriage for love which happened to bring money; research into court protocol for the novel, *Royal Highness* ('the first fruit of my married state,' Mann wrote in *A Sketch of My Life*, and 'an attempt to come to terms, as a writer, with my own happiness': critics found it 'too light'); the births of his children; the 'opera-plot' suicide of his unhappy sister Carla, a three-weeks' stay with Katia in a sanatorium at Davos (later to surface in the shape of *The Magic Mountain*); and finally the writing of *Death in Venice*.

Death in Venice, Clara Winston says, 'was the place to deal with a delicate, perhaps crucial, biographical question' which was 'like so much else in Thomas Mann's life, ambiguous'. It would seem that this delicate question concerned Mann's possible homosexual inclinations. The subject is first raised in connection with his close, even fervid, attachment to Paul Ehrenberg, a young painter and musician, around 1900. At the same time, while visiting his brother in Florence, he enjoyed a tender interlude with an English girl, Mary Smith, and there was some 'talk of marriage'. In 1910, at the age of thirty-five, he made friends with Ernst Bertram, twenty-seven years old and a teacher at Bonn University, engaged on a book on Nietzsche and composing poems in the manner of Stefan George. Mann found Bertram a highly congenial intellectual companion. Beyond that, one guess is as good as another; and none is worth much. *Reflections of a Non-Political Man* owed something to its author's correspondence with 'Dear Herr Doktor' Bertram, who incidentally was to lose his chair at Cologne in the course of denazification in 1946. However, the isolated remark in Mann's diary for 1919 to the effect that the *Reflections* was an expression 'of my sexual inversion' remains merely cryptic.

It is plain that homosexuality, a powerful manifestation of Eros, interested him deeply as a novelist and also (if we are to preserve the distinction) as a man; in a lecture on the homosexual poet Platen he adduced Nietzsche's words: 'The degree and kind of man's sexuality permeate the very loftiest heights of his intellect.' I suppose Thomas Mann could be said to be shifty, even in his very loftiest heights – in the sense that he was given to changing positions, shifting from one mode of experience to another. To talk of 'masks' in this connection is misleading, for the word suggests a procession of deliberate disguises, visors and veils held up across the face, rather than a diversity of natural expressions, expressions of feeling. Behind that stiff exterior – it needed to be stiff – danced a chameleon novelist.

(1983; 1982)

The Anti-diabolic Faith:
Thomas Mann's Doctor Faustus

The best introduction to *Doctor Faustus, The Life of the German Composer, Adrian Leverkühn, as told by a friend*, is the genuinely informative blurb on the dust-cover of the English translation:

> This novel, which has as its narrative framework a modern version of the Faust legend, is the entire life-story of a great creative musician – Adrian Leverkühn (1885–1940). It is told by his lifelong friend, Serenus Zeitblom, Ph.D.... A theological student turned composer, Leverkühn symbolically enters into a pact with the Devil (who is represented in part by an exhilarating, but wasting, disease). He sells his soul and body in return for twenty-four years of musical genius... Scarcely secondary in interest to Leverkühn himself is the narrator, Zeitblom, a scrupulous, learned, scholarly, shocked man who tells much against his will, almost by inadvertence... Through Mann's sovereign handling of his astonishing materials, *Doctor Faustus* achieves a many-layered credibility. The wonderful and terrible career of Adrian Leverkühn – including the gestation, actual writing, and inner nature of his chief compositions – is therefore thoroughly engaging as a narrative and symbolic of the purposes and dilemmas of twentieth-century man.

The most striking peculiarity of *Doctor Faustus* is its multi-stratification. It is precisely this that makes the novel so difficult to talk about. One's commentary also needs to be many-layered, and there are so many things to say about the work that, in the end, the critic will probably fail to convey the very aspect which he has set out to stress: its unity, the astounding skill with which Thomas Mann has finally merged his 'layers' one into the other in such a way that, at the time of reading, one is hardly aware of any stratification and the tragical history seems at once and without question both personal and public. The reader is only conscious of the work's steady penetrating movement: wheel engages smoothly with wheel. It is the critic's job to point to the intricate hidden system of gearing and to trace from that the various speeds within the one movement. Added to this success of unity – a success all the more astonishing when analysis has disclosed what immense amounts of energy are being released on each plane – is the success of 'credibility'. The story, in spite of everything, is dreadfully credible: quite as credible as, say, Fielding's misadventures in India or the Ramsays' trip to the lighthouse. It is true that from time to time Mann has indulged himself in a fairy story or a little allegory; but *Buddenbrooks*, published when he was twenty-five, demonstrates his sense of actuality, his early grounding in the ways of the 'realistic' novel; and this education, this quality of mind, has stood him in good stead in his later dealings with the Devil. It takes a sound realist to make a convincing symbolist.

Mann has been influenced by a number of distinguished German artists and thinkers – among them, Schopenhauer, Nietzsche, Wagner and Freud – but it is Goethe to whom he owes the greatest debt; not the borrowing of a thought here and there, but a whole cast of mind, shown most notably in a sense of balance, a remarkable spiritual poise. The sense of balance, I mean, which preserved Hans Castorp safe and sound on the perilous peaks of the Magic Mountain and which enabled the author of *Death in Venice* to describe the downfall of Gustav Aschenbach from the very position, on the brink of the abyss, from which the moral avalanche swept away that respectable man of letters. Other manifestations come to mind: the capacity to examine perversion and then to report on it with a clean tongue (unlike Dr Krokowski of *The Magic Mountain*); to sympathize with disease without exhorting to it; to commend the healthy spirit without evading the difficulty of defining that adjective; to be an artist among the bourgeoisie and then, with an agile twist, a bourgeois among the artists; to show himself, in the same moment, a thorough German and a good European; to plunge into a cloud of metaphysical speculations and then to emerge as dry and precise as ever, bearing one or two clear and very human perceptions. All this is what we mean by the name 'Goethe' – or would mean, if we still read him. Mann's *Doctor Faustus* was certainly the greatest contribution, both in itself and as tribute, to the Goethe Bi-Centennial celebrations of 1949.

The present treatment of the novel falls into four sections: the character of Zeitblom; the character of Leverkühn; the character of Leverkühn's disease; and the character of art and of the artist.

In his *History of the German Novelle*, E.K. Bennett states that

> Thomas Mann's work as a creative writer was already done in *Buddenbrooks*, and the characters which he presents in his later works are merely carriers of ideas, representatives of attitudes of mind and points of view. This is particularly true of *Der Zauberberg* which, with all its intellectual, critical and philosophical richness, does not contain a single living being. Even Peeperkorn is an idea and not a person of flesh and blood.

Not even the literary historian's urge to classify fictional characters under such headings as 'realistic' or 'symbolic' can excuse so rash a statement; though Mr Bennett might be ready to modify his comments (which were made in 1934) in the light of what has followed.

There is admittedly a great deal of discussion of ideas as such between the various characters of *The Magic Mountain*, but it is the special distinction of the novel that the expressed idea always fits the character who voices it, that the idea is used to create a character at the same time as the character serves to expound (and more, to define) an idea. To me *The Magic Mountain* doesn't mean a set of diverse points of view: it means Settembrini and Naphta and Peeperkorn and Clavdia Chauchat and a host of minor figures, among them such unintellectual creatures as Frau Stöhr, whose brightest idea is that the 'Erotica' ought to be played at the graveside of the courageous Joachim. Let the reader who has not looked at *The Magic Mountain* for some time try to remember what ideas and attitudes of mind and points of view are embodied in that novel. I am sure that he will first think of the finely substantial personages I have named and then, by a process of deduction, re-create the ideas and attitudes. There is something of Dickens, even, or Tolstoy in Mann's ability to create character by the repeated gesture or the accumulated detail, by the typical response to situation or the half-spoken sentence. This 'realism' of his – if we must use the word – this characteristic of the novelist in the grand style, is part of what preserves him from becoming the kind of novelist Mr Bennett has described. Mann's work in fiction is full of flesh and blood, it by no means suffers from anaemia of the pernicious idea; *that* diagnosis is true enough of some of the more intelligent English novelists, but there is really no point of contact between a novel by Mann and a novel by (for example) Aldous Huxley.

Zeitblom, the narrator of *Doctor Faustus*, the 'friend' of the title-page, is an admirable piece of work; and no doubt some future commentator will indulge in the paradox that it is he, really, who is the hero of the novel. But he is scarcely a hero; he is the Chorus in this tragedy (and the Messenger as well); he is a civilized German scholar of the nineteenth century mould; he is an unwilling straw on the flood of history; and musically he is the symbol of the 'good listener'. And if he, rather than Leverkühn, seems to be the hero of the book, it is because he is full of good meaty nineteenth-century character, though quite devoid of greatness, while Leverkühn, though a great artist, fails to convey much more impression of 'character' than would be given by a highly intellectual and ironic gnome. But that is quite deliberate, and not a deficiency in creativeness; it is a state of affairs which we might have deduced from the early thumbnail sketch of the artist in Tonio Kröger.

Here is Serenus Zeitblom, Ph.D. – he will do his best, against heavy odds, to live up to his name:

> I am by nature wholly moderate, of a temper, I may say, both healthy and humane, addressed to reason and harmony; a scholar and *conjuratus* of the 'Latin host', not lacking all contact with the arts (I play the viola d'amore)…

Quite something of a character already. And for the time being the picture is completed in a few further sentences which remind us of both Settembrini and Aschenbach:

> the daemonic, little as I presume to deny its influence upon human life, I have at all times found utterly foreign to my nature. Instinctively I have rejected it from my picture of the cosmos and never felt the slightest inclination rashly to open the door to the powers of darkness: arrogantly to challenge, or if they of themselves ventured from their side, even to hold out my little finger to them… But my self-satisfaction or, if you prefer, my ethical narrow-mindedness can only strengthen my doubt whether I may feel myself truly called to my present task.

Like Coleridge's Ancient Mariner, Zeitblom must tell his story, but throughout he protests against the duty which fate has so cruelly laid upon him. The tale, in a tradition 'altogether foreign to the blitheness of classical culture' (a phrase which recalls the beginning of Castorp's vision in the 'Snow' chapter of *The Magic Mountain*), is told slowly and painstakingly and always against the better feelings of this good old humanist. He is of course exactly the right man for the task: no one can tell a ghost story as well as the person who has seen too much of ghosts either to disbelieve in them or to approve of them. The reluctant Zeitblom is as aptly cast for his role as was Castorp, the colourless hero of *The Magic Mountain*, or Wilhelm Meister, the 'milksop' hero of Goethe's novel.

If Zeitblom looms larger than his subject, Adrian Leverkühn, it is not only on account of this question of character, but also because it is through him that we pass from one layer of meaning to another: it is he who so to speak is the gearbox of this great machine. In addition to the tragic life of his friend (which comprises the top layer of significance), it necessarily happens that we see the minor characters through Zeitblom's eyes (and at the same time we see him through theirs), while furthermore the aspect of the novel as a study of German character and history is revealed to us directly through Zeitblom's mind – appropriately enough, since in many ways he is a typical German of a celebrated kind, 'Gymnasialprofessor…Dozent an der theologischen Hochschule', a 'good German', to use the language of yesterday.

But the story of Germany and the story of Leverkühn are not, ultimately, separate things; the former is not the background to the latter, or vice versa. And to say that the story of the gifted tragic composer is an allegory of the fate of modern Germany, that his greatness is symbolic of hers, his sin of hers, his end of hers: this is to reduce the novelist's delicate perspicacity to the commentator's clumsiness. But the commentator must bear his responsibilities, shameful though they sometimes are, and at least the clumsiness is here patent enough and wholly unseductive. We notice firstly this passage in the *Epilogue*, purportedly written by Zeitblom after the fall of Germany:

> Germany herself, the unhappy nation, is strange to me, utterly strange and that because, convinced of her awful end, I drew back from her sins and hid from them in my seclusion. Must I not ask myself whether or not I did right? And again: did I actually do it? I have clung to one man, one suffering, significant human being, clung unto death; and I have depicted his life, which never ceased to fill me with love and grief. To me it seems as though this loyalty might atone for my having fled in horror from my country's guilt.

And then, following the account of Leverkühn's funeral, the paragraph with which the novel ends:

> Germany, the hectic on her cheek, was reeling then at the height of her dissolute triumphs, about to gain the whole world by virtue of the one pact she was minded to keep, which she had signed with her blood. Today, clung round by demons, a hand over one eye, with the other staring into horrors, down she flings from despair to despair. When will she reach the bottom of the abyss? When, out of uttermost hopelessness – a miracle beyond the power of belief – will the light of hope dawn? A lonely man folds his hands and speaks: 'God be merciful to thy poor soul, my friend, my Fatherland!'

Quite apart from the mention of the pact which Germany 'had signed with her blood', the grouping together and the tentative identification of Leverkühn and Germany in the last sentence cannot be missed:

'Gott sei euerer armen Seele gnädig, mein Freund, mein Vaterland.'
Even so, I do not think there would be any profit in reading back
through the book to check up on the implied parallel.

The first of these two quoted passages may suggest, perhaps, a
further identification: Mann identifies himself with Zeitblom occasionally, though only when it serves his purposes and no longer than
that. A good European as he is, Mann knows how much he owes to
the distinguished intellectual traditions of Germany, for more than
any other living author in our time he has embodied them and
preserved them. However much Mann may elsewhere smile at his Dr
Zeitblom, I do not think it was with any irony that he put these words
in that honest mouth:

> If it be true, as we say in Germany, that every way to the right goal
> must also be right in each of its parts, then it will be agreed that the
> way that led to this sinful issue – I use the word in its strictest, most
> religious sense – was everywhere wrong and fatal, at every single
> one of its turns, however bitter it may be for love to consent to such
> logic. To recognize because we must our infamy is not the same
> thing as to deny our love. I, a simple German man and scholar, have
> loved much that is German.

'Ich … habe veil Deutsches geliebt.' With such diverse emotions and
attitudes behind the creation of Zeitblom, states of mind ranging from
an impersonal mischievous irony to a strong emotional identification,
it is all the more striking that Zeitblom should emerge as so smooth,
rounded and consistent a piece of characterization.

Adrian Leverkühn is a musical genius – and Mann's conception of
genius is in the best sense technical, it has little in common with the
artist-hero of popular fiction – but he is not really a 'character', not in
the sense that Zeitblom obviously is. Taciturn, shy (or contemptuous)
of ordinary social life, ironical throughout, and sometimes a little
unkind to his faithful Zeitblom, he is far from sympathetic as we see
him through the eyes of his other friends. In that aspect he appears as
genius rather than human being. His failure in this latter capacity is
most plainly shown in his short and disastrous career as lover: the vain
and rather trivial Schwerdtfeger steals the girl, Marie Godeau, from
under Leverkühn's nose. In the terms of the pact, as the Devil puts it,
'Love is forbidden you, in so far as it warms. Thy life shall be cold,
therefore thou shalt love no human being.' And Leverkühn's one
requited love, for his little nephew Nepomuk, ends in the shocking
death of the beloved. Indeed it might prove rather difficult to account

for Zeitblom's close and loyal attachment to him, for it is much more than an impersonal academic respect. In symbolic terms their relationship is easily explicable, however; it is that between the cultivated audience and the original genius: what the former gives is a loving admiration mixed with a certain lack of comprehension and a firm determination not to interfere, while what the latter demands, in a spirit of detached mockery, is a fair degree of understanding, a good deal of patience, and the fact of 'being there in case of need'.

But then there comes the other aspect of Adrian Leverkühn: the human being as it emerges during the almost intolerably painful 'Last Supper', when the twenty-four years of genius-life have come to an end ('Zeit hast du von uns genommen, geniale Zeit, hochtragende Zeit, volle vierundzwanzig Jahr ab dato recessi, die setzen wir dir zum Ziel'). We have been prepared for this unimaginable eventuality by the revelation in Chapter XXV of the pact which Leverkühn has made with the Devil ... or, of course, the pact which Leverkühn fancies himself to have made (in that case betraying early signs of mental instability) ... or, of course, the allegory which Leverkühn has composed in bitter celebration of his absolute dedication to a relentlessly exacting art and his consequent withdrawal from normal human life – a process like that which Rilke to some extent underwent, of accepting art and rejecting life – here represented as a sinister compact which carries fearful danger for him who enters into it...

This is the moment to consider the episode of the pact. In return for his twenty-four years of agonizing productivity Leverkühn (it seems) has resigned his soul to Hell. In an extremely powerful passage the Devil tells him what he can expect:

One must just be satisfied with symbolism, my good man, when one is speaking of hell, for there everything ends – not only the word that describes, but everything altogether... 'here everything leaves off'. Every compassion, every grace, every sparing, every last trace of consideration for the incredulous, imploring objection 'that you verily cannot do so unto a soul': it is done, it happens, and indeed without being called to any reckoning in words; in soundless cellar, far down beneath God's hearing, and happens to all eternity ... no man can hear his own tune, for that it smothers in the general, in the thick-clotted diapason of trills and chirps lured from this everlasting dispensation of the unbelievable combined with the irresponsible. Nothing forgetting the dismal groans of lust mixted therewith; since endless torment, with no possible collapse, no swoon to put a period thereto, degenerates into shameful pleasure, wherefore such as have some intuitive knowledge speak indeed of the 'lusts of hell'...

Leverkühn asks for more information about 'what objectively and in fact must await the damned', and, after a little lecture on the distinction between *attritio* and *contritio*, his visitor replies,

> to your reassurance be it said, even hell will not afford you aught essentially new, only the more or less accustomed, and proudly so. It is at bottom only a continuation of the extravagant existence. To knit up in two words its quintessence, or if you like its chief matter, is that it leaves its denizens only the choice between extreme cold and an extreme heat which can melt granite. Between these two states they flee roaring to and fro, for in the one the other always seems heavenly refreshment but is at once and in the most hellish meaning of the word intolerable. The extreme in this must please you.

It is a fairly orthodox representation, but not unsubtle; and certainly more dreadful than the sophisticated underworld of Sartre's *Huis Clos*. And the Devil's account is susceptible of at least three interpretations: firstly, it can indeed be Hell that he is talking about; secondly, it can be a frightening description of madness, the madness which a life of tense creative effort may end in ('hell will not afford you aught essentially new... It is at bottom only a continuation of the extravagant existence'); thirdly, it can be read (in part at least) as a shocking description of the Nazi concentration camps, the madness of Germany.

Thus Chapter XXV, however we take it, has been a preparation for the moment when Leverkühn must discharge his debt; but it is not the kind of preparation that will soften the blow. The 'human' Adrian Leverkühn emerges only as the struggle between sanity and madness reaches its crisis, only in those few minutes before his mind collapses. It is a bitter thought for us to dwell on, but the hopelessly mad Leverkühn, 'creeping back broken to his mother's arms', is 'human', sympathetic, almost lovable, where the sane Leverkühn, the brilliant composer, was inhuman, antipathetic, and wellnigh hateful in his sinister ability. The crisis itself, the 'Last Supper' – for undoubtedly Leverkühn is to be seen as martyr as well as sinner – the frightful murmurings in Lutheran German of the musician, the uncomprehending, disapproving and rapidly disappearing audience, and then Leverkühn's paralytic stroke as he plays the first chords of his *Lamentation of Dr Faustus*: all this is only bearable, perhaps, because it has happened instead of something which would have been still less bearable. The appearance of the Devil himself, I mean, in flesh and blood or in sulphur and flames. For Mann has by now so firmly captured his reader that the latter cannot take shelter in time behind any of his normal beliefs or disbeliefs. The Devil comes and goes unseen; and we take refuge in Zeitblom's great grief for his friend, for this is something 'natural' and 'human', something that we are used to and can understand.

Leverkühn, human or otherwise, will remind the reader of various literary and artistic figures, in respect of both life and work. Mann acknowledges his debt in musical theory to Schönberg – who, it seems, lent himself very unwillingly – but this is the least striking of the similarities. The episode concerning the loyal lady admirer who offers Leverkühn her castle for a brief holiday but whom (by arrangement) he never meets, brings to mind both Tchaikovsky and Rilke. And these one might add to the list of resemblances already compiled by commentators. In a rather strange article entitled 'Nietzsche et le *Doktor Faustus* de Thomas Mann',[1] M. Maurice Colleville has enumerated with something stronger than distaste the many parallels between Leverkühn and Nietzsche: 'Il ne s'agit plus d'une influence de thèmes: C'est la vie même de Nietzsche que Thomas Mann a transposée dans l'existence du compositeur Adrian Leverkühn.' The chief similarities are these: both died at the age of fifty-five; both contracted syphilis which ended in madness, the progress of the disease being closely similar; both studied theology before turning in the one case to philosophy, in the other to music. The conception of inspiration which the Devil expounds during his interview with Leverkühn corresponds very closely to that given in *Also Sprach Zarathustra*. The young Nietzsche, on a visit to Cologne, engaged a dragoman to show him the sights; when asked to lead the way to a decent restaurant, the man took him to a brothel – precisely the same thing happens to Leverkühn in Leipzig, as recounted in the 'experience with the fatal porter', and the details of these unintended visits, comic in themselves but both tragic in their consequences, are also identical.

M. Colleville finds all this plagiarism not quite *comme il faut*; under great restraint he writes,

En bref, le *Doktor Faustus* fournit une fois de plus la preuve que, de tous les écrivains allemands de ce temps, son auteur est sans doute celui qui s'est le plus profondément assimilé la pensée de ses

1 *Etudes Germaniques*, Avril–Septembre 1948.

devanciers. Du passé récent ou lointain de la littérature de son pays, il a tiré la fleur de la culture dont il orne ses livres.

It is not the letter but the spirit of this judgment that is unjust. In the good sense of the word, Mann has always been a 'traditional' author, intimate with the great debates of his forebears – he derives much of his staying power, his ability to work in masses, from this fact – and as for the flowers which he has picked from other men's gardens, the way in which he has arranged them (an altogether personal way) gives him every right to be called an original author as well. One has more sympathy with the complaint of the reader brought up on a library-novel diet, that Mann is too original altogether.

A cogent answer to M. Colleville's scholarly if misguided attack has been made by Dr Hilde Zaloscer, who points out in (I believe) an unpublished manuscript that Mann nowhere makes the slightest effort to conceal his borrowings (the closeness of the Nietzschean parallels is itself a testimony of his innocence) and that there exist similarities almost as striking between his hero and two other famous Germans – Dürer (who died at the same age, of the same disease) and the composer Schumann. In fact, Dr Zaloscer sums up, 'Leverkühn est composé consciemment – comme une immense mosaïque – par des éléments appartenant aux figures tragiques des artistes damnés.' Exactly, and Mann's original genius is responsible for the merging together of these elements into the unified figure of his tragic hero; and, furthermore, in the merging of the completed Leverkühn among the other elements of the novel in such a manner that it is never submerged or distorted by, or in conflict with, the other preoccupations of the author.

In examining the structure of *Doctor Faustus* the critic can amuse himself by compiling a list of other possible tragic heroes: besides Leverkühn, the defeated artist, there is the defeat of art itself in a hostile world, there is Zeitblom, the defeated bourgeois scholar, there is the defeated figure of Germany (tragic in the way that Macbeth is, by the wastage of great possibilities and the misuse of great powers), and there is also the apparent defeat of modern civilization (Zeitblom looks in vain for the 'medicine of the sickly weal', the Malcolm who will purify and resuscitate his country). ... Under such circumstances it would be merely perverse to search out plagiarisms from reality, to try to split up the character of Leverkühn into one-quarter Nietzsche, one-quarter Schumann and so on. If one objects to Mann's peculiar dealings with actuality, then one will object to practically the whole of his work; and *Lotte in Weimar* and the *Joseph* novels must be dismissed without further ado as the impertinences of an unscrupulous crypto-biographer. Such an attitude calls to mind the good burghers of Lübeck, scandalized on the first appearance of *Buddenbrooks*.

One might smile at the phrase in the blurb – 'the Devil... is represented in part by an exhilarating, but wasting, disease' – as a nervous euphemism, were it not that the disease is never mentioned by name in the book either. The whole treatment of this delicate question is uncannily effective. The approach to the symptoms is by way of Andersen's story of the mermaid who fell in love with a human prince. The Devil first tells the story to Leverkühn, and the latter repeats it later on to Zeitblom at a time when he is suffering one of the periodic attacks of pain in and above his eyes which confine him to a darkened room. He jocularly likens his own pains to the knife-pains which the beautiful sea-maid must endure as the price of her new human legs, asking ironically whether after all it was worthwhile – wouldn't the prince, a rather trivial fellow, have loved her much more with her fish-tail? 'The sea-wife had a perfectly complete and charming organic reality, beauty and inevitability.' The allegory is simple enough: as an artist, Leverkühn has deliberately sacrificed his bodily and spiritual ease: he too walks upon knives of steel. His whimsical comments on the natural grace and aptness of the sea-maid's original form can be read as a wry reference to the healthy happiness of the ordinary citizen as compared with the seemingly gratuitous nature of the artist's sufferings: '...she became so pathetically déclassée after she had bought herself legs, which nobody thanked her for.' The knife-pains in the sea-maid's legs become the accepted symbol for the manifestations of Leverkühn's disease, and the symbol is interwoven as one motif among the other themes of the work.

The idea of using syphilis as the exponent for the disease whereby the creative artist often has to pay for his special insights was clearly a risky one, since this misfortune is more usually looked upon as the wages of something less noble. Consumption, it might be thought, would have been more tactful: it too is a sickness which is 'exhilarating, but wasting', it implies no dubious antecedents, it is the traditional artistic malady, and the author of *The Magic Mountain* would already be expert in its characteristics. But Mann chose syphilis, and he uses it magnificently: it at once dissociates Leverkühn from the novelette 'artist', it has that ambiguous flavour, both squalid and horrible, which consorts well with Mann's seedy yet sinister portrayal of the Devil, and the feeling that it might merely be the unlucky outcome of a sordid encounter is precluded by his skilful handling of the episode. Leverkühn's introduction to the brothel (the 'horrid kingdom of the sea-witch' where the mermaid acquires her legs) is comic and a little painful and quite chaste; and his later visit to his 'Hetaera Esmeralda' – with whom he insists on spending the night in spite of her warning – has the effect of a deliberate, cold-blooded act of self-immolation. As such, it is a preliminary to – or foreshadowing of – the formal pact with the Devil which is signed four years later.

The artist has always been to Mann a profoundly equivocal figure. But it must be added at once that, just as his sustained investigation of disease has been in the service of health, so his probing into the creative act and the mind of the artist has really been a preoccupation with life at the point where its problems are most acutely posed and most closely faced. Reference on this point to the short stories alone would provide matter for a substantial thesis, but here we need only mention Tonio Kröger, the 'artist with a bad conscience', the striking down of the 'strong' classical writer Aschenbach in *Death in Venice*, and Christian and Gerda Buddenbrook – the latter, in her husband's eyes, 'an artist, an individual, a puzzling, fascinating creature' – both of whom play a mysterious part in the fall of the House of Buddenbrook.[2] This old and continuous concern of Mann's is carried to a climax in *Doctor Faustus*. It comprises one of the book's most important 'layers'. And Mann has done better than merely discuss the question, as he did in several of his essays. In one of these, *Freud and the Future*, he remarks of Nietzsche,

> He will know what he owed to his morbid state, and on every page he seems to instruct us that there is no deeper knowledge without experience of disease, and that all heightened healthiness must be achieved by the route of illness.

The situation, Mann now seems to say, is not so simple as we used to suppose. What 'heightened healthiness' does Leverkühn achieve? His music is realized in the atmosphere of the sick-room, and the impression we get of it is not entirely encouraging. It is great music, but there is something dreadful about it – even the faithful Zeitblom, the good listener, regards it with a certain profound distrust. *The*

---

2 Dr Zaloscer points out that the apparition of the Devil at the beginning of the pact scene is prefigured in *Buddenbrooks* (Part Nine, Chapter II), where Christian demands of his brother, 'Perhaps it happens to you that you come into your room when it is getting dark and see a man sitting on the sofa, nodding at you, when there is no man there?'

Lamentation of Dr Faustus is the last and crowning work of Leverkühn's career, and Zeitblom takes the best part of a chapter in describing it:

> the *Lamentation* of the son of hell, the lament of men and God, issuing from the subjective, but always broadening out and as it were laying hold on the Cosmos; the most frightful lament ever set up on this earth.

He praises it in the highest terms: it is a vital work, he tells us, it is (he suggests less confidently) a work of liberation with tremendous significance for the future of music (and, on another plane, for the future of Germany, a Germany redeemed from damnation through the experience of hell). But it is obvious that what Zeitblom would desire in his heart, if only it were possible, is another Ninth Symphony – 'a hymn of exultation, a *Fidelio*, a Ninth Symphony, to celebrate the dawn of a freed Germany – freed by herself…' That it is not possible is made clear enough, for the *Lamentation* is 'as it were, the reverse of the "Ode to Joy", the negative, equally a work of genius, of that transition of the symphony into vocal jubilation. It is the revocation.' In it, as in Leverkühn's other music, Zeitblom finds to his dread 'the substantial identity of the most blest with the most accurst'. The work centres on a theme inspired by a certain passage of the text, in the *Oratio Fausti ad Studiosos*: 'For I die as a good and as a bad Christian'; that is perhaps, I must go to Hell for I have sold my soul to the Devil, yet I know what I have done, I am aware of sin. But, Zeitblom says, there is present in the work, faced and resisted, an inversion of the temptation of Christ –

> Faust rejects as temptation the thought of being saved: not only out of formal loyalty to the pact and because it is 'too late', but because with his whole soul he despises the positivism of the world for which one would save him, the lie of its godliness.

That it to say, as far as Leverkühn is concerned, there is to be no hint of a deathbed repentance. The musical work itself is entirely uncompromising: no angels appear to pelt Mephistopheles and his crew with flaming roses and snatch away the soul of this Faust. 'This dark tone-poem permits up to the very end no consolation, appeasement, transfiguration.' And yet, in spite of all he has said, at the very end of this appalling lament Zeitblom detects a ray of hope, 'ein Licht in der Nacht' – in technical language, 'the high G of a cello, the last word, the last fainting sound, slowly dying in a pianissimo-fermata'. Are we to see in this no more than Zeitblom's hopeful humanistic nature, his Goethean aversion to irreconcilable situations? I do not think it is only that. Yet certainly the hope is a difficult one, far more painful to accept than the fact of utter and passive despair.

'The route of illness' Mann has mapped out with disturbing clarity and detail, while the 'heightened healthiness' remains intangible, remote and problematical. Leverkühn has had his stroke, his acquaintances among the intelligentsia have left his chamber shocked and uncomprehending, and on the other temporal plane – as Zeitblom is nearing the point at which he can lay down his pen – the Allied armies are entering Germany's shattered towns. The experience of disease as Nietzsche knew it stands naked in the story of Adrian Leverkühn. But even Zeitblom, well equipped by nature and training to seek out the human usefulness of a thing, is hard pressed to squeeze any positive significance out of the 'deeper knowledge' which Leverkühn has presumably won for humanity. What remains with us is the possibility that Leverkühn's work *may* in some way mean a liberation of music: and, if it is that, it will be more than that. But one can only judge a liberation, of whatever kind, by its fruits. 'Free – for what?' The true value of Leverkühn's music can only emerge in the future...to slip on to another plane, the purgation by fire of the German nation will only show its full effects in the future.

But to return to the position of the artist as Mann sees it. It is now a good deal more perplexed than in the days of Tonio Kröger. In the course of the confession which he makes to his assembled friends when his last hour has come, Leverkühn says,

> it is the time when uprightly and in pious sober wise, naught of work is to be wrought and art grown unpossible without the divel's help and fires of hell under the cauldron....

These words are not to be taken as the babblings of a man already out of his mind, for they are the culmination of a series of comments and reflections on the position of the artist and the state of art in the twentieth century which have been passed by various people from the very beginning of the novel. Leverkühn has said similar things before, though coolly and ironically as was his wont, in a dispassionate tone of voice, as if he were a cotton broker remarking on the slackness of the market. Here, for instance, is Leverkühn as a schoolboy of fifteen, at the turn of the century:

> For a cultural epoch, there seems to me to be a spot too much talk about culture in ours, don't you think? I'd like to know whether epochs that possessed culture knew the word at all, or used it... Technique and comfort – in that state one talks about culture but one has not got it. Will you prevent me from seeing in the

homophone-melodic constitution of our music a condition of musical civilization – in contrast to the old contrapuntal polyphone culture?

And when the Devil appears to Leverkühn, he accuses the composer of losing his temper 'because I shewed you your despairing heart and set before your eyes with the expert's insight the difficulties absolutely inseparable from composition today':

> … it comes down to this, that his [the contemporary musician's] compositions are nothing more than… the solving of technical puzzles. Art becomes critique. That is something quite honourable, who denies it? Much rebellion in strict obedience is needed, much independence, much courage. But the danger of being uncreative – what do you think? Is it perhaps still only a danger, or is it already a fixed and settled fact?

There is a further implication. The moderate Zeitblom himself has remarked that 'genius is a form of vital power deeply experienced in illness, creating out of illness, through illness creative'. Thus the more difficult the period is for the artist, the deeper he must descend into disease to win a 'heightened healthiness' – in a sense he is the scapegoat for his civilization – and the likelier he is to succumb to disease, leaving behind him his treasure, at the best an ambiguous hoard. The extreme form of this idea is expressed by the Devil:

> … creative, genius-giving disease that rides on high horse over all hindrances, and springs with drunken daring from peak to peak, is a thousand times dearer to life than plodding healthiness. I have never heard anything stupider than that from disease only disease can come.…
>
> You will lead the way, you will strike up the march of the future, the lads will swear by your name, who thanks to your madness will no longer need to be mad. On your madness they will feed in health, and in them you will become healthy.

'Das sagt dir der unverballhornte Sammael.' And indeed only 'the venomous Angel' would seem the suitable mouth for the utterance of such a sentiment: 'The artist is the brother of the criminal and the madman.'

Even so, it is a sentiment that Mann has been working his way towards for some time. He came near to expressing it in the contentions of Naphta, the cynical anti-liberal of *The Magic Mountain*: 'the genius of disease is more human than the genius of health'. But in that novel the situation was resolved in a manner comparatively gentle and even genial: in contrast to Naphta we are given Settembrini the *encyclopédiste*, his stern opponent, who says firmly, 'Disease and despair are often only forms of depravity'. In the eventual duel Settembrini, progressive and optimist, fires his revolver into the air and offers his body (no doubt with a certain exaggerated nobility) to his rival. Naphta, the bitter authoritarian, cries 'Coward!' and shoots himself though the head. We feel that Mann only contrived to keep his sympathies, and ours, with Settembrini by an effort of will. But nevertheless we are relieved that Castorp, 'life's delicate child', has escaped from Naphta's dark influence and glad that Settembrini is left to say goodbye to him at the railway station.

From the very beginning of his career, and more clearly than is usual in the case of a major and fertile author, Mann's writings have been linked together; and the connections between *The Magic Mountain* and *Doctor Faustus* are such as to suggest that the earlier novel, with its wider scope and greater discursiveness, served to clear the ground in front of the special problems with which the later work comes more closely to grips. Thus Settembrini points the way to one theme of *Doctor Faustus* when he says, after praising art and literature as valuable aids to human advancement,

> There is something suspicious about music, gentlemen. I insist that she is, by her nature, equivocal. I shall not be going too far in saying at once that she is politically suspect.

For the Devil confirms this suspicion in his interview with the composer (and on this occasion we are not so ready with a superior smile):

> The Devil ought to know something about music ... the most Christian of all arts ... but Christian in reverse, as it were: introduced and developed by Christianity indeed, but then rejected and banned as the Divel's Kingdom – so there you are. A highly theological business, music – the way sin is, the way I am.

And Peeperkorn's remark that 'in the world of matter, all things were the vehicle of both life and death, all of them were medicinal and all poisonous' can be related to the Devil's account of how

> a whole host and generation of youth, receptive, sound to the core, flings itself on the work of the morbid genius, made genius by disease: admires it, praises it, exalts it, carries it away, assimilates it unto itself and makes it over to culture, which lives not on home-

made bread alone, but as well on provender and poison from the apothecary's shop,

and also to Zeitblom's description of Leverkühn's music ('the substantial identity of the most blest with the most accurst'), and to the words from the *Lamentation*, 'For I die as a good and as a bad Christian'.

But in *Doctor Faustus* the problems are presented more acutely, in terms less easily reconcilable. Zeitblom is a more thoughtful, more experienced and less confident Settembrini (two world wars have intervened); the Devil is a Naphta with more poise and considerably more power to his elbow; while Leverkühn – if indeed we can compare him with Castorp at all – is barred from that young man's way of salvation, the path down from the Mountain into the life of the world, the life of action. It would have seemed incredible that one should ever come to think of *The Magic Mountain* as a simple, cheerful novel of clear intentions and with a straightforward resolution. Yet, compared with *Doctor Faustus*, that is how it strikes us now.

The novel itself appears to be as uncompromising as Leverkühn's *Lamentation*. It, too, 'permits up to the very end no consolation, appeasement, transfiguration'. But the paradox of art extends even so far. At the end of *Doctor Faustus*, also, there sounds the 'high G of a cello', and 'that tone … which was the voice of mourning, is so no more. It changes its meaning; it abides as a light in the night.' Tragedy affords us no consolation or appeasement, other than itself, in itself. And Leverkühn, despite what we have said of his gnomish and highly specialized nature, is a tragic figure. But there is something else: there is the teller of the tragedy. And what Professor Heller says of Faust, that he is 'incapable of tragedy', is certainly true of Zeitblom. He is incapable of tragedy at any rate in the final and uttermost sense of the word. Zeitblom, we know, will go on, reproducing his sort. Untragic men, who know what tragedy means and who strive with varying success to fend it off. Men, 'addressed to reason and harmony', whose awareness of their own 'ethical narrow-mindedness' serves to sustain them in the effort to win from its identity with the 'most accurst' some small part of what is 'most blest'.

Doctor Faustus offers this dual experience, of indisputable annihilation and assured survival, through what is told and the way in which it is told. It is this novel itself which, changing yet again its meaning, grants us a light in the night – this novel, and the fact that such work can still be carried out. Hard, solid work which does not hesitate to be sometimes a little slow in order to be exhaustive, is not afraid of seriousness, despises fashion, prizes the detail to the profit of the planned whole, achieves what is usually left to poetry and achieves it without trying to be poetry and becoming poetic prose – work that ultimately draws its amazing energy from the author's fast hold on 'the anti-diabolic faith, that mankind has after all a "keen hearing", and that words born of one's own striving may do it good and not perish from its heart.'[3]

(1950)

---

3 The conclusion of 'Goethe's *Faust*', a lecture delivered at Princeton University in 1938, and printed in *Essays of Three Decades*.

The Stupendous Cannot Be Easy: On Robert Musil

If you were to read *The Man Without Qualities* for the story, your patience would be much fretted: you would probably not hang yourself, you would merely want to hang Robert Musil. The 'story' of the novel ostensibly concerns the preparations being made in 1913 in the Austro-Hungarian Empire to celebrate the seventieth anniversary of the Emperor's accession in December 1918. The preparations are known as the Collateral Campaign because Germany, that uncomfortable neighbour, is also planning a celebration: of Kaiser Wilhelm's jubilee, thirty years on the throne, in July of the same year. Unfortunately July precedes December, hence honour requires the Austrians to turn the whole of the year 1918 into a jubilee. Since, as the author knew (he began to write the work in the early 1920s and the first volume was published in 1930), these celebrations are never going to take place, the story in an obvious sense bears on a non-event.

The view that the work is a study of decadence, revealing the decay at the heart of the Austrian Empire, though it endows the project with a respectable-seeming significance, is a highly doubtful one. It points to what, though marvellously apt, is the least important element in the novel: its setting in time and place. By and large the dramatis personae form an exceptionally bright set – they could as well win the world as lose their little piece of it – and the tone of the work is remote from Orwellian or Brechtian allegory. The inset story of Moosbrugger the sex-murderer hardly supports the view either, despite the opening it offers for the question of whether one is responsible for one's acts, and despite Ulrich's portentous reflection in one of his grimmer moments that 'if mankind could dream collectively, it would dream Moosbrugger'. There being so much civility in evidence, someone has to stand for violence and unadorned insanity.

It says something for a country that, although it customarily regards a genius as a lout, a lout is never ('as sometimes happened elsewhere') regarded as a genius. No doubt the Empire was ramshackle, tottery and given to 'muddling through' – the hero Ulrich, we shall see, is given to thinking through: he however has no other calls of a pressing nature – but Musil was not interested in a retrospective analysis of the processes of decline and downfall. Ulrich even suggests that 'muddling through' may be Austria's world mission. And in fact, despite his virtually continuous irony, Musil is careful to forgo the hindsight wisdom which would have supplied him with irony of the cruder sort in plenty. The analysis that interests him – obsesses is a better word – is that of his characters and their situations as individual and yet (on a somewhat elevated plane) representative beings. He is the most relentlessly analytic of authors, the most sententious (except perhaps for *Wilhelm Meister*'s), and one of the most intelligent.

He did not finish his 'story' because in one sense, a minor one, history had already finished it for him, and in another and major sense it could never end. If his characters died it would be as if humanity died out. Death is as immaterial here (but how useful it is to novelists who have to tell a story and to end it too!) as in a Freudian casebook. Events too are rather crude animals, although they do happen, even to representative figures, and might be thought on occasion to be capable of representativeness themselves. Where events are concerned Musil can make Proust seem as fast-moving as James Bond: why, Mme Verdurin gets to be Princesse de Guermantes and Marcel's grandmother actually dies… Yet, like *A la recherche du temps perdu*, Musil's novel is a continuous texture, a vast weave of references back and forth, a seamless expanse of strands of thought which evince themselves at remote intervals and yet have been there, imperceptibly growing, all the while. If you skip, and it is very hard never to do so, you will be made to regret it.

'What this age demonstrates,' the novel tells us, sounding as so often as if it had been written yesterday, in some intellectually richer yesterday, 'when it talks of the genius of a race-horse or a tennis-player is probably less its conception of genius than its mistrust of the whole higher sphere.' The reader should not let himself be alarmed by that fearsome expression 'higher sphere', but merely remind himself that some spheres are higher than others. What is enjoyable in this novel is, happily, what matters most in it, and not just the sugar round the pill. To that extent the heart of the matter is worn on the sleeve and there is, until we make it, no insuperable problem: the novel is highly entertaining. Or the problem is: how sturdy is our appetite for what we are fairly overtly offered? That is to say, intelligence and insight, an 'unmerciful' shrewdness, outright comedy, wit, an all-embracing but by no means merciless irony – in short, a cast of mind, in motion, that we might think of as world-weary were it not for the sheer energy and gusto it bears and is borne by.

If the first characteristic we note of Musil's style is its leisureliness – Volume I begins with a hefty meteorological paragraph which at last summarizes itself in the words 'In short…it was a fine August day in the year 1913' – the second is its succinctness. For speed there is little to beat this sentence: 'Two weeks later Bonadea had already been his mistress for a fortnight.' And in two and a half pages we are given a living portrayal of the reluctant nymphomaniac Bonadea, the stuff of a novel in itself. 'She was capable of uttering the words "the true, the good and the beautiful" as often and as naturally as someone else might say "Thursday".' She has only one fault: 'she was liable to be stimulated to a quite uncommon degree by the mere sight of men'; a good wife and mother, 'she was by no means lustful' but 'sensual in the way that other people have other troubles, such as sweating of the hands or blushing easily'. Comic as the tone of this is, we emerge from the three-page chapter knowing that Bonadea is not merely to be laughed at or despised or condemned. Musil's starting-point, the reminder that Bonadea was a goddess of chastity whose temple suffered a transmogrification into 'a centre of all debaucheries', does not initiate the crushing send-up of a trivial, pretentious light-of-love that we might have expected. Bonadea, when she has no one in her arms, is a 'quiet, majestic woman'. Like the goddess's temple, people too are subject to queer inversions and contradictions, and the only infallible way of preserving an empire, of whatever kind, is by petri-fying its inhabitants, reducing them to programmed robots *in perpetuum*. The most perspicacious (and perspicuous) passage in Musil's early novel, *Young Törless*, touches on the boy's experience of 'the failure of language' whereby things, people and processes have been fettered to harmless explanatory words from which they may break loose at any moment.

In Chapter 99 of the Second Book the story is told, in passing, of Ulrich's adoptive Aunt Jane, whose dress resembled a soutane and who smoked cigars and wore a man's wig – not in anticipation of 'the mannish type of woman that was later to come into fashion', but because of her early and passionate admiration for the Abbé Liszt. Aunt Jane's heart was 'womanly' indeed. A music mistress, she had married against her family's wishes an improvident photographer and self-styled 'artist', who at least had a 'superb head' and drank and ran up debts like a genius. To him and then to his illegitimate child she sacrificed herself utterly. 'She seldom spoke of that past,' the author interposes: 'If life is stupendous one cannot also demand that it should be easy.' This anecdote – it arises out of a family album Ulrich is leafing through and occupies three pages – is a slice of the very body of life: again, the raw material for a substantial novel of its own, one would say, except that Musil is never 'raw'. That he over-cooks is the objection we are more likely to make. In an interesting essay, 'The Ironic Mystic' (*PN Review*, 22), David Heald varies the metaphor: 'His terrier-like habit of chewing every scrap of flesh and sucking the marrow out of every fleeting insight can irritate…'

With one sense of the word 'raw' in mind, we are provoked into perceiving before long that, for all the author's well-bred discretion, or because of it, the work carries a powerful sexual charge – in no way defused by the presence of humour, satire and pathos – and especially in the vicinity of his women characters. 'The tender aspects of masculine self-abandonment,' he remarks, 'somewhat resemble the growling of a jaguar over a hunk of meat.' But then, his women are the most original of his creations, and only brute accident, one wants to say, could bring about the downfall of an empire that had such women in it as Agathe, Diotima, Bonadea and Clarisse. It has to be admitted that Musil turns his sardonic gaze even more lovingly on his women than on his men: this detracts from them less than the reader might suppose in his innocence.

Apropos of Diotima, Ulrich animadverts on 'the mind of this woman, who would have been so beautiful without her mind', and it could hardly solace her to hear that Musil is offering her as an exemplary victim of what he calls 'the indescribable wave of skim-romanticism and yearning for God that the machine-age had for a time squirted out as an expression of spiritual and artistic protest against itself'. Diotima is the spiritual and artistic spearhead of the Collateral Campaign – culture, in the circles to which she belongs, being largely left to ladies – and in quest of a Great and Beautiful Idea, something to do with the Ideal and the eternal verities and, if at all possible, involving 'a positively redeeming exaltation of inner life, arising out of the anonymous depths of the nation'. How gratified the Emperor Franz Joseph will be by a whole year of all that! When Ulrich looks at Diotima he sees a fine woman; in his mind's eye, however, she appears in the shape of a 'colossal hen that was about to peck at a little worm, which was his soul'. Musil's women have a peculiarly potent charm, bypassing or overriding one's intellectual judgment of them; their wrong-headedness is richer than male right-mindedness, which by comparison looks cloddish, pompous or ineffectual.

In fact almost all the characters are endowed with a generous share of their creator's acuteness. Even the patently foolish ones, like those of limited brain-power, are allowed such fluent cogitation that they too strike us as preternaturally observant and self-aware. The 'tubby little general' Stumm, fallen under Diotima's sway, goes to the Imperial Library in the hope of locating a 'great redeeming idea' for the Campaign and finds himself faced with three and a half million volumes. 'You may say,' this simple soldier reflects, 'one doesn't really need to read every single book.' But that won't pass muster. 'My retort to that is – in warfare, too, one doesn't need to kill every single soldier, and yet every single one is necessary.' The Prussian industrialist Arnheim is put in his place by the author as a plausible *vulgarisateur* or at best a talented eclectic: none the less he proceeds to put neatly in their place the 'fat species' of solemn idealistic poets who 'puff out great bales of the eternal emotions'.

In conversation, as when Arnheim and Ulrich dispute together, one character's wits strike sparks off another's sagacity and, at times quite unexpectedly, intellectual honours are more or less equal at the end. What respect for – or what rare generosity towards – one's own creations this shows, among them not a single imbecile or swine! The exceptional subtlety thus implied in the differentiation between characters – levels of intelligence, degrees of good intention – doesn't make the reader's task any easier. Whose side is he meant to be on? He will need to be a reader without qualities, apart from those of insatiable curiosity and immense patience. He will need to be nearly as clever as Musil.

'At times he felt just as though he had been born with a gift for which at present there was no function.' The figure of Ulrich is obviously crucial, and also slippery: he is, one supposes, the author, in large measure at any rate, and the reader's zealous though less than wholly accommodating guide. Over this length, he will require to be more than a guide, a stance or a view-point; he will need to be of very considerable appeal, gruesome, or charming, in himself. Is he sufficiently so? He describes himself in a typical paradox as 'a man of faith, though one who believed in nothing'. More strongly he asserts (partly, one may suppose, by way of apology to Bonadea, with whom he is breaking off), 'My nature is designed as a machine for the continuous devaluation of life!'

Ulrich is or was (like Musil) an engineer and mathematician, earlier a cavalry officer, now taking a year's leave from his life in order to find out what to do with it: a youngish man of promise disillusioned with the promises, a dilettante who loves 'intellectual hardship'. He is a detached observer, a juggler with ideas, an intellectual trouble-maker – as his friends discover – and he can run to tedious sophistry and sterile elaboration – as his readers discover. If he appears sexually cold – he certainly isn't abstinent – this is in part, though only in part, because the author skips over the details (we catch a rare period glimpse of ribbons being untied or tied, hooks being unfastened or fastened) and straight into Ulrich's post-coital musings. Against his coldness we set the quickness of his curiosity, as when he pauses outside a shop window to marvel at 'the countless versions of nail-scissors' or the processes whereby a goat's skin is transformed into a lady's glove. In the barely definable relationship between him and his sister Agathe which begins to take over Volume III, he reflects, 'there was implicit not more love for each other than distaste for the rest of the world.' Yet when he is out with Agathe, discussing his dislike of the world, and they stroll through a busy market-place, he exclaims: 'Can one help loving the world if one simply sees and smells it?'

Wherever his mind may be, Ulrich has his feet on the ground, and he is less of a pedant, and in truth probably less of a world-disliker, than the windy idealists and Great Lovers whom he mocks. If he is rather too knowing about women, and – even for a personable thirty-two-year-old bachelor – somewhat over-privileged in that sphere, he likes them naturally, with a liking that can only go with a fair amount of respect, and in their company he never declines into baby-talk or sulks or masculine mysteries. He may fall into silence, however. What is exasperating to the reader, as to his female visitors, is his capacity for thinking, at such length and for the greater part so well. This is indeed quite offensive. 'Let's have more conviction!' we protest, when we really mean, 'Less superior intellection if you please!'

The reader's courage may dim a little when, in Volume III, Ulrich is reunited with Agathe ('sister …woman …stranger …friend'), for alas the siblings have long been separated and have so much to talk about. Moreover Agathe is made of sterner stuff – stuff of a less decipherable pattern too – than his other women friends, and she can give as good as she takes. We are told by Musil's expert translators – they deserve the Nobel Prize for Translation – that this is where he originally intended the story to begin, and so the previous thousand pages are only a form of prologue. What is to be narrated now, Musil declares in connection with the siblings and by way of warning to the slow-witted and hence (he assumes) squeamish, is 'a journey to the furthest limits of the possible, skirting the dangers of the impossible and unnatural, even of the repulsive, and perhaps not always quite avoiding them.' This, though one may not be absolutely sure of what it signifies, is possibly a clue to one reason for the novel's unfinishability. The man who is going to travel that far needs to travel light, and as a symbol, no matter what of, no matter how beautifully managed, incest tends towards top-heaviness.

However, this volume contains splendid material continuative of the foregoing volumes. On the one hand, such ripe comedy as Bonadea's playing truant from Diotima's high-minded academy of love, where general theory alone is taught, to taste the reality of sex in Ulrich's apartment. On the other, an unforgettably powerful scene in which – at the instigation of Clarisse, a highly-strung 'modern' version of Aunt Jane moved by fiercer artistic aspirations but a lesser loving-ness – some of the friends visit the lunatic asylum where Moosbrugger is held. As they progress from ward to ward ('this is idiocy, and that over there is cretinism') General von Stumm rambles on about the Collateral Campaign and how the War Ministry finds itself co-operating with both the pacifists and the nationalists, the former keen on universal love and human goodness and the latter on seizing the opportunity to bring the army up to scratch. The General himself is in favour of both parties.

There is no facile suggestion that it is the inmates of the asylum who are 'truly' sane while the outside world is 'truly' insane. Musil compares lunatic asylums, 'the ultimate habitation of the lost', with Hell – which 'is not interesting; it is merely terrible'. Those who have attempted to portray Hell, however imaginative they may be, have never got beyond 'oafish torments and puerile distortions of earthly peculiarities'. And Dante, more discreetly, humanized Hell by popu-lating it 'with men of letters and other public figures, thus distracting attention from the penal technicalities'. Asylums are as uninteresting, as lacking in imagination, as Hell itself, and even Clarisse, fired by self-generated excitement and a head full of Nietzschean ideas ('for her this journey was half philosophy and half adultery'), is left disappointed. On the return journey the General remarks, as he lights up a cigar, that he didn't see a single patient smoking: 'People don't realize how well off they are so long as they're in their right minds.'

The advent of Agathe brings about a new seriousness in Ulrich, or a thinning of the flippancy that has invested his seriousness. For a while we wonder whether he is going to develop qualities. He comments on his own scepticism: 'I don't believe God has been among us yet. I believe He is still to come. But only if we shorten the way for Him': that is, we have to meet God half-way. The comment is indicative of Ulrich's 'mysticism', itself a contributory reason for the novel's length. For that mysticism, in so far as it is describable, is of a scrupulously rational species which allows of no short-cuts by way of 'feeling', no leaps into the unknown, but only of hard and rigorous journeys. There follows a sustained passage of considerable solemnity on the theme of morality, which for Ulrich consists in 'order and integrity of feeling'. 'Morality is imagination' and 'there is nothing arbitrary about the imagination'. Men have introduced a degree of order into the workings of the intellect, which is at least able to weigh theories against facts. Cannot something similar be done for the feelings? For 'we all want to discover what we're alive for…it's one of the main sources of all the violence in the world.' When Arnheim interrupts: 'But that would mean an expanding relationship to God!' Ulrich asks mockingly, 'And would that be so very terrible?'

It is tempting at this point – but not especially rewarding – to turn back to *Young Törless* (*Die Verwirrungen des Zöglings Törless*, 1906), a book whose curiously high standing may owe something to the guilty sense that its author wrote another novel, much finer no doubt but very much longer and on the face of it less accessible. For it is hard, I would have thought, to distinguish between the *Verwirrungen*, the confusions, of young Törless and those of the not much older author. The unlikeable youth Beineberg – but who in the novel is likeable? – sounds like a seedy pubescent hanger-on of Diotima and her Great and Beautiful Idea when he talks about the soul and how we should restore our contact with it and make better (in his case, probably worse) use of its powers. But it is the author *in propria persona* who tells us that

> Any great flash of understanding is only half completed in the illumined circle of the conscious mind; the other half takes place in the dark loam of our innermost being. It is primarily a state of soul, and uppermost, as it were at the extreme tip of it, there the thought is – poised like a flower.

Such Freudian-style talk of light and loam may pass in a boarding school where metaphysics and masochism, soul and sadism, are jumbled up together, but the later Musil is more authentic in his aspiration and more rigorous in his scepticism.

Musil tells us that in his references to the rubble of feelings one age bequeaths to another Ulrich is prophesying the fate of Europe, though without realizing it – 'indeed, he was not concerned with real events at all; he was fighting for his own salvation.' The salvation of a representative being is a theme, a concern, which survives 1914–18 and thereafter: the end is not yet nigh, and it is wholly in character that a fourth volume of translation should be in prospect, containing (we are told) the unfinished conclusion of the work and some unfinished chapters.

Musil's mind is a brilliant, speculative and untiring one, but not precisely the mind of a novelist. Yet if such a mind applies itself to a novel – and it is difficult to think what it could apply itself to more profitably – then the result must be, if not a brilliant novel, then still brilliant. In Chapter 112 of the Second Book Arnheim reflects on Ulrich, his Viennese 'counter-influence' in the triangular relationship with Diotima and a man with whom, paradoxically, he is much taken. His diagnosis of what he persuades himself is Ulrich's weakness may stand as a criticism of Musil himself, so long as we keep in mind that it is highly paradoxical to describe as a writer's 'weakness' what is plainly of his essential strength. Ulrich is witty, 'and wit came from witting, knowing, and here was a piece of wisdom on the part of language, for it revealed the intellectual origins of this quality, and how spectral it was, how poor in feeling.' Arnheim continues: 'The witty man is always inclined to live, as it were, by his wits, overriding the ordained frontiers where the man of true feeling calls a halt.'

Yes, we think, more feeling would surely have served to inhibit, to slow down, even to tire out Musil's wits, and thus to call a halt to his novel this side of the ordained frontiers of magnitude and ambition. But therein, as we have seen, lies the burden of Ulrich's – and Musil's – complaint against 'feeling' and its soulful exponents. When they are moved by emotions they think they are moving towards truth – and never mind frontiers and halts.

The Man Without Qualities is essentially exploratory and experimental rather than programmatic or predetermined. Yet, as we expect novels to have a conclusion, so we expect thinkers to arrive at conclusions. The truth may well be that Musil couldn't end his novel because he hadn't arrived at his conclusions, he was still inching ruthlessly towards them when he died. If he had arrived – ah, then we should have more than merely a great novel, we should possess the great secret of life.

A new translation of The Man Without Qualities. *And* From the Posthumous Papers

That there should be one English translation of Musil's great novel is remarkable. That there is now a second is barely believable. Spot checks fail to establish the clear superiority of either the version by Eithne Wilkins and Ernst Kaiser (three volumes, 1953–60) or the new one by Sophie Wilkins (1995). There is little to choose between the former appellation 'Collateral Campaign' and the present 'Parallel Campaign' for 'die Parallelaktion', the Austrian preparations to celebrate the seventieth year of Franz Josef's reign running alongside the German preparations for the thirtieth year of Kaiser Wilhelm's, a joint event or non-event due in 1918: the campaign, begun in 1913, which you might say lies at the heart of the novel if you were confident of where and what the heart was.

The 1953 chapter heading, 'In a state of lowered resistance Ulrich acquires a new *chère amie*' ('In einem Zustand von Schwäche zieht sich Ulrich eine neue Geliebte zu') now reads 'In a weak moment Ulrich acquires a new mistress'. Alluding to that splendid creation Bonadea, the French locution seems right, with its anticipatory tinge of comedy, while 'in a weak moment' (Ulrich has just been mugged) may be preferred. Ostensibly enquiring after his health, Bonadea has called on him 'to continue the adventure in this romantico-eleemosynary style' (1953) or, if you will, 'to carry on the adventure in her own romantically charitable fashion' (1995). Her 'favourite idea was that of the "paragon"; she applied this expression to people, servants, shops and feelings, whenever she wanted to speak well of them' (1953) or 'her favourite phrase was "highly respectable", applied to people, messengers, shops, and feelings, when she wanted to praise them' (1995). 'Ihr Lieblingsbegriff war "hochanständig"...': if 'paragon' is slightly over the top (yet not inapt), then 'messengers' is off-centre for 'Dienstboten'. On the other hand, the new wording, 'a six-day bike race promotes international goodwill like nothing else!', is more precise ('ein Sechstagerennen') than the old 'sporting marathon'.

In the first version the tenderer feelings of the human male during mating are likened to a jaguar growling over a hunk of meat, 'and any interruption is taken gravely amiss', while in the second the snarling jaguar 'doesn't like to be disturbed'. By and large the second version is a little more colloquial or fluent, though whether this constitutes an indisputable advantage is problematic: a shade of stiffness can convey a legitimate 'period' or 'foreign' flavour. In his afterword Burton Pike remarks that the 'poetic concision' of Musil's words and their 'freight of nuances' must be 'the despair of any translator': which makes it the more surprising that the two versions keep as closely in step as they do. Considering the magnitude of the enterprise, one takes off one's hat to all concerned.

So the 'Posthumous Papers' remain to distinguish the new edition: 635 pages, including drafts of twenty new chapters, following on from where the novel seemed to have stopped, set in galleys (but withdrawn), plus sketches, fragments and notes, some of which might have been inserted or acted on in some form or sense, in one place or another. 'Like Goethe,' Pike says, 'Musil had a strange sense of having infinite time stretching out before him in which to complete his task.' One of Musil's notes for a preface reads: 'The story of this novel amounts to this, that the story that ought to be told in it is not told.' A mysterious statement, open to a number of interpretations, possibly prophetic, possibly pragmatic, what 'ought to be told' and what 'could be' sometimes being, even in the best of hands, two distinct things.

Here we are given a major selection from the *Nachlass* as printed in the Rowohlt edition of 1978, which itself is only a major selection from the extant papers. And Musil's papers were much depleted by the loss of some of them in Vienna during the war, he having left for Switzerland in 1938, and by the theft of two of his notebooks, before transcription, from an editor's car in Italy in 1970. We still have rather more than enough. The material tends to bear out J.P. Stern's comment on the question whether *The Man Without Qualities* is a great novel: 'It is great, but it is not a novel', while casting something of a shadow. Musil never authorized publication, and what doesn't add to our admiration is going to detract from it.

Perhaps the most rewarding item has General von Stumm, another fine creation, musing that in the old days you often didn't know something, but as long as it didn't occur in an examination it didn't harm anyone, whereas now, with the coming of the so-called unconscious, it is much more important to know why you don't know something than what it is you don't know. There is a considerable deal of melodramatic, not to say sensational stuff, notably a relatively explicit passage in which Rachel, Diotima's maid, is closeted for several days in a small room alone with the sex-murderer Moosbrugger, who is on the run and abetted by Clarisse ('But I'm afraid of him!' 'But, my dear Fräulein, everything great is terrible'). Elsewhere Clarisse, increasingly insane, displays a frenzied desire for a terrified Greek homosexual; and also offers her services as a hermaphrodite to Meingast, 'the Master', and his 'league of men'. The asylum scenes are stark, but lack the power and point of the madhouse visit in Chapter 33 of 'Into the Millennium'. Much the same can be said of other material here. Musil was right to keep it aside; he was no wanton fabricator of 'expressionist' nightmares. But could the protracted work on the novel be making a sick man of him? One pleasing theory might be that he was testing or immunizing himself by writing, as pastiche or parody, the kind of thing he wouldn't be found dead writing. Regarding these explorations and potentialities, more certainly valid is Michael Hamburger's observation that Musil's reflections on the behaviour of his characters often 'have the spontaneity of genuine astonishment'.

'We will be something like the Last Mohicans of love!' Agathe tells herself. In one of these potentialities the spiritual 'twin' love between Ulrich and his sister appears to be consummated in the flesh: a turn which was not wholly unheralded but is still disconcerting, since a mystical union is one thing and Agathe as swelling the list of her brother's secular mistresses quite another. 'We wanted to find the entrance to paradise!' Ulrich says later, the 'experiment' having seemingly failed. Mind you, there is much more talk than action – 'it often happened that the end of a discussion appeared to be further from its goal than its beginning' – and nothing so forthright as Donne's resounding advice on souls turning to bodies, 'else a great Prince in prison lies'. The one-liner, 'Dramatize! Make all this present!', crops up as an authorial exhortation, but one cannot see how it could be implemented in this peculiar relationship (if you cannot say the unsayable, you can hardly demonstrate or dramatize it in print) and in the siblings' journey, as Musil envisage it, to the edge of the possible, and perhaps into the impossible and unnatural, even the repulsive.

But then, isn't the novel – and it *is*, after all, more a novel than anything else – more enjoyable in its large incidentals, its rich characters and witty and wise asides, than significant in its metaphysical, moral and mystical intentions or intimations? In another passage Ulrich, in whom some very odd qualities are unfolding, empties his pistol into Agathe's piano: 'What came over you?' 'I have no idea.' And there is a violent and perverse (and, dare one say, unlikely) encounter between Ulrich and Diotima: 'You have no idea how bad I am… I'd have to be able to beat you to love you!' Whereupon he gives her a couple of sharp smacks, and – in a nice circumlocution – 'something started going the way clocks sometimes start when they are roughly treated'.

Ulrich got into trouble during his schooldays by proposing that God preferred to speak of His world in the subjunctive of possibility or potentiality: He creates the world while thinking that it could just as well be done in some other way. It was a comparable persuasion that landed Musil in trouble; and his readers in some confusion.

Diaries 1899–1941

No doubt *The Man Without Qualities* is the fullest account of what *The Man Without Qualities* is like and signifies. But it is very long, not to mention unfinished. The best short account I know of is J.P. Stern's essay in *The Dear Purchase*, and even that is rather hard to follow. We are by nature, at least when we read serious books, hot for certainties, and the answers Robert Musil gives, though by no means dusty, tend to be elusive. He was, Stern comments, the most interesting of the few Viennese writers of his time who tried (with considerable success in his case) to resist the 'irritable reaching after metaphysical certainties'. The preparations in the novel to celebrate the seventieth anniversary of the Emperor's accession, due in 1918, may bring to mind our own preparations for the millennium: lofty projects involving the eternal values, the human spirit, the institution of universal peace and brotherhood, the rearming of the cavalry, and a Greater Austrian Franz Joseph Soup Kitchen. But the campaign is only a framework supporting, not exactly a story, but a private and unofficial search for another, barely to be intimated kind of life, a millennium of a different genus, and above all the creation of some splendid characters, weird in all conscience and yet, like the finest caricature, curiously realistic and representative.

Musil's hero, engaging though not notably heroic, is (in Stern's words) 'in quest of a "second state" whose very nature it is to remain indeterminate'. (Thank heavens, one is inclined to say, for Ulrich's actual life, his first state.) In this Musil differs fundamentally from Thomas Mann, who customarily 'brings down the curtain': in *The Magic Mountain*, for instance, on a scene in Flanders. In his *Diaries* Musil, who heartily disliked him, remarked that Mann wrote for the people who were there, whereas 'I write for people who aren't there'. (His feelings softened in 1939, when Mann sought to alleviate the exiled Musils' financial worries.) This other, second state, we gather, was to be initiated through a mystical union between Ulrich and Agathe, the sister from whom he had long been separated, in a felicitous inversion of Faust's affliction: one soul living in two breasts. That mystics resort to erotic symbolism is one thing; that brother and sister should embrace incest as the way to a superior spiritual condition (see the posthumous papers) is another. 'We wanted to find the entrance to paradise!' Ulrich sums up later, wryly we take it. For all their distinction and daring, Ulrich and Agathe belong to the milieu where, as Stern remarks of Musil's Vienna, 'whatever happens isn't likely to lead to the consequences intended', and had they found that entrance it would indeed have brought down the curtain – and signalled the author's exit from his work. Perhaps we had best leave the idea, the theme of the most arid stretches in Musil's drafts, as the least probable of the possibilities that run through the novel.

For the most part the posthumous papers – chapters withdrawn at proof stage, sketches and fragments – cast more darkness than light. So what of the *Diaries*? These constitute roughly two-fifths of the *Tagebücher* edited by Adolf Frisé(1976), and extend from around 1899, when Musil was eighteen and studying engineering in Brünn, to shortly before his death in Switzerland in 1942. One of the strongest reasons for reading the *Diaries*, says the translator, Philip Payne, is that they are 'a storehouse for material that he intended to use in his creative writing', adding that since they were not meant for public consumption, 'his critical threshold is lowered, he writes fluently, spontaneously', and 'in short, he is reassuringly human' because no one was looking at him. (This might seem to imply a harsh criticism of Musil's published, public work, but such is not the intention.) 'Musil's prose addresses itself to riddles that cannot be solved in a purely "empirical world",' Mark Mirsky maintains in his touchingly enthusiastic introduction: 'Turn the ghostly key of the *Diaries* in Musil's fiction and the bolt at times clicks open to that "other" reality.' An unwieldy key for so subtle a lock, it might be felt. The efforts to say the unsayable that go on here make us appreciate how much of the sayable is finely said in *The Man Without Qualities*.

But this is a mean-spirited view of things, and we should look at what the *Diaries* have to offer. They are packed with diversely applied intelligence run riot; except that 'riot' is the wrong word: 'Something mysterious is only of value when it arises despite the engineer's aura of precision.' The result can be chilling, even repellent. '"Monsieur le vivisecteur" – that's who I am!' Musil speculates on the relationship between his mother and the family's permanent house guest, Heinrich Reiter (Herman, according to Mirsky at one point). And on two women sharing a room in the Berlin boarding-house where he took his meals (1907): 'It would be interesting to know which of them takes the lead in this relationship. The one with the Egyptian bird-face or the one with the calm, almost satiated expression? I resolved to put out feelers.' In the same year he asks an acquaintance about love between brother and sister: 'she considers that such a thing is possible. When a brother marries this is supposed to awaken certain thoughts in young girls. He is surrendered grudgingly.' He sets down the sexual tangles of his friends, as well as his own: 'all the sexual details have to be described on account of the fine soul-values that are attached to them'. More voyeurism? Or grist to the great mill of Musil's fiction?

Related at length is the story of Alice, the wife of his boyhood friend, Gustav Donath, and how she conceives a passion for a Greek homosexual, believes herself to be a hermaphrodite, and is taken into a mental hospital. In *The Man Without Qualities* Alice becomes Clarisse with Gustav as her husband, Walter. (Her madness resurfaces in lurid detail in the posthumous papers.) In 1913 Musil visits a lunatic asylum in Italy; the experience forms the basis of the grim chapter in which, at Clarisse's request, the robustly comical General von Stumm escorts her and Ulrich to the asylum where the rapist murderer Moosbrugger is held. An entry in the *Diaries* (1920) reads, 'Unleash all *criminals* that live within us. The rage of Moosbrugger to plunge a curved knife into someone's belly is comprehensible when one sees these dolled-up forms go wandering past.' (Compare Ulrich's thought in the novel, that if mankind could dream collectively, it would dream Moosbrugger.) There's no mistaking that splinter of ice in the writer's heart: 'Like a doctor who investigates the innermost mechanism of the vagina and yet, one hour later, overcome by passion, lies in its thrall. This is one of the characteristics I have given Hugo' (an earlier name for Ulrich). Nor does Musil spare himself in what Mirsky calls 'surgery upon his own limbs'. There is much evidence of a self-awareness of such intensity that if it didn't deter a man from writing at all, it would drive him to write without cease. 'My particular danger is to get caught up in theory'; and 'I too seldom know what it is that I want. In me there is no vestige of the preacher, appellant, executor of an inner preordained course.'

The *Diaries* include what might be expected of diaries: references to extensive reading of admired authors (Nietzsche, Tolstoy, Balzac, Maeterlinck, Emerson, Svevo, Husserl, Chesterton), and dissatisfaction with others; thoughts on or against politics and contemporary events; vignettes of people and places; observations both surgical and affectionate on his wife, Martha; descriptions of the behaviour of mating cats, and of flies caught on fly-paper; material for an autobiography… An obscure passage (*c.* 1921) seeks to differentiate between the moralist and the ethicist, whereby the former is concerned with rigid precepts arranged in logical order, while the latter is spontaneous, a teacher, 'related to the creative writer', and of a higher species. Ethics in this adumbrated sense, one supposes, could more easily accommodate Ulrich and Agathe (if not Moosbrugger). The idea is more persuasively broached in Chapters 11 and 12 in Part 3 of the novel, but it seems to me that Musil is following a false scent, pursuing a chimerical distinction. Which might be one reason why *The Man Without Qualities* was never completed. A more authentic dichotomy is that between the philosopher and the artist. As Musil says here, in an amusing argument with himself (1905), sometimes artists are too unphilosophical for him, and sometimes philosophers are too lacking in humanity. In the *Diaries* the psychologizing philosopher tends to have the upper hand; in the novel, happily, the artist prevails or the two of them contrive to coexist and join forces. Musil had cause to remind himself: 'Do not say "avalanche" as if it were obvious what is meant by that. But describe it as if it were an unknown happening!'

The *Diaries* are not too rich in the kind of near-epigrams, brilliantly defining and irresistibly comprehensible, that are scattered throughout the novel; for instance, the hot water Ulrich got into at school by venturing that God preferred to speak of his world in 'the subjunctive of potentiality': he creates the world while thinking that it could just as well be done in some other way. (A god without qualities?) Yet there are pithy utterances striking in one way or another. 'What the poem is about is that which can only be expressed in the poem'; 'irony has to contain an element of suffering in it. (Otherwise it is the attitude of a know-it-all.)'; 'In every organism there are functions that are degenerating and ones that are being newly formed. Thus it may be God's will to allow spirit on earth to degenerate in order to create an industrial planet. That would explain why he doesn't treat R.M. any better'; 'Look at your problem this way: that you are not famous is natural, but that you do not have enough readers, etc., to make a living is disgraceful' (1930); of a prostitute who might be brought into a novel: 'Has never used contraceptive aids; on a much-travelled road nothing grows'; the Nazis having banned 'destructive criticism': 'Since criticism is forbidden I have to indulge in self-criticism. No one will take exception to this since it is unknown in Germany.'

The translator has laboured heroically, even indicating what he has omitted; and his notes are often indispensable, though what is annotated may not always be. That there is no index is presumably because it would require a second volume. Those concerned with the creative process as distinct from the realized creation will find much to fascinate them in the *Diaries*. They 'allow us to come face-to-face with the man,' Mirsky claims. Samuel Johnson warned against the curiosity which tempts us to a nearer knowledge of an author we admire. More to the point is D.H. Lawrence's dictum: 'Never trust the artist. Trust the tale', the tale as the artist published it.

(1979; 1995; 1999)

Hesse versus *Hesse*

'Zwei Seelen wohnen ach! in meiner Brust.' And very convenient it is for the writer, for one soul can bleed on the sleeve while the other gets up to other things in other places. It is not that the breast needs to be a specially large one to entertain two souls, but rather that those among whom the two-souled move may have to be remarkably broad-minded and long-suffering. Perhaps prepared to suffer long and very painfully indeed. I will not dwell on the lowest and most horrifying depths to which double-soulness can sink – Hans Magnus Enzensberger's exemplum of the concentration-camp commandant who plays Schubert sonatas when off duty will suffice – for Hermann Hesse was obviously a good man, a good-hearted man, who recognized the onset of Germany's Faustianity at a very early date and removed himself to single-souled Switzerland.

Hesse too loved music, but like Thomas Mann he had his misgivings about the German love of it. In *The Magic Mountain* (1924), Settembrini – liberal humanist, *homo humanus*, whose musical emblem would be nothing more sinister than the wind-bag or barrel-organ – considers music 'politically suspect', and in *Doctor Faustus* (1947) the Devil points out that he ought to know something of music:

> Christian in reverse, as it were: introduced and developed by Christianity indeed, but then rejected and banned as the Divel's Kingdom…a highly theological business, music – the way sin is, the way I am… For there is true passion only in the ambiguous and ironic. The highest passion concerns the absolutely questionable.

Similarly in Hesse's *Steppenwolf* (1927) the ambiguous hero laments the hegemony which music exerts over the German spirit:

> We intellectuals, instead of fighting this tendency like men and rendering obedience to the spirit, the Logos, the Word, and gaining a hearing for it, are all dreaming of a speech without words that utters the inexpressible and gives form to the formless.

And so, he continues in one of those interesting discursive passages scattered through Hesse's work, the German spirit has intoxicated itself with beautiful sounds and

> none of us intellectuals is at home in reality. We are strange to it and hostile. That is why the part played by intellect even in our own

German reality, in our history and politics and public opinion, has been so lamentable a one.

A far cry from our good clean English music, food of love, soother of savage breasts, softener of rocks, bender of knotted oaks, and server of other social functions! But let us have done with the commandant and Schubert, and also with Enzensberger's equally double-souled SS officer who carries Hölderlin (though a word-user and not a dreamer of music) in his knapsack. Hesse's novels, and especially his largest and least readable, *Magister Ludi* (*The Glass Bead Game*, 1943), are much nearer to the ivory tower than to the concentration camp, albeit an ivory tower which bustles with enigmatic activity. The 'Treatise on the Steppenwolf' pokes fun at Faust's pathetic claim, 'in a line immortalized among schoolmasters and greeted with a shudder of astonishment by the Philistine', to possess *two* souls:

> The breast and the body are indeed one, but the souls that dwell in it are not two, nor five, but countless in number. Man is an onion made up of a hundred integuments, a texture made up of many threads.

Duality can be dull enough, but think of the potentialities of plurality! Why I compared Hesse's novels to ivory towers or palaces of philosophy is that customarily they *talk* a lot about man's many souls yet they rarely or only briefly *show* us any one of these souls or selves in action. Thomas Mann is the greater novelist in that, though he too is ever ready for a long, abstract and learned excursus, he surrounds his lecturing with characters who are irresistibly 'flesh and blood'. Hesse, however, falls back on 'the East', 'the ancient Asiatics', the Yin and the Yang, that unholy pair of twins, or points encouragingly to 'India' or 'China' (an India empty of Indians, a China without Chinese), or to the Buddha, or 'the return into the All'. *Magister Ludi* is an exhausting account of the minutiae of an aristocratic, highly spiritual secret society; the theme, much beloved of earlier German writers and categorized in the formula *Bundesroman* or 'League Novel', is treated also in *Demian* and *The Journey to the East*. But the odd thing about this secret society is that it doesn't *do* anything. It simply *is*. The secret is in the secret, perhaps.

Theodore Ziolkowski describes the book admiringly as an attempt on the grand scale 'to project the ideal into reality',[1] but the Magister himself retires from the Order because of its aestheticism, its

1 *The Novels of Hermann Hesse*, by Theodore Ziolkowski.

ignorance of the outside world. In fact we see little of any 'commit-
ment to life' *within* life and the outside world: this is only more
highflown talk. When Magister Knecht leaves the Castalian Order, so
Ziolkowski glosses, 'his representative life is over. He is now free to
live or to die as an individual.' In the story he dies, pretty promptly.
But then, life in Hesse is mostly a shabby business; he could never
have achieved anything comparable to Thomas Mann's Mynheer
Peeperkorn, ludicrous and majestic, gone to seed and full of seed, a
symbol and a particular Dutch coffee-planter from Java, 'Life' itself
and yet 'an out-and-out personality'. Mann sounds like a novelist, if
discernibly a German one then the most 'Dickensian' of them, where
Hesse sounds like a commentator on somebody else's novels, as when
in *Magister Ludi* he instructs the reader that the Bead Game 'represented a select, symbolical form of the quest for perfection, a sublime
alchemy, a self-approach to the inherent spirit beyond all images and
pluralities – and thus to God'. Ziolkowski, a devotee writing at length
on the master, carries the process of abstraction and rarefaction to the
point at which the reader's (or this reader's) mind fails to get a foot-
hold or a nail-hold on the discourse and can only suppose that the
exegete speaks with the tongue of angels perhaps, but certainly not
with that fleshy muscular organ given to man.

Two at least of Hesse's novels are exceptions or partial exceptions
to what I have said or implied above. I must have given the impression that Hesse is an extreme case of Teutonic heaviness and
humourlessness, and yet *Steppenwolf* is quite funny in some of its discursive passages and in some of its incidents. Harry Haller, a lonely,
wretched intellectual, pacifist and lover of Mozart, 'a most refined and
educated specialist in poetry, music and philosophy', falls in with a
strange and seemingly bisexual dance-hostess called Hermine
(Hermann). Hermine takes his re-education or de-education in hand,
makes him buy a gramophone and some jazz records, teaches him to
dance, and generally introduces him to a new world. 'Marble-topped
tables, jazz music, cocottes, and travelling salesmen!' She also provides
him with an attractive mistress, Maria, who 'taught me the charming
play and delights of the senses' and brings him to view less priggishly
'the world of the dance and pleasure resorts, the cinemas, bars and
hotel lounges'. The account of a late flowering of sexual love is quite
charming and tender, but Harry somehow knows that this new life
cannot last and some new 'unwinding of fate' is at hand: 'It was my
destiny to make another bid for the crown of life in the expiation of
its endless guilt. An easy life, an easy death – these were not for me.'
No such luck! In the course of the book's lively yet enigmatically phan-

tasmagoric dénouement, Maria and Hermine disappear and Harry is left with 'all the hundred thousand pieces of life's game' in his pocket:

> A glimpse of its meaning had stirred my reason and I was determined to begin the game afresh. I would sample its tortures once more and shudder again at its senselessness. I would traverse not once more, but often, the hell of my inner being.

In 1961 Hesse complained that *Steppenwolf* had been violently misunderstood, especially by its most enthusiastic readers who identified themselves with Harry in his sufferings and failed to realize that 'the story pictures a disease and crisis – but not one leading to death and destruction, on the contrary: to healing'. But it is the tale we have to trust; the sheer phantasmagoria of the ending and the obscure 'healing' which it is alleged to point towards simply cannot stand up to the weight of melancholy, the realistic and documented misery, of the book's first half.

I complained that we rarely saw any of Hesse's 'souls' or fragments of souls in action. Rare in that respect, then, is *Narcissus and Goldmund* (1930), which Ziolkowski describes as the most popular and most imperfect of Hesse's later novels, but which I would say is the best of all. The duality here is very plainly exemplified in Narcissus, the scholarly and austere monk, and Goldmund, the artist, adventurer and lover. It is Narcissus, as befits 'mind', who expounds with Hesse's customary explicitness the differences between the two of them. 'The difference between mother-heritage and father-heritage, the difference between soul and mind'; 'we are sun and moon, dear friend; we are sea and land'; 'you sleep at your mother's breast; I wake in the desert. Your dreams are of girls; mine of boys.' Where Narcissus looks to God the Father and teaches in the monastery school, Goldmund looks to the Earth-Mother and becomes a sculptor. Hesse spells out the message in large lettering, reminding us for instance that pain and joy resemble each other closely (we would like to remind Hesse that sometimes they don't, too), and that while it is good to lead a disciplined life of intellect, religion and meditation, it is also good (for all manner of things shall be well, though some of us may not always think so) to 'suffer sun and rain, hunger and need, to play with the joys of the senses and pay for them with suffering'. Goldmund is brought back to the monastery and dies in Narcissus' arms, and to Narcissus is given the bulk of the moralizing, the explication of the novel and the directing of the reader's intellectual responses. But the adventures are given to Goldmund, and it is these which count.

Ziolkowski complains that the title of the first English translation referred only to Goldmund, thus by implication ignoring the signifi-cance of the counterpart, Narcissus, and he quotes Hesse's own protest against readers who made the same mistake: 'The book and its world become meaningless if one splits it like that: Narcissus must be taken just as seriously as Goldmund; he is the counterpole.' We will silence our doubts as to whether, in that case, the monk is altogether happily named, but again it is the tale we must trust, not what its author says about it. I maintain that the reader to whom this Narcissus can *mean* as much as this Goldmund must have come to the book with an entrenched predisposition in favour of thin-lipped philosophizing and cloistered virtue and a gross lack of interest in the life of the world and the life of the senses. For one thing, if we agree to think of the two poles in question as 'Nature' and 'Spirit' (Ziolkowski's sugges-tion), then where Narcissus is spirit alone, we come to feel that Goldmund is both nature and spirit. Ziolkowski contends that something has gone wrong 'technically', and this he attributes to a structural flaw in the novel arising from the fact that Hesse conceived Goldmund before he conceived Narcissus and the former thus had an unfair start in life. I would say, though, that something has gone right – despite Hesse. (We should note that in *Siddhartha*, 1923, the most tract-like of the novels, the eponymous hero who has been a merchant, lady's man, epicure, gambler and ferryman, and who distrusts doctrines and teachers, ends up holier than his friend Govinda, ascetic monk and disciple of the Buddha.) Where generally Hesse's persons merely dent the walls of the ivory tower on the inside, here Goldmund breaks clean through them – and goes on what seems a *real* journey through a reasonably real medieval Germany.

Goldmund's adventures are largely erotic, and in a recent piece in *The New Republic* Stephen Koch remarked irreverently that what the novel is really about is not Artist *versus* Intellectual or what have you but 'wanting women'. Good for Goldmund, then, for he not only wants, he gets. His success rate is perhaps unrealistically high. 'Everywhere women desired him and made him happy… Without knowing it, he was to each woman the lover she had wished for and dreamed of.' He begins to feel that

> perhaps his destiny was to learn to know women and to learn love in a thousand ways, until he reached perfection, the way some musicians were able to play not only one, but three, four, or a great number of instruments… Here he had no difficulty learning; he never forgot a thing. Here experience accumulated and classified itself.

All the same, women don't stay with him very long, and the two he most desires elude him altogether. But what impresses is the *goodness* of the eroticism, its naturalness, indeed its pleasurableness. This endows Hesse's accounts with an effect of quite startling novelty at a time when the chief attraction of much current fiction is its analysis of the repulsiveness of physical intercourse. Goldmund enjoys making love to women, women enjoy having Goldmund make love to them, and Hesse knows how much of love-making can be justly conveyed through words and how much cannot. His easy, sure touch in physical matters (even the highly spiritual *Siddhartha* has some wise remarks on the subject) contrasts oddly with his over-heated meta-physicality, his lasciviously loose talk about destiny, the abyss, the longing for death and for the All.

But wanting and getting girls is not the whole of Goldmund's adventures. He kills twice, under provocation. And to rectify the balance further, Hesse follows Love with Sickness (the scenes of the Black Death are stark enough but not manipulated morbidly) and then with the persecution of the Jews in the wake of the plague. In this book too he makes excessively free with such large, question-begging concepts as 'the demands of fate', but despite the author's assiduous and finally tedious interventions, the balance of the novel's sympathy tips in favour of nature, art, action and the flesh, as against spirit, religion, contemplation and asceticism. The novel does have a tapestried air about it, a faint but distinct smell of fake-medieval alle-gorizing, yet there is still more of the feel of life in it, of experience not solely cerebral, than in any other work of Hesse's.

Of the other books recently published in translation there is less to be said. *Rosshalde* (1914) is an essentially *gemütlich* mixture of idyll and anguish, of talk about life and talk about art, with some talk about the erotic East thrown in. The chief duality here seems to be the old one of life and art which Mann treated so much more comprehensively, pointedly and professionally.

> The intellect of man is forced to choose
> Perfection of the life, or of the work …

Johann Veraguth is a famous artist who hardly exists at all as a man. He resides on the beautiful estate of Rosshalde, coolly estranged from his family, which is only held together by Pierre, the seven-year-old son uneasily shared by the parents. Of Veraguth we are told plainly,

> he, who never sent a bungled drawing or painting out into the world, suffered deeply under the dark weight of innumerable bungled days and years, bungled attempts at love and life …

One of those beautiful, over-sensitive, precocious children who are too good to live, Pierre dies. And Veraguth prepares to leave for the East, where (he believes) he will be able to unite his art with a 'new life, which, he was resolved, would no longer be a groping or dim-sighted wandering, but rather a bold, steep climb'. New life will nourish new art: it is the old Gauguinesque dream. What is most convincing here is the harrowing account of the child's sickness and death, an event merely incidental to what is presumably the novel's central concern.

Demian (1919) is considered the 'break-through', the first of the maturely meaningful novels. I would say it is insufficiently cryptic for its own good. Hesse jeopardizes the novel by tactlessly tying his vague prophecies to a particular occurrence, the First World War. Thus we hear of 'a great chain of events' commencing with the war, about 'a new world' which is beginning to emerge and 'something akin to a new humanity' which is taking shape 'deep down, underneath' – as it were, something like Wilfred Owen's 'Strange Meeting' without that poem's conditional tense and its elegiac tone and tenor. The novel's schoolboy pranks, quasi-mystical visions and admixture of sexual stirrings account for its appeal to adolescents of all ages.

Halfway through *The Journey to the East* (1932) the narrator, H.H. (Harry Haller, Hermann Hesse), cries out, 'But how can it be told, this tale of a unique journey, of a unique communion of minds, of such a wonderfully exalted and spiritual life?' Towards the end, at a judicial assembly of the League, its Speaker announces that the League is ready to pass judgment on the narrator,

> who has now realized how strange and blasphemous was his intention to write the story of a journey to which he was not equal, and an account of a League in whose existence he no longer believed and to which he had become unfaithful.

The catch is that the League can only be spoken of in public by those who have left it, and those who have left it cannot remember what the League was all about! Therefore, as Ziolkowski puts it, all the narrator can do now 'is to narrate his own *attempt to narrate* the journey to the East: the act of narration has become the subject of the story'. Ending as it does with what is blatantly a symbol, but a symbol amenable to any number of interpretations, the book can be said to be open-ended. In that sense it can also be said to be open-beginninged and open-middled as well. It seems to me an amusing piece of higher chicanery (indeed it seems to me rather like a parodic send-up of *Magister Ludi* in particular and of armchair 'journeys' in general), but Hesse apparently took it very seriously, and there have been and no doubt are and will be plenty of readers ready and eager to supply their own beginning, middle and end, and in effect to write Hesse's book for him.

Beneath the Wheel (1906), Hesse's second novel is more honest and more sad, the story of a gifted boy of humble birth who is sent from his village to a theological academy, sinks to the bottom of the class, breaks down, goes home, and dies. Ziolkowski claims that, just as the school is the same as the one in *Narcissus and Goldmund*, so is the duality of the later novel anticipated here in the school friendship between Hans Giebenrath and Hermann Heilner (another H.H., though here a rather fleeting Hitchcockian presence), between the grind and the poet, the quiet worried scholarship-boy who is destroyed and the 'checkered and striking personality' who runs away and lives to fight another day. Unalerted to this parallel, we should read *Beneath the Wheel* as simply a straightforward warning, touching and telling, against the evils of subjecting a boy to the academic grindstone at a time when he should be giving himself up to the beneficent sway of nature. The slight smell of metaphysical *Lederhosen* which pervades Hesse's work is rather less metaphysical than usual here and more physical. And none the worse for that – but why must Hans die? Surely not that Hermann may live?

It is not so much that Hesse dramatizes or even popularizes ideas as that he takes the stiffening out of them, sandpapers the sharper edges away, and hands them over to his readers to play with as they will. A highly cultivated person, he is the ideal second-order writer for the sort of serious-minded reader desirous to believe that he is grappling successfully with intellectual and artistic profundities of the first order. Best among his books, I would say, are *Steppenwolf* for queer fun and mystification and some shrewd comments on the bourgeoisie, and *Narcissus and Goldmund* for a fairminded (if not consciously intended) assessment of some of those polar opposites so interesting to us all (for who wants to feel himself under-privileged in the matter of souls?) and so obsessively fascinating to the romantic German mind.

(1968)

Svevo's Progress: or, The Apotheosis of the Poor Fish

Each of Italo Svevo's three novels is a 'Life'. But the difference in liveliness between the first and the last is striking. *A Life* (1893) is a simple and sad story, predictable and yet – while obviously a superior work by the standards of current fiction – not altogether cogent. It is difficult to present convincingly the sort of character who is utterly lacking in convictions: the weak character tends to emerge as a weak characterization. And unhappily Svevo makes his character commit suicide for reasons which are almost – the official formula is not so ironic in its effect as Svevo may have intended – 'quite unknown'.

The simplicity of approach is intimated on the first page, in Alfonso's letter to his mother. The country boy has come to work in a Trieste bank: 'I feel such a need to breathe some of our good pure air coming straight from its Maker. Here the air is thick and smoky.' Poor Alfonso, he is doomed from the start, though (one would have said) doomed to tuberculosis or malnutrition rather than death by his own hand. And 'country boy' is a misleadingly robust description of him, for he is handicapped by an education and a degree of culture. 'Generally he read serious works of criticism and philosophy, which he found less tiring than poetry or art.'

For Alfonso his 'culture' is an escape from life, an unsuccessful attempt to escape: it returns him to life even less qualified to cope than he was before. 'A well-written book gave him megalomaniac dreams, not due to the quality of his brain but to circumstances; finding himself at one extreme, he dreamt of another.' Unhappily he strikes up an acquaintance with the boss's daughter, a young lady whose interest in culture derives from something worse than enervation of character or unfriendliness of circumstance – from vanity and snobbishness. When there is no more spring in their emotions than in a snail, plainly a mutual taste for novels or for talking about novels is not likely to bridge the social and economic gap between them, not in Trieste at the end of the nineteenth century.

Macario warns Alfonso about Annetta's true nature at the very beginning of their tepid relationship, indeed before their relationship begins. None the less, for some unexplored reason, Alfonso pays half-hearted court to her. They even collaborate on a novel, Annetta's role being to write it, Alfonso's to admire what Annetta has written. Alfonso despises Annetta, Annetta despises Alfonso, and they continue to court each other quarter-heartedly.

Other well-meaning persons warn Alfonso, plainly enough. Annetta, one of them says, is 'a vain little thing who wanted to see someone die of love for her, but had not succeeded so far'. But an irresistible lack of force drives him on, and eventually they make love, or some shadow of it. Admittedly this happens only once, but the vague talk about Annetta's sensuality doesn't explain how she came to 'give herself' – the expression is peculiarly incongruous – to someone of inferior class, and one moreover whose physical presence, hero though he is, remains so indistinct. He is described at the outset as 'tall and strong', but later, in the company of Macario (himself 'tall and strong'), we hear that in size Alfonso was 'so small and insignificant that Macario felt fine beside him'.

The act of sexual collaboration proves too much for them, and mutual indifference sets in forthwith. 'His love for Annetta and his repugnance for her both seemed colourless.' Alfonso returns to the village, but only to be present at his mother's sick-bed. Her doctor now begins to show more interest in her, and Svevo comments sadly that perhaps this was a benefit Signora Carolina derived from her son's arrival, 'for a person's life seems precious mainly because of the value others put on it'.

Returning to the city after his mother's death, Alfonso finds Annetta engaged to Macario and himself in indefinably bad odour with his employer. After a curiously obscure brush with Annetta's brother and an ensuing challenge to a duel – presumably a social transgression cannot be dealt with except obscurely – Alfonso gases himself; the country boy chooses a metropolitan way of death. 'He knew neither how to love nor to enjoy; he had suffered in the best of circumstances more than did others in the most painful ones.' Suicide might be thought to be Alfonso's one successful act in life, except that by this time we are so used to him failing that we cannot accept the author's ruling. The case is altogether different with Guido Speier in *Confessions of Zeno*, since Guido is not the chief character and, though he too may lack sufficient reason for suicide, he was in truth hoping to win sympathy and respite from the burden of financial failure. By a mischance the stomach pump which Guido was counting on failed to arrive in time.

Though this account of *A Life* indicates the novel's self-imposed limitations, it fails to do justice to the quiet clarity and decency of the writing, and above all Svevo's gift for making plain the mediocrity of a character without the least trace of a sneer. Svevo is always at his best in the vicinity of a death-bed, and the mother's last days are movingly related. He is almost as good in the vicinity of finance, and the atmosphere of the bank is evoked with the minimum of documentation, by a scattering of light hints and natural touches.

Svevo's second novel, *As a Man Grows Older* (1898), though its hero is similarly a poor fish, is a marked step forward. It has a good deal of charm, often what seems a deliberately faded charm, and it is innocent of straining after effect or significance. Emilio, a bachelor of Trieste who has once published a novel, falls vaguely in love with Angiolina, not definitely enough to marry her, but just enough to feel hurt and indignant when she deceives him, as (it is clear to the reader) she is practically bound to do in the circumstances. There are foretastes of Zeno. For instance, Emilio has banished religion from his home, but is gratified and reassured to find that his intended mistress is a believer: 'What a blessed thing religion was!' Zeno tells us repeatedly that, if *he* were religious himself, he would spend all day in church, nothing else in the world would matter. But, worldlier than Emilio, Zeno would never have attributed rapid progress with a new lady friend solely to the fact that 'she had found him so reasonable that she felt she could trust him completely'. Before long Emilio and Angiolina come to despise each other hardly less than do Alfonso and Annetta, and Emilio's reflection that 'he had possessed the woman he hated, not the woman he loved' could well come from Alfonso at the corresponding stage in his courtship.

Yet in the central relationship of *As a Man Grows Older* there is a strong and credible element of sensuality, of natural appetite. Moreover the novel contains a powerful character, Emilio's sister Amalia, colourless in her life but powerful in her decline and death, a process described at length and in lucid and dramatic detail. There is nothing elsewhere in Svevo's work to compare with this, not even the death of Zeno's father, for he exists chiefly as an adjunct to Zeno, or to Zeno's 'disease'. Certainly Amalia's death-bed throws the rest of the book (as I suppose the moral requires) into the shade. Svevo's sense of irony is developing; and Emilio, having lost both his mistress and his sister, settles down to 'a love of quiet and of security' and 'the necessity of looking after himself'. As the years pass, Angiolina merges in memory with Amalia, the physical beauty of the one with the spiritual qualities of the other, to become a 'lofty, splendid symbol'. Emilio's taste for literature has, after all, proved to have its uses. He survives.

The hero of Svevo's last novel, *Confessions of Zeno* (1923), not only survives, he triumphs. Third in this sequence of poor fishes, Zeno is the one who gets away. He gets away with quite a lot. It is as if Svevo has revolted against his earlier attitudes, or against their one-sidedness, their excessive simpleness. Perhaps, under his cod's clothing, the poor fish may be something of a dolphin, even at times a bit of a shark? And here it is Guido, robust and successful, the proficient violinist who understands Bach better than Bach himself, the Tuscan-speaking dandy, the charmer who wins the beautiful and virtuous Ada – it is Guido who kills himself, while Zeno, invalid and dilettante, goes on to recover the family fortunes and build a family and a fortune of his own.

The sickliness of Svevo's heroes, their physical enervation, is gloriously caricatured in Zeno. Continuously beset by mysterious aches and pains, he lives on avidly while strong characters die off all around him. His nerves, it seems,

> were so sensitive that they already gave warning of a disease from which possibly I was going to die only twenty years later. They might in fact be called perfect nerves, their only disadvantage being that there were very few days when they left me in peace.

The *Confessions* were written at the suggestion of Zeno's analyst (who supplies a nicely pompous and uncomprehending preface), or rather his ex-analyst. Towards the end Zeno cries,

> How can I any longer endure to be in the company of that ridiculous man, with his would-be penetrating eye, and the intolerable conceit that allows him to group all the phenomena in the world round his grand new theory?

For Zeno's trouble has been diagnosed as that of Oedipus: which enchants him (what an impressive pedigree that disease has!) but doesn't, even in 1915, deceive him. The association with Sophocles may titillate his vanity, but neither his common sense nor his sense of humour nor his status in the Triestine bourgeoisie nor indeed his vanity will permit for long this assimilation to a barbarous, dead mythology. Zeno is alive, civilized and very real. He remarks of his analyst, 'He must be the only person in the world who, hearing that I wanted to go to bed with two lovely women, must rack his brains to try and find a reason for it!' It is really the analyst who is sick, who is abnormal.

The truth is, Zeno is an extraordinarily normal and healthy man. He is one of the toughest characters in fiction: he needs to be, if he is to think about himself so minutely, so intensively, so protractedly, without turning into an absolute monster or dissolving into thin air. Rich enough not to have to do any real work, he has plenty of time to suppose that there must be something wrong with him. He is the most cheerful type of *malade imaginaire*, since his maladies never prevent him from doing or not doing whatever he would have done or not done otherwise. The 'search for health' is equally imaginary, a device for occupying the intervals between adventures and for justifying (Zeno enjoys big words and large conceptions even though he doesn't exactly trust them) his immense and unremitting interest in himself. 'Health cannot analyse itself even if it looks at itself in the glass. It is only we invalids who can know anything about ourselves.' It must be his 'illness' (or it might be his 'search for health') which leads him to take a mistress, seeing that he genuinely loves and admires his wife. It must be this too which causes him to give up his mistress – or causes him to cause her to give him up – seeing that she is a wellnigh perfect mistress. *He* is ready to tell us as much, but he declines to hear the same explanation from his analyst: common sense is all against it, and in any case one expects better things from a doctor.

When the *Confessions of Zeno* first appeared in English translation, in 1930, Frank Swinnerton spoke aptly of its 'amusing and mischievous illustrations of the adjustments of conscience by which sinners are able to continue respecting themselves'. When Zeno is about to take a mistress, he falls ill with conscience, and his wife assumes that his suffering is caused by the imminent marriage of Ada, her sister and Zeno's first love, to Guido. Zeno's indignation is such that it at once dispels the pangs of conscience. 'I honestly felt that she was wronging me; I was not guilty of such a crime as that.' A similar touch occurs in *As a Man Grows Older*, when Emilio taxes his mistress with infidelity: she has been seen with another man, in a café, drinking chocolate. Angiolina flares up in righteous indignation: 'Chocolate! I simply can't endure it! The idea of my drinking chocolate!'

Much of the humour of the *Confessions* derives from the fact that Zeno *sometimes* deceives himself or errs in interpretation. During his honeymoon, 'I was prone to assume the dignified pose of an equestrian statue,' he tells us, amusedly, complacently. The honeymoon was spent in Italy, visiting the galleries, and Zeno misses the point of Augusta's remark, reported directly after: 'It is lucky one only has to visit museums on one's honeymoon, and then never again!' Any interpretation of that remark other than the obvious, superficial one, wouldn't fit in with his settled conception of his wife as 'the personification of health' – that is, a splendid woman, but not too bright.

But if Zeno always, or mostly, deceived himself – or was tediously striving to deceive us – his company would prove intolerable over four hundred pages. A genuine *malade imaginaire* is deceiving himself: Zeno is an imaginary *malade imaginaire*. The *Confessions* move nimbly to and fro, from self-deception to engaging attempts at deceiving the doctor (and the reader) to truth-telling. (An instance of the latter is when he, the great self-analyser, the foremost expert on Zenology, points out that 'to explain to somebody how he is made is only another way of authorizing him to do as he likes'.) And what emerges from this agile to-and-fro is, not a very sublime character admittedly, but the truth about Zeno.

Like his predecessors, then, Zeno is a self-examiner, but on a vaster and minuter scale, and what he sees, far from depressing and disabling him, keeps him vastly stimulated. He is not the narrow, exclusive kind of egoist, for the egos of others amaze him almost equally. As a tragic figure a poor fish cannot amount to much, however humane his creator: but his comic potentialities are enormous. Zeno has been described as a Triestine Charlie Chaplin, but he is much further removed from the tragic, or pathetic, than this would suggest. In some respects he resembles Falstaff – witty in himself and a notable cause that wit is in other men – except that he is thoroughly Triestine and bourgeois and in little danger of having his heart killed by anybody. For a hypocrite, he is a relatively honest man. Thus, during the period of his rivalry with Guido he consoles himself by playing the Kreutzer Sonata. And pretty well, too: the battle for Ada is not hopelessly lost. 'One's own violin,' he adds, 'resounds so close to one's ear that it reaches the heart very quickly.' The truth is sometimes too harsh to be faced squarely: Zeno will then squint sideways at it. In this way he is enabled to carry on with the battle of existence – but before long he will himself demolish the consolations and vindications which he has fabricated. There is much of the rascal about him, but nothing of the prig.

Tottering on the brink of death, as he likes to imagine, Zeno maintains a zest for living, is endlessly fascinated by all the sad and lovely contradictions of human life. Ada, the perfect woman, makes the mistake – as Zeno sees it, though not the reader – of preferring Guido: in fact, as things turn out, it *is* a mistake. A succession of mistakes and misapprehensions leads to Zeno affiancing himself against his conscious will to Augusta, Ada's plain though kindlier sister: as things turn out, this is no mistake, for Ada loses even her good looks, while Augusta gains them. Zeno has more luck than he deserves: he makes up for poor Emilio and poorer Alfonso. Yet the luck is not wantonly bestowed by a doting author, for Zeno's disposition is such as to attract good fortune. Towards the end of the novel he informs Guido, now patently the under-dog, that 'Life is neither good nor bad; it is original.' Alfonso and Emilio might well have produced a set of melancholy and flaccidly 'cultured' variations on the first part of that epigram, but neither could have delivered himself of the second part.

Having already switched from law to chemistry, the young Zeno asked his father's permission to change back to law. The father remarked good-naturedly that Zeno must be mad. The grateful son, wishing to amuse his parent, underwent a thorough examination in order to obtain a certificate of sanity, which he then carried in triumph to his father. The latter, 'in an agonized voice and actually with tears in his eyes', exclaimed, 'Ah, then you really are mad!' But *Confessions of Zeno* is not only much funnier than Svevo's other novels, it is richer in very nearly every way, a splendid complex of wit, irony, shrewdness, tenderness and dry compassion. If the earlier books derived from Flaubertian realism and from the confusion of literature and life called *bovarysme*, the *Confessions* are nearer to the nobler and larger tradition of the *Bildungsroman*, and at the point where this genre overlaps with the picaresque. There are similarities with Thomas Mann's *Confessions of Felix Krull* and even with *The Magic Mountain*. And just as the equivocal hero of *Wilhelm Meister's Apprenticeship* is finally likened to 'Saul the son of Kish, who went out to seek his father's asses, and found a kingdom', so Zeno, incredulous paterfamilias, goes out to seek roses for his daughter, inadvertently crosses a military frontier, is prevented by the confused outbreak of war from rejoining his family, and later – with the help of the war – finds himself become a successful speculator in his own right. 'I really am well, absolutely well.… Of course I have pains from time to time, but what do they matter when my health is perfect?' It was business, his business, that has cured him, and, he says, he would like his late analyst to know it.

James Joyce, who encouraged Svevo to persevere in the face of public neglect, remarked in a letter to his widow, 'The important thing is that Svevo be read and written about.' Had Joyce managed to overcome his reluctance to set up as a literary gent and written about Svevo himself, perhaps the English might have overcome their ingrained suspicion of the European novel and actually read the *Confessions*, at least, this masterpiece of a period rich in master-novels.

(1963)

The Ghosts of Apes

Franz Werfel's *The Forty Days of Musa Dagh*

Days of misfortune pass and are gone,
Like the days of winter, they come and they go;
The sorrows of men do not last very long,
Like the buyers in shops, they come and go.

Persecution and blood lash the people to tears,
The caravans, they come and go,
And men spring up in the garden of earth,
Whether henbane or balsam, they come and they go ...

(Armenian folk-song)

Before we can achieve the heart of this remarkably rich novel,[1] something must be said about its 'story', the historical events of the Forty Days which make up the skeleton. More truly the inner history of individual spirits is so inextricably bound up with the outward events of the narrative and their ethical implications that even to speak of them under the metaphor of different parts of the same body is misleading. The novel is so little known, however – even in comparison with lesser works by the same author – that the critic is forced to make use of the anatomical approach.

The years 1894–5 were marked by the first wholesale massacres of Armenians in Turkey, under the Sultan Abdul Hamid. There were, of course, various reasons for the persecution, and probably the difference of religion was the least of them. Stateless since the Middle Ages, the Armenians had never been assimilated into the Ottoman Empire. An ancient race, with a tenacious culture of their own, they had retained their language, their customs and their crafts. King Tiridates of Armenia, who was converted to Christianity during the latter part of the third century, is said to have been the first ruler in the world to adopt the Christian faith as his state religion. And since that time an extensive Armenian literature has accumulated, mainly of a religious nature, in both poetry and prose. A monument of later Armenian culture is the thesaurus of the language, compiled in 1836, which gave Latin and Greek equivalents for every word, and of which the

---

1 *Die vierzig Tage des Musa Dagh, Roman des Armenischen Volk* (1933), by Franz Werfel, translated by Geoffrey Dunlop.

Encyclopedia Britannica remarks that there was at that time no dictionary of any language comparable for exhaustiveness and accuracy. To the more warlike Turks the Armenians seemed, in Werfel's words, 'a race of bookworms'; and Toynbee comments that 'the Armenians may be trusted to establish a school in every hamlet'. The very individuality and tenacity of culture of the Armenians might be expected to arouse the resentment of their neighbours and rulers. And, as in the case of other stateless peoples, this was aggravated by their adroitness both in the peasant crafts and in business.

Official justifications of the late nineteenth-century massacres revolved around the growing pro-Russian feeling among Armenians (several of the leading Russian generals in the 1877 war against Turkey had been Armenian) and the existence of a revolutionary movement within the Empire. The European Powers took exception to the bloodshed, and Gladstone denounced Abdul Hamid as 'the Great Assassin'.

That there was an element of truth in Abdul Hamid's arguments was indicated by the happenings of 1908, when Armenian intellectuals joined with the Young Turkish Movement (the 'Committee for Union and Progress') to overthrow the Sultan and the old régime. The reward for their revolutionary co-operation was that the Armenians suffered far worse treatment, with the outbreak of war in 1914, under the Young Turks. The declared policy of the government was 'extermination of the race'; Armenians everywhere in the Ottoman Empire were deported to the uninhabitable regions of Mesopotamian deserts; the young men were generally murdered at the outset and, of those who travelled in the convoys, more than half died before reaching their destination. The story is familiar enough to our generation, and it lacks only the gas chamber. The reasons given for the extermination are familiar too: the Armenian communities were accused of fifth-column activities and of intriguing with the advancing Russian forces. Again there were protests from some of the European Powers, and they were stronger this time since France and Britain were at war with Turkey. But they were of little practical use to the victims. And indeed the pre-war statesmanship of the Great Powers had served to worsen the lot of the Armenians. Italy, France, Germany, Austria, Russia and Britain had all intrigued over the body of the 'sick man', and their intrigues had naturally involved the one large Christian minority. Moreover, a staff of German officers had helped in the reform of the Turkish army after the counter-revolution of 1909, a British admiral had occupied himself with the navy, and French and Italian officers had reconstructed the gendarmerie. In the political and moral confusion which prevailed in 1914–15 the Armenians could expect actual assistance and relief only from non-official bodies – American missionaries and teachers, German pastors, British residents and Turkish peasants. The end of it was that of the pre-war Armenian population of Turkey roughly one-half died during the deportations and accompanying slaughter.[2]

In a collection of documents laid before Parliament by Viscount Bryce in 1916 and published under the title *The Treatment of Armenians in the Ottoman Empire* there are papers referring to the defence of Musa Dagh, which the editor, Arnold Toynbee, described as 'the single happy incident in the national tragedy of the Armenians'. The Armenians living in Yoghonoluk and the other villages on the slopes of Musa Dagh, the 'Mountain of Moses', rising sheer from the sea on the Syrian coast near Antioch, received their deportation orders at a later date and therefore had had an opportunity to see and hear what happened to their friends. They consequently chose to die on their own mountain, rather than during the ghastly journey to the deserts. With a few guns, flocks and some food, they took refuge behind the natural fortifications of Musa Dagh. They numbered roughly four thousand persons, of whom less than a quarter were grown men. In spite of their deficiency in the military spirit, they resisted full-scale attacks by the Turkish army for forty days (for fifty-three according to the documents), and just as their supplies had finally given out and it was clear they could survive no longer, a French cruiser which had noticed a banner hung out over the sea came to their rescue and took them to a British refugee camp at Port Said.

The moral we are meant to draw from the official documents – presumably they were published chiefly as propaganda against the enemy – is that the gallant outnumbered Armenians had triumphed over the cruel Turks. It was to be seen as one of those simple heart-warming adventure stories where a downtrodden right emerges amazingly victorious over a tyrannical might. But for Werfel the novelist, the moral is something quite different, for he knows that two brands of intolerance do not make for peace and justice, and his intention is to convey an experience which is less 'pure' than propaganda and much more authentic.

2 European estimates were between 500,000 and 700,000 out of a total population of 1,300,000; Turkish estimates between 200,000 and 300,000. Muslim historians, it should be added, claim that after the Russian Revolution between thirty and forty thousand Muslims in the area under Russian occupation were murdered by Armenians.

The main incidents of the novel correspond to events mentioned in the documents: the apparently insuperable difficulties of the undertaking; the storm which ruins a great part of their provisions at the outset; the election by ballot of a committee of defence; the surprise attack by the besieged upon the besiegers; the primitive battering-ram used to propel boulders down the slopes; and the banner with its inscription, 'Christians in Need. Help'. But it is in those points where the novel departs from the documents that the importance – the special quality – of the novel lies. Differences relating to the invented characters may be left for the moment, while we glance at the difference in tone and intention, in explicit comment and implicit belief, between the compilers of the documents and the writer of the novel.

The first distinction (and it implies the others) has to do with the mastery of the artist – art as distinct from documentary. Here is an extract from a 'Statement by two Red Cross Nurses of Danish nationality' describing events at Erzindjan, in east-central Turkey:

> A soldier attached to our staff as cobbler said to Sister B.: 'I am now forty-six years old, and yet I am taken for military service, although I have paid my exemption-tax regularly every year. I have never done anything against the Government, and now they are taking from me my whole family, my seventy-year-old mother, my wife and five children, and I do not know where they are going.' He was especially affected by the thought of his little daughter, a year and a half old; 'She is so sweet. She has such pretty eyes'; he wept like a child. The next day he came back; 'I know the truth. They are all dead.' And it was only too true. ...

With this we should compare the following passage from the novel:

> A shifting carpet woven with the threads of blood-stained destinies. It is always the same ... Here, for instance, a man of forty-six in good clothes, an engineer. It needs many cudgel blows to get him away from his wife and children. His youngest is about one and a half. This man is to be enrolled in a labour battalion, for road-making. He stumbles in the long line of men and shuffles, gibbering like a half-wit: 'I never missed paying my bedel ... paying my bedel.' Suddenly he grips hold of his neighbour. 'You've never seen such a lovely baby.' ... A torrent of sentimental agony. 'Why, the girl had eyes as big as plates. If only I could, I'd crawl after them on my belly like a snake.' And he shuffles on, enveloped in his grief, completely isolated. That evening they lie down to rest on a hillside. Long after midnight he shakes the same neighbour out of his sleep. 'They're all dead now.' He is perfectly calm.

It seems more than likely that Werfel's passage is based on the extract from the document (even to retaining the ages of the man and his daughter), but the two belong to different classes of writing. In short, the novelist's treatment is more real – it is *too real*, too complete, to serve as effective propaganda. The document, on the other hand, is well presented, in an official, informative and apparently impersonal style; and yet it does provide wartime propaganda, of a comparatively decent sort. For the neutral tone does not exclude emotional cliché: the soldier 'wept like a child' – that, one suspects, is the prerogative of our allies. The soldier of the novel, however, was 'gibbering like a half-wit': and his 'torrent of sentimental agony' tends to sweep away the distinction between ally and enemy, between Muslim and Christian, between political right and political wrong. Werfel does not marshal us into righteous anger, but shows just what reprisals and counter-reprisals amount to, in human terms.

Then there is this extract from a letter sent by members of the German Missions Staff in Turkey to the German Ministry of Foreign Affairs, describing conditions in Aleppo:

> All this happens under the eyes of high Turkish officials. There are forty or fifty emaciated phantoms crowded into the compound opposite our school. They are women out of their mind; they have forgotten how to eat, when one offers them bread, they throw it aside with indifference. They only groan and wait for death.

This may well have served as scaffolding for the description of the desert concentration camps which Werfel puts into the mouth of the shocked Turkish officer in the second 'Interlude of the Gods' (the title given to the two chapters in which Johannes Lepsius, the German pastor who is working for Armenian relief, interviews the various powers):

> THE CAPTAIN: 'Battlefields are horrible. … But the worst battlefield is nothing compared to Deir ez-Zor. … Nobody could ever imagine it.'
>
> THE OLD SHEIKH: 'And what was worst?'
>
> THE CAPTAIN: 'They're no longer human. … ghosts. … But not the ghosts of human beings … the ghosts of apes. It takes them a long time to die, because they chew grass, and can sometimes get hold of a piece of bread. … But the worst thing is that they're all too weak to bury their tens of thousands of corpses. … Deir ez-Zor is a horrible cloaca of death …'
>
> THE OLD SHEIKH (*after a long pause*): 'And how can they be helped?'

THE CAPTAIN: 'Helped? The best anyone could do for them would be to kill them all off in one day. ... I've sent a letter to all our brethren. ... We've managed to find homes for over a thousand orphans in Turkish or Arab families. ... But that's scarcely anything.

The document is horrible, but the extract from the novel is terrible. The former, though not intended as propaganda against a secular enemy, is likely to rouse our feelings against the Turks as anti-Christians; the latter conveys a different warning, that it *is* possible for man to turn his fellow-men into animals. In the novel the victims are not injured innocents: they are dehumanized creatures who cannot now be helped, 'the ghosts of apes', for whom right and wrong, friend and enemy, have no longer any meaning. We have arrived at the far edge of humanity, and at the edge of Hell as the Devil describes it in Mann's *Doctor Faustus*:

'*here everything leaves off.*' Every compassion, every grace, every sparing, every last trace of consideration for the incredulous, imploring objection 'that you verily cannot do so unto a soul': it is done, it happens. ...

Occasionally one hears in the documents the overt tones of the proselytizer. The Armenian mission at Van had first harboured Armenians and later, when the advancing Russians had taken the town, was asked to look after Turkish refugees. 'The effect on its followers of the religion of Islam was never more strongly contrasted with Christianity' –

Where the Armenians had been cheery and hopeful, and had clung to life with wonderful vitality, the Muslims, with no faith in God and no hope of a future life, bereft now of hope in this life, died like flies of the prevailing dysentery from lack of stamina and the will to live.

The attitude we are conscious of in *The Forty Days of Musa Dagh* – and Werfel was a Jew (he left Vienna for America in 1940) and hence would have no casual, dilettante interest in persecution – is nearer to that of the impersonal, scientific historian on this point:

The atrocities have been revealed in their true light, as crimes incidental to an abnormal process, which all parties have committed in turn, and not as the peculiar practice of one denomination and nationality.[3]

3 Arnold Toynbee, Introduction to *The Western Question in Greece and Turkey*.

Werfel puts forward the Turkish-Muslim case in all fairness. When Lepsius attends a meeting of the mystical order of dervishes called 'the thieves of hearts', the Türbedar – the 'guardian of the tombs of sultans and holy men', who represents the more fanatical kind of Muslim – throws the blame for the massacres on the Western powers whose experiments in 'progress' inspired the Young Turks to overthrow the Sultan:

> At the [*Berlin*] Congress you Europeans began to meddle in the domestic affairs of the empire. You urged reforms. You wanted to buy Allah and our religion of us, for shabby sums. The Armenians were your commercial travellers. ... You tell us our government is guilty of all this bloody injustice. But, in truth, it is not our government but yours. It went to school to you. You supported it in its criminal struggle against our most sacred treasures. Now it carries out your instructions, in your spirit. ...

The strength of the Türbedar's arguments helps to preserve the essential balance of the novel, which otherwise might seem weighted in favour of European and Christian values. 'Do we send you missionaries, as you us?' he cries. 'You only send out the cross before you so that the Baghdad railway and the oil trusts may pay better dividends.' And his reasoning is backed up by the more sympathetic figure of the old Sheikh Achmed, a moderate, who ascribes the inability of the well-intentioned to help the Armenians to the fact that 'we are weak because these lackeys of Europe have stolen religion from our people.'

Yet when, after describing the Armenians in Turkey as an electric wire which 'conducted your devil's restlessness into the midst of our peace', the Türbedar concludes, 'Can't you yourself see the justice of God in these events?', we are reminded that there are always as many gods as there are combatants. If this is logic, then logic is of no use here: neither the Türbedar's logic nor the logic which the Christian lady brought to bear upon the incidence of dysentery among Muslims. And more hopeful than argument or generalization or logic of any kind is the unofficial, human behaviour of the Turkish villagers as related in the chapter called 'The Great Assembly':

> Often, as he rode about his district, a surprised müdir would pull up in the village street, where he had just read out his decree of banishment, to watch Turks and Armenians mingle their tears. He would marvel as, before an Armenian house, its Turkish neighbours stood and wailed, calling after its dazed and tearless

inhabitants, who without looking back were leaving the doors of their old home: 'May God pity you!' And more, loading them with provisions for the road, with costly presents, a goat or even a mule. The amazed müdir might even have to see these Turks accompany their wretched neighbours for several leagues. He might even behold his own compatriots casting themselves down before his feet, to beseech him: 'Let them stay with us. They haven't the true faith, but they are good. They are our brothers. Let them stay with us.'

All this is ground which must be measured out and cleared before Werfel can properly come to grips with the real problem of the novel. And this, we find, is no problem at all. ... For the theme is persecution. Not a debate as to the rights and wrongs involved, but simply a painfully detailed 'psychology' of persecution. Systematically breaking down all those defences – of false logic, cultivated scepticism, sentimentality – which we erect against the attacks of unpalatable knowledge, Werfel brings us face to face with it: the experience of the victim.

But first, the experience of the persecutor. How does persecution begin? A governmental order cannot take all the responsibility. And the stages by which the common emotions of irritation at another's nonconformity or smarter business sense, or jealousy of his house and furniture, or suppressed desire for his 'foreign' wife – the stages by which these feelings pass into murder, looting and rape, are dramatically realized in 'The Great Assembly'. This short passage describes the state of mind of the Turkish police in charge of the convoys:

> Those saptiehs were not all brutes. It is even probable that most of them were good, plain, middling sort of people. But what can a saptieh do? ... His heart may be in perfect sympathy with the screaming mother who tries to snatch her child out of a ditch, flings herself down on the road, and claws the earth. No use to talk to her. She's wasted minutes already, and it's still six miles to the next halt. A convoy held up. All the faces in it twisted with hate. A mad scream from a thousand throats. Why did not these crowds, weak as they were, hurl themselves on the saptieh and his mates, disarm them, and tear them into shreds? Perhaps the policemen were in constant terror of such an assault, which would have finished them. And so – one of them fires a shot. The rest whip out their swords

to beat the defenceless cruelly with the blades. Thirty or forty men and women lie bleeding. And, with this blood, another emotion comes to life in the excited saptiehs – their old itch for the women of the accursed race. In these helpless women you possess more than a human being – in very truth you possess the God of your enemy. Afterwards, the saptiehs scarcely knew how it all had happened.

Man's recognition of humanity, of the worth of human life, of being a man, is – the novel tells us – so easily lost. And once lost, it is difficult to recover. In its stead are erected flimsy standards of political expediency, to be replaced in their turn by still flimsier ones. Talaat Bey, the Turkish Minister of the Interior at the time of these events, is said to have made the following statement in an interview for the *Berliner Tageblatt*:

The sad events that have occurred in Armenia have prevented my sleeping well at night. We have been reproached for making no distinction between the innocent Armenians and the guilty; but that was utterly impossible, in view of the fact that those who were innocent today might be guilty tomorrow.

In the given circumstances, Talaat Bey was quite right. Supposedly the instrument for exterminating the guilty, force has the habit of turning into an instrument which produces guilt, and in ever-increasing ratios. And this, it seems to me, is a way of describing one of the themes of *The Forty Days of Musa Dagh*.

In the course of projecting the experience of persecution, Werfel demolishes our various modes of mental defence. One of these defences lies in the distinction postulated between the regular soldier and the 'thug', between the bombing plane and the Turkish saptieh. Werfel is concerned chiefly with atrocities committed at close quarters, in hot blood and against defenceless victims, but he makes no suggestion that this is in some way more disgusting than the warfare in Europe. He reminds us of Europe as the villagers prepare for their secret exodus to the mountain:

there the dog-fight was being conducted with all modern conveniences. According to the most advanced scientific principles, not with the innocent blood-lust of the beast of passion, but with the mathematical thoroughness and precision of the beast of intellect.

Another protective skin for the conscience is the notion that 'suffering refines', and therefore cannot be absolutely and altogether deplorable. The victim emerges as the hero. But even the writers of the eye-witness accounts in *The Treatment of Armenians in the Ottoman Empire*, however inclined to praise the Armenians, were too close to the reality for this. And Werfel blows this scrap of consolation sky high. Part of the novel's uninsistent poetic symbolism lies in the quiet suggestion that Musa Dagh is an exemplar of the Garden of Eden:

> The flower-strewn meadows of its eastern slopes, the fat pasturage of its many-folded flanks, its lithe orchards of apricot, vine and orange around its feet; its quiet, as of protecting seraphim – all this seemed scarcely touched by the fall of man, under which, in rocky melancholy, the rest of Asia Minor mourns. ...

But the fleeing Armenians bring with them to Musa Dagh the angel of the flaming sword who turns Paradise to a gutted wilderness: the last desperate device of the defenders is to set fire to the mountain which has sheltered them. And their settlement, right from the start, is by no means a Utopian community: they cling desperately to their social and financial class-distinctions, and very soon spy fever, food stealing, disloyalty, apathy, personal antipathies and jealousies prove to be enemies just as dangerous as the Turkish army.

On the thirty-third day of the defence, the Agha Rifaat Bereket, a pious Muslim of pre-revolutionary sympathies and one of 'the thieves of hearts', obtains admission to the settlement and, though he has visited the worst of the deportation camps, is sickened by what he sees:

> The savage, feverish masks of men grimaced round him avidly. Waving arms, as thin as twigs, thrust out of tattered sleeves, held children close to his face, as the women begged. Nearly all these children had swollen heads, on the thinnest necks, and their huge, staring eyes had a knowledge in them forbidden the children of humankind... He believed that now he could understand how much this draining off of the spirit exceeds in cruelty even the massacre of the body. The most horrible thing that had been done was, not that a whole people had been exterminated but that a whole people, God's children, had been dehumanized. The sword of Enver, striking these Armenians, had struck Allah. Since in them, as in all other men, even unbelievers, Allah dwells. And whoso degrades His dignity in the creature, degrades the Creator in his victim. This, then, is God-murder, the sin which, to the end of time, is never forgiven.

Suffering on this scale does not strengthen or refine: it dehumanizes. But the effects of persecution – the spiritual disasters resultant on this inhuman testing – are most persuasively and poignantly brought out in Werfel's depiction of the people of his story. Before we pass on to this we should note the author's avoidance of overt moralizing (the critic is likely to be less successful in this) and his use instead of a telling irony.

Irony, Werfel's most effective stratagem in his attack on muffled sensibilities, is integral to the book, but there are several instances which may conveniently be quoted here. The Armenian camp has been unmolested for over a week; the reason, unknown to the refugees, is that the authorities have something more pressing to contend with – a violent outbreak of spotted typhus originating with the masses of Armenian corpses in the Mesopotamian deserts:

> The worldly wisdom of Talaat Bey, in the Serail Palace of the ministry, might well have been confounded by the perception of what strange results may emerge from any attempt to exterminate a whole people. But neither he nor Enver let it perturb them. …

A singular gloss on the text, 'Any man's death diminishes me, because I am involved in mankind …'

Then there is Werfel's ironical protest against the reader who will accuse him of exaggerating the horrors, of grinding some private axe. When Lepsius intervenes for the Armenians with Enver Pasha, the Minister of War, he refers to an account of the atrocities drawn up by the American ambassador: '"Mr Morgenthau," said Enver brightly, "is a Jew. And Jews are always fanatically on the side of minorities."'

But the finest example of this irony – it invests what is a crucial development in the plot – is Werfel's account of how the rescue of the survivors came about; this, of course, is a complete departure from the historical facts. One of the village teachers, Hrand Oskanian, off his head with jealousy, hurt pride and the general desperation, has become the leader of a small suicide cult. There is no God – he teaches – and the world is a lump of dung spinning in space. But there is one way whereby man can show his power and spite this non-existent God: suicide. This will also spite the Turks. On the fortieth night Oskanian and his four converts gather on the edge of the mountain, ready to throw themselves into the sea. The three women are induced to jump first, leaving the prophet with his stern male disciple. When Oskanian refuses to jump until sunrise, the follower suspects his leader of back-sliding. In the ensuing struggle the follower is flung over the cliff. Oskanian, hopping about insanely, falls over a flagpole – the banner, 'Christians in Need. Help', which the wind had blown over long before. He picks it up, shoulders it without knowing what he is doing, and continues his antics. The French cruiser *Guichen* notices these mad wavings and signals an answer back. But Oskanian, consumed with the desire to escape the consequences of his guilt, steps too far and the weight of the flagpole drags him over the cliff-edge: 'At that minute the twelve-inch guns of the *Guichen* halted the Turks with a shell that crashed down into Suedia.' That such a significant event – yet what does it signify that the Armenians are to be rescued now? – should hang on the inglorious twitchings of an almost mindless body is itself an indication that the novel is more than the exciting adventure story which it contains.

The final ironical situation – it is part of the personal tragedy of the chief character – occurs with the subsequent landing of the fleet-commander, the French rear admiral, and his ceremonial inspection of the locale of this heroic action: 'The rear admiral was a pious, indeed a celebrated Catholic, and this fight of Armenians in defence of the religion of the Cross had really moved him.' As the Armenian commander, Gabriel Bagradian does his best to meet the occasion by asking the admiral, 'in the name of the French nation', to accept the two howitzers captured from the Turks by his young son (who has since been caught and killed). It is found impossible to move them to the ship, however, and they have to be blown up:

So much the better, Gabriel thought, two pieces of artillery less in the world. And yet he was sorry. For Stephan's sake. The admiral proffered consolation: 'You have done the good cause most signal service, Monsieur le Commandant, even though these howitzers are destroyed.'

The admiral then asks for an account of the defence, while Gabriel grows more and more impatient –

The three battles? They had been by no means the reality. What did these electro-plated bigwigs know of the Armenian destiny, of the gradual, slow undermining of every individual life up there? His impatience became tinged with disgust. Couldn't he simply turn his back on them and walk away? … No – in Christ's name! The French, after all, were miraculous saviours; they had a right to eternal gratitude.

The admiral makes a short speech in honour of Gabriel: 'You, Monsieur, have given proof of the most exalted of all heroisms –

Christian heroism, which defends something more precious than hearth and home…' But all this talk of victory, unforgettable deeds, Christian heroism and *la gloire* is utterly out of place on Musa Dagh at the end of the Forty Days. Gabriel has broken irrevocably with the world in which such words can be spoken and have a meaning:

> As Gabriel bowed the deepest gratitude in answer to this sincerely felt little speech, cordially grasping the rear admiral's small, thin hand, he casually thought: 'Port Said? Alexandria? I? What should I do there? Live in a concentration camp? Why? …'

The fate of the four main characters: that is what I have called the 'heart' of the novel. All that can be said here of the many lesser persons is that all of them are portrayed with skill and economy and their individualities and idiosyncrasies are pressed unobtrusively into the service of the theme. Of the four outstanding figures, one – the priest, Ter Haigasun – may be quickly dismissed. For, monumental as he is, his function is simple enough: he is the 'man of God', iron in his faith and fire in his enthusiasm. Without him and the powerful religious sanctions which he is able to invoke, the camp on Musa Dagh would not hold together for longer than a day. Yet against his account of the rescue – 'the evil only happened … to enable God to show us His goodness' – we have to set the unedifying, bitter farce of Oskanian's suicide cult. Werfel clearly has the greatest respect for Ter Haigasun, the Moses of the mountain, but he does not advance him as a typical representative of persecuted humanity. The priest is 'a giant of inspiration', and he cannot be persecuted – he could only be martyred. If he is greater than Gabriel Bagradian, he is less complex and also less human.

Gabriel Bagradian is the true hero of the novel, both as adventure story and as tragedy. Of the adventure story because he has the qualities of a secular leader and some technical knowledge of warfare; of the tragedy because he is civilized, aware and thoroughly articulate. Born of wealthy parents in an Armenian village which he left at the age of twelve, he has spent twenty-three years in Paris, at a lycée, at the Sorbonne, marrying a French woman and living the life of a cultured déraciné – 'a scholar, a *bel esprit*, an archaeologist, a historian of art, a philosopher'. He has almost forgotten that he was ever an Armenian:

> At present he was more French than ever. Armenian still, but only in a sense – academically. … He was a thinker, an abstract man, an

individual. What did the Turks matter, what the Armenians? …
Massacre and torture he only knew through books and stories.

Together with his wife and son he returns to Yoghonoluk on family
business and is trapped by the outbreak of war in Europe. His
Armenian blood quickly begins to reassert itself and the Parisian years
fall away. It is he who first senses the coming persecution:

> I heard all kinds of disturbing things – but that's not the point.
> Perhaps, really, very little may have changed. But it always comes
> suddenly, like a desert storm. It's in my bones. My ancestors in me,
> who suffered incredible things, can feel it. My whole body feels it.
> No, Juliette, you can't understand! Nobody could understand who
> hasn't been hated because of his race.

And it is he who leads the exodus to Musa Dagh and takes responsibility for the camp's defence.

Gabriel's wife, Juliette, who can feel little but antipathy for the
unpolished Armenian villagers, may stand for the 'average person',
unacquainted with persecution, confident in the rectitude and protec-
tion of her country, and with little beyond that confidence to depend
upon. She cannot adjust herself to the way of life of a refugee; and,
more as an act of pitiful defiance than anything else, she commits
adultery with the other outsider on the mountain, a nomadic Greek-
French-American journalist. This, the most unpornographic adultery
in literature, is made almost intolerably painful by the doubt as to
whether she is in her right senses or in the early stages of fever. At
the end, her self-respect gone, her marriage in ruins, her son –
who was only too Armenian – dead, and her beauty destroyed,
she searches madly for a dress in which to greet the French naval
officers. There is for her this happy ending, or rather this bitter
imitation of one, for 'would any frock have been the right one in which
to welcome rescuing brothers, since for broken lives there can be no
rescuer?'[4]

Sarkis Kilikian, the fourth of these symbolic figures, joins the camp
as a deserter from a Turkish labour battalion. Throughout his life,
since earliest childhood, he has suffered atrocities of the ghastliest
kind, and his quietest years have been spent in Turkish prisons. This
great, dead, personality, coffined in a fleshless shrunken body, is the

4   There is here a reference back to the beginning of the novel, before the trouble
    begins, when Juliette has to decide in which clothes she shall receive the local
    Armenians, 'her new fellow-countrymen'.

very type of the lost Armenian, the Wandering Jew. In him we see dehumanization in an extreme form:

> The skin of his face, livid for all its tan, seemed to be tightly, thinly stretched over a sardonic skull. His features appeared less to be hollowed out by endurance than by life itself, lived to its very last dregs. Sated – satiated with life, that was the word!

Kilikian is Enver, the Minister of War, in reverse: the one the emotionless oppressor, the other the emotionless victim: 'His secret lay in his being nothing at all explicit, in his seeming to belong nowhere, to be living at some zero-point of incomprehensible neutrality.' For Gabriel he means what Tom of Bedlam means for Lear: 'Thou art the thing itself.' By now he is a sort of robot, conditioned by his history to perform just one action, whether useful or not – to defy authority. In the end, 'restless with longing to break out of one jail into the next', he leads a revolt within the camp, and Gabriel is forced to execute him: 'those indifferent eyes as little expressed the wish to live as the wish to die'. Kilikian, who has suffered more cruelly than anyone else, who seems immune to Turkish bullets, has to be killed by his friends, because he is so fearful an example of what they are becoming – non-moral, non-human, barely living.

At the close of the novel, when the miracle has happened and the survivors are being taken on board the ships, Gabriel falls asleep. When he wakes up the ships are already leaving, each supposing that the Armenian hero is on one of the others. He signals to them, but 'the movements were not those of a desperate man', and he stands in the shadow of a rock. He is surprised at his own calmness in the face of this ludicrous disaster. Then, 'in one clear flash, he realized – that *he did not want the ships to see him*'. We remember his answer, during the siege, when the Agha Rifaat Bereket had offered him a chance of escaping alone from the mountain: 'No one who stands where I stand can begin again from the beginning.' After what he has seen and done and undergone, there can be no return to human society. It could not tolerate him, nor he it. Nor can he settle down to be 'an Armenian', a refugee in a nation of refugees. For he has now become in full fact the 'abstract man', the 'individual', which he once considered himself.

But that is not all. At the last – the final irony, perhaps, and yet at the same time that sign which in *Doctor Faustus* appears as 'the high G of a cello … a light in the night' – he hears the ships' sirens and 'life raged within him'. Leaving his son's grave, he starts back to the sea. There is a flash of rifles:

Gabriel Bagradian was lucky. The second Turkish bullet shattered his temple. He clung to the wood, tore it down along with him. The Cross of the Son rested upon his heart.

The Forty Days of Musa Dagh jolts us, flesh and blood and spirit, into 'the extravagant existence' where, as Mann's Devil says, 'everything leaves off', but of which later historians will make their theories. This is what it is to *be* history. 'Every man and every nation at one time or another becomes "the weak",' pleads Johannes Lepsius.

(1949)

II

Democracy of Gods

Life and Works of Heine

We continue to hear that biography is the most esteemed, indeed the most popular, of literary forms nowadays. If this is true, then, first of all, it is a pity, since the novel – the form of literature which can wield the widest and strongest influence – ought to occupy that position. (Poetry may cut sharper, but one doesn't use a razor to chop down trees.) Secondly, if it is true, it is incredible. For biography is a highly dubious enterprise. Its author is concerned with, concerned to re-create, another person, a real (even if dead) one, of whom he is bound to know less than all and whom, with insufficient sure evidence to go on, he is bound to keep judging whether or not he intends or desires to. Dissatisfaction with the pious memorial class of biography, Great Sexless Lives and so forth, led (once the world was made safe) to all sorts of imaginative reconstructions or 'imitations' (a word suggested by Robert Lowell's 'free translations' of verse), sometimes entertaining, often impertinent. Girls Galore, and latterly Boys too. Perhaps one comforting thing about 'the truth' in this sense of the word is that you can only tell it when it doesn't matter, it can't do any harm: 'revelations' even turn out to be a latter-day form of piety. As for it bearing witness to a new, liberated and vivid interest in the ways of humanity – tell that to the vexed ghosts!

It was perhaps the suspicion that God alone knew the whole truth about a man and He was too busy to write it out which provoked the theory that biography should and would aspire towards the condition of fiction or poetry. Some years ago Richard Ellmann (whom we have to take seriously) asserted that we now 'ask of our biographers the same candour that our novelists have taught us to accept from them'. One hardly dare object to candour. But the candour of a novelist is something different in nature from the candour of a biographer. The novelist tells us frankly (this seems the sense of 'candour' intended here) about his own inventions. And so he should: it is up to us to decide whether or not we want to listen. The biographer however is being candid about objective verities. Naturally the novelist's candour is intended to serve some general truth about mankind, but the biographer is talking about a specific, actual human being. The biographer is a historian, and we still expect historians to get things right, or at least aspire to: the real deserves a special respect. No doubt this respect is difficult to ensure – the historian wasn't there, whereas the novelist *is* there, in the middle of his creation – but difficulty is no excuse for confusing genres. One extreme to which the ostensibly liberalizing theory of biography has led is 'psychobiography', a practice which bears much the same relation to truth-telling as necrophilia does to love.

These remarks are not intended for Jeffrey L. Sammons's full and painstaking biography of Heine. Though he subtitles it 'A Modern Biography', he intends, he tells us at the outset, to avoid 'the derring-do of psychobiography', and he ventures the hope that the reader 'will accept more or less on faith my conviction that it is the works that make the life important, and that the purpose of literary biography is to be a handmaiden to a more informed and alert apprehension of the works'. That 'more or less on faith', though it follows on from Sammons's announcement that he will be 'characterizing' rather than interpreting Heine's writings, betrays a nervous recognition of the state of opinion on biography as outlined above. Taking it for granted that only men and women who have *done* something qualify for biographical treatment and that therefore a better understanding of the things done will be of the essence, an earlier generation of readers would not have needed such a plea for acceptance.

But Heine himself calls up another general thought about biography: the inclination in some biographers to grow ratty with their subjects. This, I take it, is a separate phenomenon from the mounting impatience often to be observed in doctoral theses, where the candidate simply wants to get away and lead his or her own life at last. Here, it appears as a resentment provoked by the subject's inconsistencies or irrationalities, his recalcitrance to pigeon-holing. What makes the subject interesting turns out to make him exasperating: he is dead but he won't lie pinned down. It might be felt that such biographers ought to approach the condition of fiction sufficiently closely to read some of it – and then ask themselves this question: if in major novels a fictional character, made up freely by its unconstrained author, can be so complex, why should they expect a real person to be straightforward, transparent, comfortable to cope with? Reality is stranger – and untidier – than fiction can afford to be.

It is not always realized – or if realized, not sufficiently allowed for – just how 'unscrupulous' a writer can be in the pursuit of his vocation and obsession. I don't mean in the sense of listening at keyholes, turning friends into figures of fun, burning the baby's fingers to see exactly how it will react. Nor the sharp practices he may consider necessary to promote his own survival: those shabbinesses referred to by Heine on one occasion as 'often praiseworthy when they put us in a position to serve the great idea of our life the more worthily', but which Sammons describes as 'disconcerting to the biographer'. Rather, I have in mind the cool remorselessness with which the writer exploits everything in himself and everything that comes his way, by 'acting it out', sucking whatever can be sucked from it. After all, this is an aspect of the respectable faculty we call 'imagination'; and it is related to Keats's shrewd professional depiction of the chameleon poet who has no identity because he is 'continually filling some other body', who 'has no character' and is 'everything and nothing'. The process is less deliberate, less willed, than a general account must make it seem; less a conscious matter than Sammons's term 'the fictive persona' may suggest. One might say that, at such moments, the writer needs to be deceiving himself first of all. Deliberateness vitiates the process, and the individual who courts some grand personal distress in order to enhance his art through suffering is likely to procure nothing but personal distress. The protean capacities of every writer have their limits, narrow or broad: he can only make use of what touches on a nerve maybe hidden from his awareness but alive in him. To class him as an actor is less than apt, though to his biographers he may seem, alas, exactly that: in serious eyes, a hypocrite. The best biography of an artist, I incline to think, would take the form of a critical commentary on his work plus a *Who's Who* entry.

Heine is a prime irritant in this connection. Not only do his biographers regard him askance, or else askew, but they come close to hating one another as well. A maker of trouble for himself and his contemporaries, now he makes trouble for them. To confine oneself to the more manifest externalities of the man: he was a German who spent the greater part of his adult life in France; he was a Jew, a baptized Christian, and a free-thinker; 'a brilliant soldier in the war of liberation of humanity' (Matthew Arnold) and 'a modern Tannhäuser' loitering in the salons of the Venusberg (Engels); an egalitarian and an intellectual aristocrat ('we are all brothers, but I am the big brother, and you are the little brothers, and I am entitled to a more substantial portion'); a lyricist and a satirist; highflown and piercingly raw; egregiously active and enormously invalid ... In short, it has been suggested, a schizophrenic: for what the diagnosis is worth. True, if poetry comes out of the quarrel with ourselves, Heine was abnormally well endowed with selves to quarrel with.

But what hair-raising contradictions, what incongruities, what shabbinesses, will the biographer uncover once he penetrates below the surface? What hope can he entertain of establishing – the natural ambition of all who lay pen to paper – 'a pattern'? There is undeni-

ably 'something peculiar' about the case of Heine. 'In moments of
exhaustion,' Sammons confides, 'I sometimes wonder if there is not
a strange curse lying on the topic.' It is not merely that Heine is
surrounded by 'rough debate' (would it be fit and proper to name a
new university in his home town of Düsseldorf after him?) or that he
engages 'allegiances, prejudices, antipathies, and ideological commit-
ments of all kinds'. It is worse than that, for he attracts extremists and
crackpots and 'can generate the most eccentric styles, not only of
public altercation, but sometimes of scholarly discourse'. It doesn't
seem quite fair to visit the sins of the children upon the father, but all
the same, in this case… Sammons then cites some unseemly incidents
that have marred the calm and civility of scholarly conferences – one
of them involving a Düsseldorf policeman of an artistic bent who took
the platform by storm: quite Grassian, that – which may not produce
the shock horror effect he anticipates.

Heine was an awkward cuss, given to saying a lot, and also given to
saying nothing; and the latter habit has created greater hardships for
the biographer even than the former. 'Over large and important areas
his silence is downright deafening.' And hence, one supposes, his
deafened biographers have been forced to shout loudly, and possibly
incautiously, in their attempts to say 'what he would have said if he
could have said what he meant'. (The proposal suggests that he was
an unusual subject for biography: an inarticulate illiterate.) Stage-
managing reality to suit himself, Heine created one 'Heine', and from
Heine's 'Heine' the biographer must make 'yet another "Heine"
devised for our own purposes and to suit our own notions of what
we would like him to have been'. This process, Sammons remarks with
immoderate temperateness, has shown signs of getting out of control,
and he warns or assures us that 'my own purpose cannot be to present
the "true Heine", for I do not know what that is'. In the event we
perceive that behind this declaration of non-intent lies a decent and
apposite modesty rather than an abject admission of incompetence.
Happily, the adjective in Sammons's subtitle means nothing – or only
that the book was published in 1979.

Heine's troublesomeness starts very early, with his date of birth.
1797 (as is generally accepted)? 1798? 1799? 1800? 1779? – no,
obviously a slip of Heine's pen in applying for admission to the
doctoral examination… 'If we were to recapitulate the problem in all
its details, it would take him almost as long to get born as Tristram
Shandy.' But why did he give different dates on different occasions?
Was he concealing the fact that he was born out of wedlock? Did he
deceive in order to dodge the draft? Seemingly no in both cases: he

was born in wedlock, and he was too young anyway for the Napoleonic wars. Sammons thinks it possible that Heine actually didn't know when he was born: 'one's birthdate is not, after all, a datum of experience.' We shall have to rest content with the knowledge, beyond dispute, that he *was* born.

However, Sammons views the matter as an omen of wider import, presaging Heine's carelessness with the truth. 'He did not strike his contemporaries as a person of integrity, and it must be said in frankness that he cannot always appear so to his biographer today.' Integrity is a point a biographer may properly concern himself with. One curious implication is that only those bodies interested to make a hero of revolutionary morality out of Heine have managed to find him a man of integrity – and this doesn't say much for either the ingenuity or the devotion of campaigners on the side of reactionary morality.

When we look into the question of Heine's Jewishness we encounter a similar disorderliness. As a young man, Sammons suggests, he 'did not feel very uncomfortable about his Jewishness'. (Ought he to have done? No, Sammons doesn't mean that.) Later he was to feel uncomfortable – uncomfort was his forte – but uncomfortable in his Heineishness rather than his Jewishness. I suspect he felt Jewish when he felt like feeling Jewish, or when it suited his purpose and, for instance, he could use Jewishness as a stick to beat something else with. His interest in the subject seems to have constituted one form of self-exploration and explanation (he was fascinated by himself) and, in the manner of all creative writers and particularly poets who more than others spin out of their own guts, of self-exploitation. He upheld Jews against brands of nationalism that discriminated against them, but when it came to denouncing bourgeois commercialism and philistinism he did not discriminate between Christians and Jews. In any case his inability to take religious sentiment seriously for long at a stretch would have inhibited any very profound Hebraism.

In politics also, for all his socialistic beliefs and busyness, he is equivocal, more obviously so than Brecht, evincing that final scepticism towards ideologies to be detected in the majority of intelligent people, poets or otherwise. His most effective satire is directed less at wealth or privilege or capitalism than at puritanical elements in the party of progress and the 'universal kitchen-equality' (as he put it in a letter of 1840) of grey, grudging proletarianism. Nor are such shafts discharged wholly in the spirit of 'whom the Lord loveth he chasteneth'. For him, the purpose of revolution was to bring about the lineaments of gratified desire. He spoke of fighting for 'the divine rights of humans' (*not* 'the human rights of the people'), for a democracy of equally blissful gods – a levelling-up of some magnitude – and answered the 'censorious reproaches' of the 'virtuous republicans' with Sir Toby's tag: so 'there shall be no more cakes and ale'? Though he became a notorious dissident and the object of Metternich's special attention, he insisted that 'the true poet is the true hero' while 'the true democrat writes like the people, sincerely, simply and badly'. Interestingly enough, in *Atta Troll* ('A Summer Night's Dream'), 1841, the bear personifying the radical poets is summed up in a phrase reminiscent in a contrary sense of Keats's passage on the chameleon poet: 'Kein Talent, doch ein Charakter!'

Sammons reports Heine's political skirmishing in slightly suffocating detail, possibly in order to avoid any hint of tendentious selectiveness. True, he was a great fighter – that is, bellicose by nature – and 'a brilliant soldier in the war of liberation of humanity', but he fought for a republic not of this world. He ran into that 'very modern dilemma' (as S.S. Prawer termed it some time ago) whereby intellectuals come to realize the likely effects on *them* and the things they hold dear of the cause they have been championing. While Marx seems to have preserved a degree of fondness for the 'old dog' (from whom he derived the famous analogy between religion and opium), after his death in 1856 Engels likened him – not altogether felicitously – to an earlier poet who incurred the tyrant's frown and then 'crawled up Augustus's rear'. The redoubtable radical journalist Ludwig Börne had earlier held much the same view, while expressing it more genteelly: Heine kept a set of mouseholes in his opinions, and if you tried to pin him down, he escaped through one hole and peeped out of another. To compound the offence, Heine has proved the cause of mouseholes in others, and it is typical of him and his phenomenon that since the Nazis could not possibly exclude his famous early poem 'Die Loreley' (so Germanic!) from their songbooks, they attributed it to 'author unknown'.

Professor Sammons may not know what the 'true Heine' is, but he knows what it isn't, and he comes out firmly against the 'scripting of soap-opera' that has afflicted much writing on the theme. He comments, amusedly rather than aggrievedly, that 'Heine's erotic life has been a great deal more frustrating to his critics and biographers than it probably was to him.' While one would have liked him to develop and support his summary verdict that Heine was 'a complex but not really a profound writer' (cf. Günter Grass: 'In a devious way I'm uncomplicated'), he brings out well the element of 'play', as for instance in the 'camel problem' propounded by the poet. If the rich had more hope of passing through that needle's eye, perhaps they would be less grasping and hard of heart while on earth? Heine lent a helping hand towards this desirable outcome by lampooning the friendly Rothschilds and simultaneously (as a deserving man of letters) extracting financial aid from them. The protean are bound to want it at least both ways.

'Play' is not the right word, of course, hardly more so than 'deviousness' or 'duplicity'. Sammons uses the word 'multiplicity', implying an honest acknowledgement of the real difficulty of his task, and he certainly adduces a multiplicity of evidence. Heine made poetry out of politics – where others made poetry into politics. That proposition could be repeated in other fields. His 'return' to religion following his physical collapse in 1848 hardly took the edge off his tongue, since he could ask God for the pleasure of seeing a few of his enemies dangling from the trees outside his window. 'Yes, one must forgive one's enemies, but not before they are hanged ...' Earlier, and proteanly, he had written, 'I am accused of having no religion. No, I have them all.' To observers not wholly committed to a party line of one sort or another, it must be reasonably clear what Heine's priorities were. 'Ultimately,' Sammons concludes, 'Heine was of his own party.' Yes, and his party was poetry.

What we now need is some good criticism of Heine, a cogent exposition of what in Heine's work is worth knowing and why. And, if possible, some translations more convincing than we have seen so far, and not only of the romantic and lyrical verse.[1] Outside the scholarly conference hall and the political arena ('Wherever books are burnt, in the end people are burnt too') Heine must be one of the most misconstrued of famous writers, taken in small arbitrary doses, and outside Germany surely the most shadowy. Now that we know so much about his life, perhaps we could get to know something about the works which make that life important to us.

'A bad man, my dears': Heine in English

As Jeffrey L. Sammons had indicated in his judicious 'modern biography' of 1979, Heine's critics and biographers have re-created their subject in the image of their own tastes or (he has latterly become

---

1   A desideratum admirably met by Alistair Elliot in *The Lazarus Poems* (1979), while a respectful bow is due to Hal Draper for *The Complete Poems of Heinrich Heine* (1982), an immensely brave undertaking.

a hot political property) their doctrines; in this they have been encouraged by Heine's protean self-projection or production. The
phenomenon, not so very rare, isn't necessarily the sign of a difficult,
sophisticated, or recondite author. When Sammons judges that Heine
is 'a complex but not really a profound writer', he is conveying a truth
about him, though we might want to substitute 'obscure' for
'profound'. He can always be understood, with reasonable immediacy,
though this isn't to deny that we are grateful for the notes Hal Draper
appends to *The Complete Poems of Heinrich Heine: A Modern English
Version*, for Heine was a great namer of names and instancer of
instances. What is truly hard to come to terms with is the overall para-
doxicality, the unnerving juxtaposition of opposed and seemingly
incompatible attitudes and feelings, and the unheralded switching
from one to another.

Heine habitually introduces himself as a man of sorrows and
acquainted with little but grief ('For me the world has been a torture
cell'); and the next moment he is thumbing his nose at the respectful
reader: 'Usually you're not such a donkey, / Dearest friend, in such
affairs!' Or more often at somebody or something else; after what
sounds like a stirring night spent on the Drachenfels, scene of
Siegfried's slaying of the dragon, 'What I brought back with me was
a cough and cold', while in a poem about the Devil as a professional
diplomat we come across the lines

> He's somewhat pale – no wonder, I vow,
> For he's studying Sanskrit and Hegel now…
> He'll put reviewing on the shelf
> And do that job no more himself.

The only English poet he can be likened to is Byron: all those ready
and often rough rhymes, the gentlemanly casualness attending a blow
to the solar plexus, or lower down… In which case, we must agree,
Heine is a proletarian model of that lord, or (to avoid an adjective
which would arouse his wrath) a much less lordly one. And more intelligent, in that you couldn't say of him, as Goethe said of Byron, that
as soon as he reflects, he is a child. Heine is at his best when he sobers
up and reflects; to do this, it appears, he needed strong draughts of
fairly violent excitement in advance.

Hal Draper has a shrewd passage in his foreword on the subject of
Heine as 'freedom fighter' and in relation to Marx: 'He was against
oppression because he thought the people should have *good* masters,
the benevolent type. He preferred that society be controlled by
bankers he could scorn than by a democratic mass movement he

would fear.' The sight of complacent burghers made a crusading socialist of him; when he considered the grey masses at his back he turned into an intellectual élitist. (Which he more whole-heartedly was.) 'We are all brothers, but I am the big brother, and you are the little brothers, and I am entitled to a more substantial portion.' In a similar spirit, although baptized a Christian, he could summon up his Jewishness when it provided extra momentum in attacking Christian hypocrites. Some have seen this as itself hypocritical, as opportunism, egotism, play-acting; to me it seems part of a free-ranging individual's survival kit.

Varying Heine's own self-description, Matthew Arnold termed him 'if not pre-eminently a brave, yet a brilliant, a most effective soldier in the war of liberation of humanity'. One may wonder why 'brave' has yielded to 'brilliant', that suspect epithet; surely not because Heine failed to get himself killed on active service (the Continent was a more dangerous place for intellectuals than England, then as later), or because he conducted himself with prudent obliqueness. That was clearly not the case, nor would Arnold have thought along those lines. To be brave in Arnold's sense it was necessary to be less intemper-ately susceptible (to offence, to female charms), less 'unscrupulous in passion' (whatever the passion), less given to 'incessant mocking' – and to possess a larger or less adulterated share of 'self-respect', of 'true dignity of character', 'moral balance', and 'nobleness of soul and character'. Rather more explicitly, and more lightly, George Eliot spoke of Heine's great powers serving to give 'electric force to the expression of debased feeling', and recommended the use of a 'friendly penknife' before handing his works to immature minds.[2]

After that summary of what Arnold saw as Heine's 'crying faults', it is necessary to remind ourselves that he considered him the chief successor to Goethe. All the same, when he pronounced Heine 'profoundly *dis*respectable' he was not simply getting in a dig at Carlyle for overlooking Heine in favour of the romantic school. He meant it as a distinct reproach; for him, as he makes plain, 'respectable' was too valuable a word to subvert through ironic usage. But his views on the subject were remote from the feelings of Charles Kingsley;

---

2 'German Wit', *Westminster Review*, January 1856. In this article, published a month before Heine's death, and seven and a half years before Arnold's essay, George Eliot is highly amusing on the topic of German humour and finely perceptive about Heine's prose: in his hands 'German prose, usually so heavy, so clumsy, so dull, becomes, like clay in the hands of the chemist, compact, metallic, brilliant; it is German in an *allotropic* condition.'

according to the story, when Kingsley was asked by his children who Heine was, he replied: 'A bad man, my dears, a bad man.'[3] In fact '*dis*respectable' is a fair description of Heine, and one to bear in mind when forging through Draper's bumper volume, sometimes suppressing and sometimes admitting its pejorative connotations.

Heine delighted in rhythms – and in jingles – and in playing with them, often disconcertingly, in a variety of poetic forms. His translator has to be correspondingly nimble and versatile, coping with ballad, folk-song, narrative, the tremulously yearning, the heroic-rhetorical, the *Hiawatha*-stutter, and the low-life (verging on doggerel, yet scanning and rhyming nattily no matter what the diction is up to). Other problems stem from Heine's application of solemn or pensive-promising metres to light-hearted or deflationary material, as when a poem evokes the springtime sun, flowerets, moon and stars, and 'two beautiful eyes', and terminates thus:

> *Wie sehr das Zeug auch gefällt,*
> *So macht's doch noch lang keine Welt,*

which Draper translates:

> No matter how much you like such stuff,
> To make a world they're just not enough;

or as in a three-stanza poem which begins in trite distress – 'once you were mine only / In body and in soul' – and modulates into this:

> I still want your body, the merry
> Tender young body I know;
> Your soul you can go and bury –
> I've soul enough for two.

Such sudden reversals of tone or – when generalized meditation shifts into specific abuse or debunking – of matter are found cheek by jowl with the dark-side 'romantic' paraphernalia of faithless loves, *belles dames sans merci*, funeral bells, hauntings, wounded knights, howling

---

3 And he wouldn't have known this poem, uncollected until the *Sämtliche Schriften* of 1968–76:

> Last night, in a dream – too bad, too bad! –
> I enjoyed the dirtiest girl yet seen:
> Yet for the same price I could have had
> The loveliest princess or fairest queen.

Most un-Goethean? No; see Goethe's 'un-Goethean' *Venezianische Epigramme*. One difference is that Goethe hived off his naughtinesses.

winds, the Devil, and (more often than not figurative) prison cells.

In the opening poem of the early sequence, *The Homecoming*, Draper rhymes more royally than his original, which has one pure rhyme and one approximate (e.g. *Dunkeln/bannen*) in each stanza:

> In my life so dark and jaded,
> Once a vision glistened bright.
> Now the vision's dim and faded –
> Once again I'm wrapped in night.
>
> In the dark a child, dissembling
> While the fearsome phantoms throng,
> Tries to cover up his trembling
> With a shrill and noisy song.
>
> I, a frantic child, am straining
> At my song in darkness here.
> What if the song's not entertaining?
> Still it's freed me of my fear.

This involves a slight misrepresentation in that the 'I' is 'straining' instead of simply singing, and Draper makes the song 'not entertaining' rather than not delightful. But one wouldn't quarrel with this latter shade of difference: 'entertaining' (less private in suggestion) carries us on from the child singing to keep up its spirits to the poet singing to entertain – perhaps – other people.

Alas, the following poem – and one so famous – collapses at the very outset:

> I do not know what it means that
> I am so sadly inclined;
> There is an old tale and its scenes that
> Will not depart from my mind.

The original sings itself:

> *Ich weiss nicht, was soll es bedeuten,*
> *Dass ich so traurig bin;*
> *Ein Märchen aus alten Zeiten,*
> *Das kommt mir nicht aus dem Sinn.*

Draper follows the rhythm closely, except for the second line, and 'means that' / 'scenes that' is a purer rhyme than *bedeuten/Zeiten*, but the loss of the end-stopping and the inapt stress given (twice) to 'that' turn a sweetly grave lyric into something approaching a pop song. The translation rises from the dust in its final verse:

> I think, at last the wave swallows
> The boat and the boatman's cry;
> And this is the fate that follows
> The song of the Lorelei.

The third line, submitting (with fairly good grace) to rhyme's importunity, sounds like a warning against harmful practices, yet the second line has a nice synecdochic variation on the original's boatman and boat, and Draper too contrives to leave the naming of the fatal siren until the very last.

In Heine, as in Goethe, the 'pure' lyric, with its bare, fragile but precise simplicity, has generally proved impossible to carry over into another language. A notable exception here is the third poem in the group entitled *In der Fremde* ('Abroad'):

> Oh, once I had a lovely fatherland.
>   The oaks grew tall
> Up to the sky, the gentle violets swayed.
>   I dreamt it all.
> I felt a German kiss, heard German words
>   (Hard to recall
> How good they rang) – the words *Ich liebe dich!*
>   I dreamt it all.

Draper's departures are minimal: the initial 'Oh'; the harmless 'grew tall up to the sky', compensating for the discrepancy in length between *Eichenbaum* and 'oak', instead of the undecorated 'grew so high'; and, to preserve the essential rhyme, 'Hard to recall' for the literal 'One can hardly believe'.

Heine's translators are faced by an extra problem, one not encountered in Goethe outside the squibs and parts of *Faust*. The poet is frequently slapdash and (to put it mildly) over-hearty. We may not altogether admire such behaviour in him – *dis*respectable indeed! – but we know that it is wholly deliberate, whereas when we are reading a translation we may well ascribe such effects to the translator's inadequate resourcefulness in the face of formal exigencies. The expression 'dizzy dame' affects us as just *too* American, or stage-American, for *tolle Dirne* (not that 'whimsical wench' would sound much better); in fact the immediate context goes far to condone it, but it still looks odd in the vicinity of so many a 'lo' and 'ere' and (which isn't quite the same as *Und sieh!*) 'Behold!' Vulgarity, sincere vulgarity, is the most difficult of styles to carry convincingly into another tongue; or the next trickiest after simple sincerity.

Similarly, in translation self-caricature can easily emerge as evidence of near-imbecility, unless the reader is already fairly intimate with the poet. An instance of this form of parody – and also of the poet's mixed mode – is the poem from *Lyrisches Intermezzo* which begins:

> *Ich steh' auf des Berges Spitze,*
> *Und werde sentimental.*
> *'Wenn ich ein Vöglein wäre!'*
> *Seufz' ich viel tausendmal.*

> I stand on the mountain summit
> And sentimentalize.
> 'If I were a birdie, dearest!'
> I say with a thousand sighs.

Draper renders this virtually word for word, except that 'sentimentalize' tips us off rather more forcibly than does the German expression. The second and third verses appear wholly conventional and well-meaning, untouched by irony: 'If I were a swallow', 'If I were a nightingale' … The final verse, however, runs:

> *Wenn ich ein Gimpel wäre,*
> *So flög' ich gleich an dein Herz;*
> *Du bist ja hold den Gimpeln,*
> *Und heilest Gimpelschmerz.*

> If I were a boobybird, dearest,
> I'd fly to you straight as a dart;
> You're partial to boobies and able
> To heal a booby-heart.

The traditional accessories, swallow and nightingale, have slumped into boobybird. The original *Gimpel* is a bullfinch, but the word also means 'ninny'; Draper's boobybird – albeit a marine species not, as far as I know, notable for stupidity – speaks for itself, and the designation takes on a further felicitousness if we think of the probable derivation from *balbus*, stammering.

Here Draper has scored a triumph, improving on Heine. It is all the stranger, then, that in his dealings with another poem in this collection –

> *Aus meinen grossen Schmerzen*
> *Mach' ich die kleinen Lieder;*
> *Die heben ihr klingend Gefieder*
> *Und flattern nach ihrem Herzen… –*

he should rest content with a sad travesty of those famous lines:

> Out of my great unrest
> I make little songs and things;
> They lift their tinkling wings
> And flutter off to her breast.

The more tolerant may allow 'unrest' to pass for *Schmerzen*, and accept that Heine's songs do sometimes tinkle – but 'songs and things'! What sort of things? Just things that happen to rhyme with other things.

Yet Draper displays considerable brio in such darker items as 'The Silesian Weavers', a poem which was banned in Germany and led Engels to claim that 'the most eminent of all living German poets has joined our ranks':

> A curse on this false fatherland, teeming
> With nothing but shame and dirty scheming,
> Where every flower is crushed in a day,
> Where worms are regaled on rot and decay –
>   We're weaving, we're weaving!
>
> The shuttle flies, the loom creaks loud,
> Night and day we weave your shroud –
> Old Germany, at your shroud we sit,
> We're weaving a threefold curse in it,
>   We're weaving, we're weaving!

And in general he copes pretty well with Heine's rather fearful fluency, or facility of imagination, in those many lyrics that promise to tell a story and then tail off into banality or vague longings and regrets – though not without offering fine incidentals, like this, from 'The Shepherd Boy' in *Die Harzreise*, done into English faithfully and well:

> At his feet the sheep are lying,
> Fleecy flatterers, prinked with red;
> Calves are cavaliers, and pertly
> Strut about with legs outspread.

Draper cannot be held responsible for the poet's glib or reiterative cynicism, neatly replicated in

> Friendship, love, philosophers' stones –
> These are praised in reverent tones;
> These I praised and sought to get –
> Ah, but I've never found them yet,

or for his crude self-dramatization (a posturing which later was transmuted into something more authentic and moving), his zestful but hammered-in moralizing on the degeneracy of the age, or the sitting ducks he scuppers. Or his gratuitous outbursts, as when chiding some harmless woman for possessing a tepid soul (unlike his adventurous one) and wanting to lead a life

> Hanging on your husband – cosy,
> Just a proper pregnant wife.

Pregnancy – rather common among wives at that time – was one of the trials that, though he suffered many, Heine didn't have to endure.

From 1848 till his death eight years later, Heine was paralysed by a disease of the spinal cord. Written from his 'mattress-grave', the *Lazarus* poems and those in the supplementary group, *Zum Lazarus*, are sardonic yet spirited, bitter but humorous, and even affectionate, less evidently personal than the mass of his verse and yet more deeply so, originating in 'self' but invulnerable to Arnold's charge of insufficient self-respect and dignity of character. They are relatively modern in sensibility, closer to current poetic preferences and practice, and have been reproduced in English quite brilliantly by Alistair Elliot. More relaxed, more idiomatic, Elliot generally has the edge over Draper, but the *Lazarus* poems are a fraction of Heine's output. Far harder to make readable, though Draper does his swashbuckling best, are the two early verse tragedies. The production of a tragedy, George Eliot remarked in this connection, is the 'chicken-pox of authorship'. *Almansor* is an exercise in the Spanish/Arab exotic, and *William Ratcliff* an attempt at Scottish Gothic. Both are largely claptrap, while both display the sudden trenchancies typical of their author. 'Here within my breast I bear my turban,' declaims Almansor, a Moor disguised as a Spaniard, to which the faithful old Hassan ritually replies, 'All praise to Allah! Allah's will be praised!' But when Almansor reports the burning of the Koran by the Inquisition, Hassan speaks the celebrated, reverberating words: 'Where men burn books, they will burn people too in the end.'

Other stumbling-blocks for the modern reader are the mock epics, *Atta Troll: A Summer Night's Dream* and *Germany: A Winter's Tale*, long, ambitious works, over-long and ambitious to cram rather too much in. Heine, one inclines to feel ruefully, was more a force of nature than a force of art. For the well-disposed reader the famous 'problem' settles into the simple and sheer difficulty of distinguishing with much assurance between verbosity and vivacity. Both these works, I suspect, are more significant as documents in the 'case' of Heine than as poetry.

In *Atta Troll* the radical poets are satirized in the figure of a clumsy, sententious bear,

> Atta Troll: bear with a cause.
> Moral, pious. Ardent husband.
> Led astray by our Zeitgeist,
> Primitive sansculotte of the forest.
>
> Dancing: bad. But strong opinions
> Borne within his shaggy bosom.
> Sometimes also stinking strongly.
> Talent, none; but character, yes!

Elsewhere Heine averred that artists who busy themselves with the great idea of freedom are themselves customarily unfree in spirit.

In *Germany*, another banned work, which George Eliot found 'exquisitely humorous', the main thrust of the satire is directed against German feudalism and nationalism and the absolutist state, with Heine present in person ('My head is a twittering nest of books / Good enough to be confiscated') as a radical or at any rate forthright poet, advising the Prussian King: 'Offend the gods both old and new / ... But the poets – don't offend them!'

> A little girl was playing the harp
> and singing with genuine feeling
> and out of tune, but still the song
> she sang was most appealing.
>
> She sang of love and sacrifice,
> of pain and a tomorrow
> when all shall meet in a better world
> beyond this vale of sorrow ...
>
> I know the tune, I know the words,
> I know every single author;
> I know they tippled wine on the quiet
> while publicly preaching water.
>
> A different song, a better song,
> will get the subject straighter:
> let's make a heaven on earth, my friends,
> instead of waiting till later.[4]

---

4   These four stanzas are taken from a more recent and splendidly rollicking translation by T.J. Reed: *Deutschland*, 1986.

In the end, from the beginning, the party Heine belonged to was a 'party of one'.

To sum up, Draper handles satire, polemic, and abuse proficiently, at times with an ingenuity approaching genius, but is (understandably) less at ease with the elegance and the plangency of Heine at his more delicate and lyrical. This generous volume is the outcome of some thirty years' labour; it is not as perfect as it is courageous, but then, it is breath-takingly courageous.

Printer's Ink: Heine's Prose

Matthew Arnold considered Heine significant because he was 'if not pre-eminently a brave, yet a brilliant, a most effective soldier in the war of liberation of humanity'. Despite the truth in it, this testimonial may not cut much ice these days: which particular war of liberation was that? Perhaps George Eliot's essay on German wit, appearing a month before Heine's death in 1856, is more persuasive. German wit, she said, generally shows 'no sense of measure, no instinctive tact', and is either as clumsy 'as the antics of a leviathan' or as interminable 'as a Lapland day'. And German comedy resembles a German sentence: 'you see no reason in its structure why it should ever come to an end, and you accept the conclusion as an arrangement of Providence rather than of the author.' Heine, though she deplored his occasional coarseness and lack of scruple in attacking others, is the great exception, an artist who has shown even more fully than Goethe the possibilities of German prose. He combines French esprit with Teutonic imagination and sensibility, and in his hands 'German prose, usually so heavy, so clumsy, so dull, becomes, like clay in the hands of the chemist, compact, metallic, brilliant; it is German in an *allotropic* condition.'

Ritchie Robinson's excellent selection, beautifully translated and indispensably annotated, bears out much that George Eliot noted, happily including that lack of scruple, and shows how the lyrical and the satirical, commonly kept separate in Heine's poetry, are found side by side in his prose, and for the most part at ease. In *The Harz Journey*, along with rural idylls, we come across this: 'By and large the inhabitants of Göttingen may be divided into students, professors, philistines, and cattle; which four classes are by no means sharply distinct. The cattle are the most important class.' And the account of dining at an inn on the Brocken is both elaborate and succinct, mixing the amiably bizarre with the deftly mocking. 'This man dated from the days when lice had a good time and hairdressers were afraid of starving… He looked like a life-sized reproduction of a fool.' The most amusing incident concerns Dr Saul Ascher, a deceased philosopher whose watchword was 'Reason is the supreme principle!' Dr Ascher appears to Heine at midnight in his lodgings in Goslar, wearing the same clothes as ever, 'the same abstract legs, and the same mathematical face', the latter somewhat yellower than of old. Ascher tells Heine not to be afraid, and proves by logic that there are no such things as ghosts. Absent-mindedly the doctor pulls a handful of worms out of his pocket instead of his watch. As he is declaring 'Reason is the supreme – ', the clock strikes one and the ghost vanishes.

'A Catholic priest strolls along as if heaven belonged to him, a Protestant priest, on the other hand, bustles about as though he had taken a lease of heaven,' Heine writes in *The Town of Lucca*. Featured here is a theological triangle consisting of the beautiful, pious, uncomprehending Francesca and the witty, free-thinking Briton, Lady Matilda, seemingly erstwhile ladyfriends of the poet, with Heine as the not wholly impartial umpire. He represents himself as, with certain reservations, a supporter of both throne and altar, but deems an established religion a 'monster born of the coupling of secular and spiritual power', a 'mule sired by Antichrist's white horse on Christ's she-ass'. Left to itself, the German state would be strong and united, instead of being split into warring sects: 'while we quarrel about heaven, we are perishing here on earth'. Religions are admirable only when they have to compete with one another, and when they are victims of persecution rather than agents of it.

On the History of Religion and Philosophy in Germany is intended to enlighten French readers misled by Mme de Staël, seen as the mouthpiece of the Romantics, nationalists and obscurantist reactionaries. In the preface to the second edition, 1852, eighteen years later, Heine describes the work as a fragment, and says that though he has since changed his mind, notably on the subject of God, the word once spoken, let alone printed, is no longer the property of the speaker. He could of course tone down his language, but 'I hate ambiguous words, hypocritical flowers, cowardly fig-leaves, from the depths of my soul'. Fragment though the piece may be, it is pretty substantial. True, he is no scholar, yet if any great German philosophers reckon his observations paltry, they should note that what he says is at least clearly expressed, whereas their own words, undeniably profound, stupendously profound, are unintelligible. 'What good to the people are locked granaries to which they have no key?'

The *History* is enlivened by anecdotes, often funny, at times grim, of a kind no doubt eschewed by the philosophers. Of Luther's story about throwing his inkwell at the Devil when interrupted in his translating of the New Testament, Heine remarks that ever since then the Devil has felt afraid of ink, especially printer's ink. (Latterly the Devil may have had second feelings on the subject.) It was thanks to Luther that the German people attained freedom of thought. He created the German language by translating the Bible: 'In fact, the divine author of this book seems to have known as well as the rest of us that it is not a matter of indifference by whom one is translated, and he chose his translator himself, and endowed him with the wondrous power of translating from a dead language, which was, so to speak, already buried, into another which was not yet alive.'

Intensely personal and sharply public, *Ideas: The Book of Le Grand* is a monologue ostensibly addressed to a charming lady who will need some help in following the digressions, and has a distinct flavour of Laurence Sterne about it. One chapter begins 'The German censors' and thereafter consists solely of dashes, except for one word, 'idiots', halfway through. The Le Grand of the title leads us to expect something akin to the pathetic history of Lieutenant Le Fever in *Tristram Shandy*; it turns out that Le Grand was a possibly fictional French drummer, quartered on the family when the narrator was a boy, who taught him the meaning of French words: for instance, of *liberté* by drumming the *Marseillaise*, of *égalité* by drumming the march 'Ça ira, ça ira, les aristocrates à la lanterne!' Returning from imprisonment in Siberia after the Russian campaign, Le Grand drums a dead march for the battle of Borodino, and dies; in a gesture worthy of a man of sentiment, the boy punctures the drum so it may never 'beat a servile tattoo for any enemy of freedom'. In the *Memoirs* a more curious story has it that an executioner's sword which has lopped off a hundred heads must be buried ceremoniously because it has acquired a sort of consciousness and possibly a thirst for more blood.

There isn't as yet a plaque on the house in Düsseldorf where he was born, Heine admits in *Ideas*. His fame is 'still sleeping in the marble quarries of Carrara', and noble Englishwomen on their travels, swathed in green veils, must content themselves with the equestrian statue of the Elector Jan Wilhelm in the market-place. Egoism is relieved by irony, in Heine commonly a positive force, and by choice quotation and allusion (a few learned references 'adorn the whole man'), while sentimentality is habitually subverted, as in the ominous evocation of little Wilhelm, a schoolfellow who drowned in the Düssel while saving a kitten: 'The kitten had a long life.' Similarly a standard nostalgia for his schooldays is checked by a schoolboy joke: the

Romans would never have had time to conquer the world if they had had to learn Latin. And the repinings over unrequited love are marked more by vivacity than anguish. About to shoot himself, the narrator passes over 'To be, or not to be', the conventional formula on such occasions, in favour of speeches from 'the immortal *Almansor*', Heine's verse tragedy. It is only natural to prefer your own words, even to Shakespeare's, and such speeches by 'people graduating from life' are useful in distracting you from your intention, and allowing time for another lovely lady to come along. Like much else of Heine, *Ideas* is encapsulated in one sentence: 'So long as my heart is full of love and the heads of my fellow-men are full of folly, I shall never lack something to write about.'

(1979; 1983; 1993)

Cavafy: Poet-Historian

In introducing Rae Dalven's *Complete Poems of C.P. Cavafy* in 1961, Auden remarked that a poem by Cavafy, whoever the translator, was at once recognizable as a poem by Cavafy. This he attributed to 'a tone of voice, a personal speech' characteristic of the Alexandrian-Greek poet. It is difficult to say very much more than that. Though my admiration for Cavafy has continued to rise ever since John Mavrogordato's important volume of translations came out in 1951, I have never found an adequate way of describing his peculiar attractiveness, or of analysing the relevance one senses, somewhat unexpectedly, in reading his poems set in the remote Panhellenic world. Cavafy himself died in 1933.

Yet there can hardly be a tone of voice divorced from subject-matter, a personal speech without something being said. And in many of his best poems Cavafy is saying something true and moving about the stoicism and fortitude demanded of losers. Sometimes the situation he sketches has a humorous aspect. Thus, 'In a Township of Asia Minor':

> The news of the outcome of the naval battle, at Actium,
> was most certainly unexpected.
> But there is no need to compose a new address.
> Only the name needs to be changed. There, in the last
> lines, instead of 'Having liberated the Romans
> from the ruinous Octavius,
> that parody, as it were, of Caesar',
> now we will put, 'Having liberated the Romans
> from the ruinous Antony.'
> The whole text fits in beautifully...[1]

With some adjustment to the terminology, this could describe public attitudes in a Vietnamese hamlet which has been held in turn by the South Vietnamese and the Vietcong. An attitude of prudential adaptation to forces which cannot be met head-on – though in the case of the Vietnamese villagers, so much nearer the storm centre, the humour would be somewhat less in evidence, the desperation more.

The Alexandrian underdogs did occasionally have their day out,

---

1 All quotations are from Rae Dalven's translations. See also *C.P. Cavafy: Collected Poems*, translated by Edmund Keeley and Philip Sherrard, 1975.

perhaps enjoying the spectacle of Cleopatra's children being made kings, among them Caesarion, 'all grace and beauty':

> they grew enthusiastic and they cheered
> in Greek and in Egyptian and some in Hebrew,
> enchanted by the gorgeous spectacle –
> knowing full well the worth of all these,
> what hollow words these kingships were.

A pathetic sequel is the poem 'Caesarion', in which Cavafy evokes the figure of the young man, another if slightly more glamorous victim of power politics, about whom history says little:

> in vanquished Alexandria,
> wan and weary, idealistic in your sorrow,
> still hoping that they would pity you,
> the wicked – who murmured 'Too many Caesars.'

Also 'relevant', also (and not exclusively) Asian, is a poem about political reformers. Things are not going as well as they might, so experts are called in; but

> the handicap and the hardship
> are that these Reformers make
> a big story out of everything …
> they inquire and investigate,
> and immediately they think of radical reforms,
> with the request that they be executed without delay.

'They also have a bent for sacrifices', to be made by other people, and when at last they have finished their work and left, 'carrying off their rightful salary', you may feel that after all it is preferable to go on as before. More obliquely pertinent is 'The First Step', in which the young Eumenes complains that after two years of labour he has only completed one idyll. Theocritus reproves him: he should feel proud that he has advanced so far, for it means

> you must rightfully be a citizen
> of the city of ideas.
> And in that city it is hard
> and rare to be naturalized.
> In her market place you find Lawmakers
> whom no adventurer can dupe.

Besides what Theocritus is saying about the privilege of creativity, we receive – largely through the word 'naturalized' with its load of associations – a sense of contemporary political engineering, of our own world of new and old states, our age of passports, and the helpless victims of nationalism and nationality.

One of the finest of Cavafy's stoic poems is 'Thermopylae', about those who keep faith with what they believe and tell the truth 'without rancour for those who lie', even though they foresee – 'and many do foresee' –

> that Ephialtes will finally appear,
> and in the end the Medes will go through.

Another is 'The God Forsakes Antony', which is also adroitly generalized into speaking for all who see the failure of their work. Do not be fooled, Cavafy says, do not deceive yourself that your ears deceived you, but show yourself worthy of what you are losing, worthy of the success for which you strove unsuccessfully:

> approach the window with firm step,
> and listen with emotion, but not
> with the entreaties and complaints of the coward,
> as a last enjoyment listen to the sounds,
> the exquisite instruments of the mystical troupe,
> and bid her farewell, the Alexandria you are losing.

There is a dignity and a tenderness about these unrhetorical exhortations to courage and fortitude which save them from the faintest suggestion of the stiff upper lip or the hearty scout-master. Yet they are equally free from self-indulgence, the 'firm step' is there as well as the 'emotion'. In other circumstances Destiny is seen wryly as an artist; two lovers are separated by brute necessity, 'the needs of a living', but their grief is palliated, just a little, by the thought that Destiny has divided them before Time could change them,

> so each for the other will remain for ever as he had been,
> a handsome young man of twenty-four years.

Cavafy once said that while many poets were exclusively poets, he was a poet-historian. In this case we must agree with Sidney that 'the best of the historian is subject to the poet', for whatever action the historian is bound to record, 'that may the poet with his imitation make his own, beautifying it both for further teaching and more delighting, as it pleaseth him'. The young and vigorous Nero sleeps soundly on his ebony bed, while his small household gods fall over one another in panic as they recognize the iron footsteps of the Furies on the stairs. A travelling salesman in Alexandria, 31 BC, can't sell his

Brylcreem or Old Spice because of the inexplicable noise and excitement, the music and the parades; finally someone in the crowd

> hurls at him also the gigantic lie
> of the palace – that in Greece Antony is victorious.

At Delphi the priests are delighted with the gifts presented by the envoys of the two rival Ptolemies, but sorely embarrassed by the consideration that one party or the other must inevitably be displeased by the oracle's verdict. While they are deliberating, the envoys suddenly depart, happily leaving the gifts behind. The envoys have heard, as the priests have not, that 'the oracle was pronounced in Rome; the division took place there'. It seems so casual, so easy to do, this historical-poetic miniature painting, yet very few people have done it with anything like Cavafy's neatness, lucidity and unemphatic force.

His poems on the subject of homosexual love form a less interesting section of Cavafy's work, I think. It is true, as Auden said, that Cavafy is an exceptionally honest witness who 'neither bowdlerizes nor glamorizes nor giggles'. But for all their typical terseness these poems are repetitious where the 'historical' ones are not; and, not surprisingly when emotion is recollected in age's untranquillity, there is an element of gloating in the references to 'the ardour', 'the supreme pleasure', 'the delightful stored-up sensual emotion'. More business-like, certainly, are the poems in which the poet relates his physical pleasure to his art. Out in the street, the young men are uneasy, as if something about them must reveal what sort of bed they have just risen from:

> But how the life of the artist has gained.
> Tomorrow, the next day, years later, the vigorous verses
> will be composed that had their beginning here.

Auden felt it was all very well for the poet, who could exploit such experiences – but what would be the future of the artist's companion? One takes the point, yet it is only fair to remark that the protagonists are consenting and adult and moreover the possibilities of pain are not played down. Cavafy describes the fate of one handsome boy:

> Of course, no statue or painting was ever done of him;
> cast into the filthy old ironmonger's,
> quickly, by heavy labour,
> and by common debauchery, so wretched, he was destroyed.

The best of this group is 'He Asked about the Quality', where the keen, economical, simple-seeming presentation of a small drama – a young man is drawn into a shabby shop by a glimpse of the assistant – reminds us of the historical pieces:

> They kept on finding something to say about the merchandise –
> but their only aim: the touching of their hands
> over the handkerchiefs; the coming close
> of their faces, by chance their lips;
> a momentary contact of their limbs.
>
> Furtive and fleet, so that the storekeeper
> who sat in the rear would not notice anything.

That I have quoted copiously is further recognition that Cavafy's charm, so hard to analyse, speaks best for itself, his poems are the only description of themselves. The combination of tenderness with irony, the cool confrontation of disaster, the gift of nimbly enlarging a specific historical incident into general applicability, give him the right to that touch of arrogance which he ascribes to 'A Byzantine Noble in Exile Writing Verses':

> Let the flippant call me flippant.
> In serious matters I have always been
> most diligent…
> it is not at all peculiar that I amuse myself
> composing sestets and octets…
> and that I compose impeccable iambics,
> such as – permit me to say – Constantinople's men of letters
> > > cannot compose.
> This very accuracy, probably, is the cause of their censure.

(1970)

Echt Brecht

Bertolt Brecht: Poems 1913–1956

The first thing to say about this scholarly production, which includes notes both by the poet and by the editors, is that it is vastly enjoyable. The second is that it is scholarly – and all that prevents one from regretting the sparsity of explanatory, interpretative glosses (i.e. a little more help with meaning) is that there is patently no room for them in a volume already bumper.

The volume takes in roughly half of the approximately one thousand poems in the 1967 Suhrkamp Verlag collected edition. The editors tell us that Brecht felt his poetry to be private to him, and they suggest that he also felt it to represent 'a dangerously seductive distraction from the real hard work of writing and staging the plays'. If, as they say, this consideration discouraged him from letting his verse be seen, it certainly failed to inhibit him from writing verse. Indeed, he was so continuous, so 'natural' a writer that he could hardly have had the time to arrange for the publication of so immense an output. It could be that what the editors term 'his staggering indifference to much of his own work' was in part sheer forgetfulness.

Even so, I think the editors overstate our ignorance of Brecht as a poet. True, not very much has hitherto been available in English: in fact, as we now see, a mere fraction of the whole. But what there was – notably though not solely H.R. Hays's *Selected Poems* (1947), the poems scattered through John Willett's *The Theatre of Bertolt Brecht*, the selection in *Modern German Poetry 1910–1960* (Michael Hamburger and Christopher Middleton) and in Hamburger's *Tales from the Calendar* – has been much read and (usefully or not) influential. More than a few English readers have at least realized – or come to think, or to suspect – that Brecht is more considerable as a poet than as a dramatist, despite (or in some cases because of) his cult as theorist of the theatre. Obviously not many will have had much idea of the sheer volume and variety of his poetry until now.

Brecht on the run from the Nazis, with his combative and barbed poems, is of course a stirring figure. Brecht *in situ* as a Communist, with his combative and barbed poems, becomes, as the years go by and Nazism recedes while Communism doesn't, if not a sinister at any rate a suspect figure. In her *Unwritten Memories* (published in 1974) Katia Mann remarks, apropos of his defence before the Committee on Un-American Activities in 1947: 'Brecht was very sly indeed'.

(Possibly the comment was meant to have a wider application, but either way we might note her next words: 'he pretended to be stupid, and the others *were* stupid'.) Some of Brecht's admirers remoter from the *haute-bourgeoisie* than Katia Mann (there was something lordly even about the Manns' late Leftism) must wonder over the nature of their admiration – and whether perhaps Brecht wasn't a trifle sly and shifty over and above the call of survival.

His poetry is less likely than the plays to arouse such suspicions. Aside from the simple-minded propagandist pieces ('Only in Karl Marx and Lenin could we workers / See a chance of life ahead') and occasional outbreaks of silly bad temper, it has other weaknesses. Notable among these are repetitiousness, the over-insistent and vain effort to make minority art look like *vox populi*, and what we might call an excessive fluency in laconicism. What mostly kept Brecht out of danger as a poet, and what is most potent in him, is that – whether or not you share his attitudes – he talked about his times, he was plugged firmly into a particular reality. This kept him, generally, on the right, decent path. It also preserved him from the mere vapid egotism of poets who pride themselves on their concern with the so-called 'eternal verities' while actually busying themselves narcissistically with themselves. (No offence is intended to the said verities, who, like Brecht's gods, tend to evince themselves in disguise. And not much to Narcissus: the poet does look into his own heart, to find something more than himself there.) But perhaps this is to say no more than Brecht's favourite slogan says: 'The truth is concrete.' His 'Little Epistle' begins, solemnly and mischievously,

> If someone enjoys writing he will be glad
> If he has a subject.

In the early poems Brecht's liking for catastrophe, for 'strong meat', already comes out strongly; and later he was to find plenty of it to hand. Even around 1922 we read this:

> When the tables of the law broke, so did all vices.
> Even sleeping with one's sister is no fun any more.
> Murder is too much trouble for many
> Writing poems is too common...

Similarly, his taste for strong cigars, brandy and damnation (all those drowned girls who weigh on his sturdy conscience!): for rotting timbers and 'pestilence and puke and piss'. This goes along with his amusing and surely self-amused 'persona' poems, such as 'Anna speaks ill of Bidi' (*c.* 1919):

> Smokes cigars and reads the papers
> Swigs schnapps, haunts the billiard hall
> Ice-cold, with his airs and capers
> No humanity at all

or, 'You smoke. You shit. You turn out some verse', or of course the famous 'Of Poor B.B.' (in its present form, revised *c.* 1925, when Brecht was twenty-seven):

> Before noon on my empty rocking chairs
> I'll sit a woman or two, and with an untroubled eye
> Look at them steadily and say to them:
> Here you have someone on whom you can't rely.

The comical 'woman or two' is sufficient to modify the horrid 'machismo' of the lines, while the whole poem – despite the newspapers, the tobacco, the brandy – has less to do with any form of virility than with a growing sense of self-chastening unease.

And elsewhere the toughness of the persona is in a fairly undeceptive way 'deceptive', as we give due weight to lines like 'all that lives, lives frailly' and the allusion in a seemingly hard-headed secular version of the Nativity to Mary's

> bitter shame
> Common among the poor
> Of having no privacy.

The two strands, tough subject-matter and tough persona, develop and combine into Brecht's 'news-item' poems. Some of these relate to the past, like the coarsened-Cavafy of 'The Gordian Knot' and 'I'm not saying anything against Alexander' –

> Only
> I have seen people
> Who were remarkable –
> Highly deserving of your admiration
> For the fact that they
> Were alive at all.
> Great men generate too much sweat.

(Incidentally, 'The carpet-weavers of Kuyan-Bulak honour Lenin' reads like a *bien-pensant* version of Cavafy's *mal-pensant* 'In a Township of Asia Minor', where the citizens adroitly switch their honouring from the defeated Antony to the victorious Octavius.)

Other poems in this genre are drawn from the fairly immediate present: the poem about the eight thousand unemployed miners and their families camped outside Budapest (seemingly written two years after the event), and the one, also written in 1926 and carrying as epigraph 'A dispatch from London says…', concerning the three hundred coolies who froze to death in China. I don't know whether the eternal verities feature in these reports; and probably to claim that the truth, besides being concrete, is topical, isn't to make out much of a case for them. 'Letting the facts speak for themselves' is hardly an adequate definition of poetry. Still, at the least such poems are likely, for as long as history survives, to retain some historical interest. And that, if one thinks of the short life-expectancy of the great mass of verse, is something.

> When the wound
> Stops hurting
> What hurts is
> The scar.

This book raises a number of questions of radical concern, not only to Brecht's work but to literature in general, its subject-matter and form and tone, the relationship between writer and reader, between the transitory and the permanent and between *Wahrheit* and *Dichtung*. For instance, the temptation common among poets to 'point up', to make a good story even better (which often means making it worse), as when an injured man in history becomes a dead one in the poem, or the Moscow Metro, exemplifying 'the builders in the role of proprietors', is said to have been built in one year instead of the actual three. In some sense the phenomenon is, if not justified, at least acknowledged in 'Bad time for poetry' (1939):

> Why do I only record
> That a village woman aged forty walks with a stoop?
> The girls' breasts
> Are as warm as ever.

'Only an idiot lives without worry': at times Brecht strikes us as worrying mechanically. His didacticism exacted a price, various prices. The Svendborg and other satires are a mixed bunch; the eternal nastinesses certainly haunt some of them. 'Praised be doubt!' he said, and perhaps this tip which he offers us – a defence against his sloganeering – was one of his own defensive measures. If so, it is effectively, and movingly, deployed in 'To those born later':

And yet we know:
Hatred, even of meanness
Contorts the features.
Anger, even against injustice
Makes the voice hoarse. Oh, we
Who wanted to prepare the ground for friendliness
Could not ourselves be friendly.

Then there are the love poems, highly individual, and the Buckow Elegies of 1953. The latter, with the other late and last poems, suggest that the old Adam in Brecht couldn't for long have toed a line, and wasn't likely ever to locate an Earthly Paradise, however constituted and administered. For one thing, he was too well aware of the old Adam in other people.

Another question raised here has to do with the translation of verse. Technique being more important in Brecht's case than with many modern poets, the editors say, 'we felt it essential to match the original forms as closely as possible': not, that is, to rest content with a flat literal translation hopefully intended to supplement whatever in the way of 'sound and structure' the reader can deduce from the originals. The 'many hands' involved in these translations chose the hard way, and it has paid off in the simplest and purest of currencies: readability.

Bertolt Brecht in America

Chased from my country now I have to see
If there's some shop or bar that I can find
Where I can sell the products of my mind.
Again I tread the roads well known to me

Worn smooth by those accustomed to defeat.
I'm on my way but don't yet know to whom.
Wherever I go they ask me: 'Spell your name!'
And oh, that name was once accounted great…[1]

The poems Brecht wrote in America between 1941 and 1947 tell us much about his mental and emotional life during those years. Now James K. Lyon tells us all, or what seems like all, or even more than all in some departments, drawing on unpublished letters and

---

1 'Sonnet in emigration', translated by Edith Roseveare, in the volume discussed above.

documents, FBI files, and interviews with the subject's friends, relatives, associates and collaborators.

Brecht's American years were, in his own words, an 'exile in paradise' – he thought of himself throughout as an exile, not an immigrant – and to this we might add, with partial truth, that Brecht was himself the serpent in the garden. The experience of exile is peculiarly hard on one whose life centres on language, and no easier if he finds he has little fame in his new land. (There was a sharp contrast in this respect between Brecht's lot and that of the much-translated Thomas Mann.) The situation is aggravated if the exile is a playwright, and hence in need of a theatre; still further aggravated when he has very strong and unshared ideas about 'theatre'. Brecht had lost his natural public, his true students – temporarily at any rate, for much of his writing at this time he saw as lessons laid up in advance for the postwar German people.

As for America, his feelings might have been expected to reflect those conveyed in Goethe's verse: '*Amerika, du hast es besser*', better than our old continent with its ruined castles, its fruitless memories and vain strife – even allowing that for Brecht hardly any strife was in vain. In fact his view approached Rilke's: America was a country of nomads who built homes without intending to stay in them and changed jobs like boots, rootless, lacking a cultural past. Nine days after arriving he wrote in his journal of 'this mortuary of easy going'; a week later, referring to Hollywood, 'Tahiti in metropolitan form'; eight months later: 'I have the feeling of being like Francis of Assisi in an aquarium, Lenin at the Prater (or the Oktoberfest), or a chrysanthemum in a coal mine.' What America could offer him – peace and security – was something he never really wanted, something his nature would soon reject or pervert.

Setting out on his previous visit to America, from Denmark, in 1935, Brecht had compared himself to Columbus, with the implication that it was the New World that was to discover *him*, along with his new kind of 'learning play'. Now, at the age of forty-three, he was stuck in that new world, faced with the prospect of causing himself to be discovered, or (as Lyon puts it) with the necessity of 'producing' himself. That the 'production' failed was largely due to his unyielding didacticism, his emphasis on that un-American activity, class conflict, and his self-will, or what seemed to his indigenous contacts a European 'superiority complex'.

Bertolt Brecht in America details the nature of that failure, in instance after instance, while indicating that in another, longer-term and no doubt more important sense, these years *were* productive. Although

135

Brecht described Hollywood as the 'world centre of the narcotic trade', he was alive to the enormous power films could wield in forming or modifying opinion, and he played some part in the writing of more than fifty film stories, the most fruitful of which (though it is impossible to say how much of Brecht's work survived in the end) issued in Fritz Lang's *Hangmen Also Die*. More often such projects foundered: film-making was collective work, but not (as Lyon observes) collective work of Brecht's kind. Early and late he insisted on collaborative effort, but with himself as the Boss, having the whip-hand. Hollywood declined to hand the whip over.

Most engaging was the plan to turn his poem 'Children's Crusade' into a film, with the ballad-story told in a snowbound New England schoolroom. The project failed, seemingly in that it was 'by extension' an anti-war film and would have had to compete with the successful and more wholehearted war pictures then being put out by Hollywood. Another story on which he worked, 'Silent Witness', appears to have had the requisite ingredients to carry it through to the silver screen, notably a strong plot and a happy ending. A French woman, unjustly accused of collaboration with the Germans, is vindicated when recognized as the model for a stained-glass window of Joan of Arc commissioned by a dead but impeccable abbé who worked for the resistance… However, Brecht insisted that the leading lady should appear with her head shaven – and no star could be persuaded to do that! Then there was his comedy, *Schweyk in the Second World War*, probably written with an eye and a half on Broadway: but alas, its hero was too unheroic, its humour too European, and the play did not receive its first professional American performance until 1977.

During 1943–4 Brecht wrote *The Caucasian Chalk Circle*, in which the celebrated Austrian-born actress Luise Rainer was to star on Broadway. Their ideas on acting failed to coincide and – even though at this stage only one page of the play actually existed – a violent row blew up. Luise Rainer remembers it thus:

Brecht (roaring): Do you know who I am?
Rainer (calmly): Yes. You are Bertolt Brecht. And do you know who I am?
Brecht: Yes. You are nothing. Nothing, I say!

The customary tangle ensued, with collaborators and translators set one against another and only Brecht's right hand knowing what his left was doing. Having been told by the dramatist that *any* actress would jump at the chance to play the role of Grusha, Luise Rainer withdrew, and two decades passed before the play was seen in New York. Two minor successes – minor in Brecht's table of priorities at the time, one guesses – were the publication by New Directions in 1944 of seventeen scenes from the play *The Private Life of the Master Race*, as translated by Eric Bentley, and of *Selected Poems*, in the fine English versions of H.R. Hays, by Reynal and Hitchcock in 1947.

For Luise Rainer, Brecht was 'cruel, selfish, vain – an awful man'. Apropos of the confusion into which Brecht had thrown the staging of *Master Race* in 1945, Eric Bentley wrote to a mutual acquaintance, with considerable discernment: 'He has neither good manners nor elementary decency. He lives out his own theory that it is impossible to behave well in this society...a scoundrel but an artist.' Bentley and Hays both suffered from his blend of the dictatorial and the devious, both retained an unwavering admiration for his writing. And both of them attest to this charm. Not so, however, Auden ('an odious person') or Isherwood ('Brecht simply had very bad manners'). Isherwood also remarked how 'ruthless' Brecht was where his own projects were concerned. Here lies the overriding cause of the many quarrels, complaints and wounded feelings recorded in this book. Brecht was intransigently Brechtian. He knew nothing of the fashionable uncertainty about 'identity': he had it in excess. His attempts to 'depersonalize' professional or political disagreements were not uniformly successful; he got up people's noses, and generally stayed there. His works were to be produced the way he wanted, not how Broadway or Hollywood or the rest of the United States wanted. He was his own worst enemy, at least in the short run. But he was the best friend of his own beliefs and principles.

George Grosz, a friend of Brecht, remarked in his autobiography that 'he would have preferred a good electric calculator where his heart was, and the spokes of a car wheel in the place of his legs.' Professor Lyon is a well-disposed ringside commentator, but still somewhat hard pressed to make out a case for Brecht's warmth of heart. He cites a poem, written in 1947, which begins with a reference to the 'swamp' of Hollywood, or conceivably of drugs:

> I saw many friends
> And the friend I loved most
> Among them helplessly sunk
> Into the swamp...

and ends thus:

Now I watched him leaning back
Covered with leeches in the shimmering, softly moving slime

Upon the sinking face
That ghastly blissful smile.

The poem was apparently about Peter Lorre, addicted to morphine
and now suffering a sharp decline in reputation, and since it was found
among his papers we may assume the author gave it to him. Lyon
claims, not altogether convincingly, that the poem reveals a concern
for the actor extending beyond his professional usefulness to the
dramatist: 'the poem is for Lorre as a human being whom he wanted
to help.' Aside from the one brilliant phrase in it ('that ghastly blissful
smile') it savours of the coolly didactic and depersonalized.

Yet it is probable that Brecht was genuinely attached to Lorre, as
also to the politically timorous Charles Laughton, whom Lyon
considers the single most important person for him during his
American exile. If Brecht hid his feelings, he must have had them. He
customarily preferred to voice a professional reason for admiring
someone rather than a merely personal one; to admit to an objective
cause for affection (in Lorre's case, for pity or regret) rather than a
subjective one. This was the case at times with his women friends too;
they were of interest and significance to him in more ways than one.
There is a comical-naughty poem written in America in which he
praises an ample peasant-style skirt for its ancient associations and its
grace – 'Your lovely movements bring to mind Colchis / The day
Medea strolled towards the sea' – adding that there are other reasons
for favouring such a skirt, however: base and lustful ones, which 'will
do for me'.

In his chapter on 'Brecht's Women' Lyon is relatively reticent,
confining himself to Ruth Berlau and Brecht's wife, Helene Weigel,
both of them actresses (though then unemployable) and therefore
collaborators, as being the only two women in America who counted
in terms of his work. Certainly there would be little point or propriety
in leading us through the list of members of the 'harem'. Sufficient on
this aspect of Brecht's briskness (and his distaste for the bourgeois/
capitalist notion of love-as-ownership) is Joseph Losey's comment
that he 'ate very little, drank very little, and fornicated a great deal'.
Ruth Berlau ('Brecht's backstreet wife' she called herself) returned his
devotion but, by this account, gave him dreadful trouble by her
exigency, hysteria and utter lack of discretion. A story told here about
Helene Weigel is particularly refreshing since it was commonly Brecht
who came out on top in arguments with his intimates. She had maintained that women possess greater fortitude than men since they have
to put up with menstruation and childbirth. Brecht, who was

notorious for his permanent stubble, countered with: 'Men shave.' To which his wife retorted: 'How do you know?'

That Brecht, who could put his hand to practically anything, was obliged to abandon the idea of rendering the *Communist Manifesto* into classical hexameters may suggest that there were limits to his ideological manœuvrability, and that – for all his foxiness and for all that the old fox had nowhere eminently desirable to run to – he would not have lasted much longer in the bosom of the German Democratic Republic. (At least in East Berlin he had an appreciative audience, even if much of it came from the bourgeoisie of West Berlin.) During his earlier visit to America he reportedly answered Sidney Hook's protest against Stalin's persecution of innocent people with the shocking epigram, 'The more innocent they are, the more they deserve to die.' Alert though Lyon is to Brecht's trickiness, he is content to ascribe the saying to annoyance at Hook's attack on Stalin and the desire to stupefy his opponent – without exploring the possible implication that those who were innocent of plotting against Stalin deserved to die for that very reason.[2]

Lyon is enlightening on the subject of Brecht's relations with the 'Frankfurt School', also evacuated to America. He might have been expected to find the group's self-critical, dialectical procedures congenial. However, he regarded them as introverted mandarins, spinning verbal subversions of the capitalist society in which they (unlike Brecht) lived in some ease, while they saw him as a 'vulgar' Marxist, a crude and retarded materialist still committed to the stuffy proletariat. Both camps had a point to their credit: Brecht in that his politics were at least down to earth, 'concrete', unlike the school's disembodied theorizing, and Theodor Adorno in the element of truth behind his gibe that Brecht spent two hours every day pushing dirt under his fingernails to make himself look like a worker.

The quarrel between Brecht and Thomas Mann – the greatest German novelist and the best living German poet, both of them exiles – is less edifying. According to Katia Mann's *Unwritten Memories* hostility was born early on, when somebody showed Mann one of Brecht's plays and the novelist's comment – 'Just imagine, the monster has talent' – was passed on to the dramatist. The latter came back with a sharper quip: 'As a matter of fact, I always found his short stories quite good.' Bad feeling intensified in America. Mann referred to Brecht as a 'party-liner', Brecht described Mann's works as 'clerico-

2   See Martin Esslin, 'Brecht: Icon and Self-Portrait', *Encounter*, December 1977.

fascist'. Mann was a pessimist, seeing the Faustian two souls as Siamese twins native to the German breast; Brecht was an optimist, readying himself to foster a single-souled Germany just as soon as he could get back there. Mann was an 'Establishment' figure, or figurehead, in America; Brecht, as ever, was a rebel, a 'professional "anti"', in Elsa Lanchester's words. Yet neither was exactly single-minded or transparent, and it is possible that what each of these masters of irony most disliked in the other was his public image. The one dirtied his fingernails every day, the other cleaned them.

We may still be in doubt as to what Brecht really intended by his remark about Stalin. He was himself devoted to the play of thesis and antithesis, but what he generally expected from other people was synthesis, or plain simplicity without the frills. When Hans Viertel, a Trotskyist, asked him what would happen to those who declined to accept his views, he answered: 'They have to be shot.' Given his dialectical nature, not very many would be left alive in that case. Lyon remarks that it was Viertel who came as near as anybody to realizing the complexities of the Brecht enigma when he termed him 'a one-man political party'. The description continued: '…in close coalition with the Communists', which now gives it a strong air of paradox. But paradox was in order for Brecht, while orthodoxy was for other people. And what in him was the licence of the 'chameleon poet' would in others be the mark of the turncoat.

Katia Mann's comment on his appearance before the House Un-American Activities Committee is worth repeating: 'He was very sly indeed: he pretended to be stupid, and the others *were* stupid.' Brecht politely stressed his consciousness of being a guest in the United States, freely admitted that he was not nor ever had been a member of any Communist party, and courteously corrected the Committee regarding the date of his birth. Martin Esslin has compared the proceedings to the cross-examining of a zoologist by apes. In which case the apes, too, were courteous. 'They weren't as bad as the Nazis,' Brecht joked. 'The Nazis would never have let me smoke.' Finally the Committee pronounced him an honest and cooperative fellow and a good example to others, one whose links with known Communists were principally on an artistic level – a judgment which normally would have infuriated him but presumably, on this occasion, merely amused. It was undeniably convenient. As it happened, the hearing was held immediately before Brecht's previously arranged departure from the country – a coincidence which, as Lyon notes, gave his going a dramatic appearance. It was as if he were escaping from a witch-hunt. (A hunt from which, in reality, he had just been officially exempted.) He was pursued hotly by an award of a thousand dollars from the Academy of Arts and Letters. And behind him, like a bomb timed to go off later, he left his dramaturgy. 'In one form or another, it was theatre until the very end.'

(1976; 1980)

The Lord's Song

On Paul Celan

Paul Celan – originally Paul Antschel, in its Romanian form Ancel, whence the anagrammatic name he took later – was born in 1920 to a German-speaking Jewish family in polyglot Czernowitz ('Little Vienna'), in present-day Romania. When his parents were taken by the Nazis in June 1942, he was either away from home or forcibly separated from them. His father died of typhus in a camp, his mother was shot as unfit for work. Celan spent some two years in Romanian labour camps, and then either escaped or was released and made his way to Bucharest, now occupied by the Red Army, where he worked as a translator of Russian literature. He 'saw little future in Romania as a German-language poet under the aegis of socialist realism', and in 1947 he moved to Vienna and the following year to Paris.

In *Paul Celan: Poet, Survivor, Jew*, John Felstiner, the perfect guide, describes Celan's celebrated 'Todesfuge' ('Deathfugue') as 'the *Guernica* of postwar European literature'. The poem appears to have been written in 1944, and was first published in Romanian translation in Bucharest as 'Tango of Death', a reference to the playing of tangos by Jewish musicians during tortures, grave digging, executions, and other camp functions. Wherever Celan found 'the facts', from survivors or from printed reports, the poem is so dramatic, real, immediate in impact, that it is no wonder it was widely thought to derive from someone who had direct experience of the death camps. Celan could have said of 'Deathfugue' what Picasso said when a Gestapo officer in Paris asked, 'Did you do *Guernica*?': 'No. You did.'

If at first sight the poem looks surrealistic, it soon reveals itself as starkly realistic. 'Black milk of daybreak we drink it at evening': perhaps an initiatory point-blank contradiction in terms, perhaps the smoke from the crematoria. 'We shovel a grave in the air there you won't lie too cramped': those incinerated find a grave in the air (which supports the reading of black milk as smoke), a grave more commodious than the narrow (*eng*) camp bunks. The obscurer passages are illuminated by the plainer ones: the man who 'lives in the house' (a camp is not a house) 'whistles his Jews into rows', he shouts 'jab this earth deeper you lot there you others sing up and play'. It is graves in the earth that this lot are digging: music while you die. And as he points out the difference in weight between the German words and his English and the added pressure of Hebrew allusion, Felstiner reminds us of the psalm: 'For they that carried us away captive required of us a song… How shall we sing the Lord's song in a strange land?'

The man who whistles his Jews (and his dogs) writes to Deutschland… 'Your golden hair Margarete your ashen hair Shulamith': Germanly romantic, though less Goethe's Gretchen than Heine's siren of the Lorelei (a poem which, since they couldn't wipe it out of people's minds, the Nazi cultural experts represented as an anonymous folksong), Margarete can only be his wife or sweetheart back home. Shulamith hardly needs any gloss, even if we know nothing of the Song of Songs ('Return, return, O Shulamite'): she is obviously no Aryan ash blonde, and there follows a repetition of the words 'we shovel a grave in the air…' Concerning 'der Tod ist ein Meister aus Deutschland', now 'a tag line' gracing many a monograph, documentary and work of art, Felstiner notes that while 'master' is the only possible translation, bearing equally such senses as Christ, rabbi, teacher, champion, overseer, maestro, it lacks the specific German connotations of Goethe's *Wilhelm Meister* and Wagner's *Meistersinger* (of Nürnberg, i.e. Nuremberg). (Maybe it gains with our 'master race' rather than 'Herrenvolk'.) 'This Death is a master from Deutschland his eye it is blue / he shoots you with shot made of lead shoots you level and true': apropos of this 'childlike' rhyme, the only rhyme in the poem, Felstiner mentions something we could well miss, that Goethe too rhymes on *genau*, 'true', 'exact' (though with *grau*, not *blau*, a grey clump of willows, not a blue eye) in his ballad of the 'Erlking', who steals away children.

The poem, the fugue, ends with a further recurrence of 'der Tod ist ein Meister' and then of the two women, 'dein goldenes Haar Margarete / dein aschenes Haar Shulamith'. Felstiner comments, 'Darkened by ash, "Shulamith" ends the poem holding onto what Nazism tried to erase: a rooted identity. Archaic, inalienable, she has the last word, not to mention the silence after.' Some were later to see in the coupling of Margarete/Shulamith a sign of forgiveness and reconciliation. True, the poem was being taught in German high schools, but there is no evidence in the poem for this agreeable conclusion.

Celan came to resent the way 'Deathfugue' overshadowed his other poems. That could hardly be avoided; it was as if the reality, the directness had gone into this poem and the rest could be little more than glimpses and cross-references, cryptic gestures, intimations or gasps.

One might wonder whether there isn't something mechanical in the multilingual wordplay, the 'semantic explosions', the crowding allusions, Hebraic and other; mechanical, or despairing: these poems could barely be written, how can they be expounded or criticized? Outwardly surrealist, yet breaking into such explicit clarities as 'No one / witnesses for the / witness', in a poem titled 'Aschenglorie'. (It may be that 'There's nothing in the world for which a poet will give up writing', but the many translations Celan made, taking up 1,500 pages in the collected works, of Mandelstam, Michaux, Valéry, Ungaretti, Marvell, Shakespeare's sonnets, Emily Dickinson, Housman, among others, may have come as a blessing, a sharing of the psychic burden.) Felstiner deals minutely with the later poems, many of which carry more power than I have suggested, notably 'Tenebrae', with its inverted echo of Celan's much loved Hölderlin, and 'Psalm', where the translator achieves the bonus of an English-only pun: 'No one kneads us again out of earth and clay'. Of another poem Felstiner remarks that 'Tausendwort' has been mistranslated as 'myriad-word', and must be 'thousandword', as in 'Thousand-Year Reich', since the subject is words that have been lost and need to be salvaged. He sheds light on – or derives light from – Celan's prose as well, for instance the speech he gave on receiving the Bremen Prize in 1958, with its mixture of conventional gratitude and pointed obliquities.

Celan drowned himself in the Seine in 1970, at the age of 49. Recurrent depression and a sense of loneliness may have been exacerbated by renascent anti-Semitism. And then, he wrote in German, a seeming paradox which has been much aired. It was the language of the Nazis, but it was his language too (and Goethe's, and Hölderlin's); he himself declared: 'Only in the mother tongue can one speak one's own truth. In a foreign tongue the poet lies', but there is no telling what toll this 'paradox' exacted. And there was the searing knowledge that while he had survived, his parents had perished; his mother is a persistent presence in the poems: 'And can you bear, Mother, as once on a time, / the gentle, the German, the pain-laden rhyme?' Felstiner doesn't speculate, observing only that it is no coincidence that Primo Levi too took his own life.

Throughout this portrayal of a writer's life by way of his writing, the tone is faultless, free from gratuitous pathos, emotional bullying, and any trace of self-regard. With his own difficulties in mind, Felstiner suggests that translators resemble the beggar employed to wait on the outskirts of town and watch for when the Messiah might come. Asked how he liked his work, the beggar said, 'Well, the pay's not so hot, but it's a steady job.' Probably the only joke in the book, but surely a good old Jewish one.

Celan's Collected Prose

'After Auschwitz, to write a poem is barbaric,' Theodor Adorno dogmatized in 1951. In 1966 he seems to have changed his mind: 'Perennial suffering has as much right to expression as the tortured have to scream, hence it may have been wrong to say that no poem could be written after Auschwitz.' Paul Celan's poetry shows how wrong Adorno's original opinion was, but also, by its agonized manner, how almost right, in a sense, Adorno had been. So does Celan's prose, both in its style and in its meagre quantity: it occupies some forty-six pages in Rosmarie Waldrop's translation.

'For Celan, whose poems moved ever closer to silence,' Waldrop says, 'prose was too noisy a medium.' Equally, the poems (hundreds of them) appear to have been squeezed by grievous force out of silence. She observes that his prose is a poet's prose in that 'it often progresses by sound association and puns which must suffer in translation': and suffer all the more because these devices (and Celan needed devices desperately) are less expected in prose. In all Celan's writing, elusiveness is tempered (or fed) by allusiveness: nervy, pain-laden, disjointed, gestural, always about to arrive, *en route* at least, the outcome (what does come out) resembles surrealism in that what is hinted at is such an enormity, beyond our ability to comprehend and make sense of.

In an early essay on the surrealist painter, Edgar Jené, Celan rejects the idea that words have remained the same or can readily be cleaned up; he cannot help seeing the persistence of 'the ashes of burned-out meanings (and not only of those)'; we don't need to be alerted to the 'ashen hair' of Shulamith in 'Deathfugue'. Replying to a questionnaire from a Paris bookstore in 1958, he had his own poems in mind when he declared that German poetry ('with most sinister events in its memory') could no longer speak the language many people expected of it, but instead a language which distrusted 'beauty', sought to be truthful, posited rather than rendered 'poetical', whose 'musicality' had nothing in common with the 'euphony' which, as he puts it, 'more or less blithely continued to sound alongside the greatest horrors'. Finally he loses patience: 'These poets! One ends up wishing that, some day, they might manage to get a solid novel on to paper.'

The most resounding statement occurs in the speech Celan gave on receiving the City of Bremen Literature Prize in 1958, with its opening double-edged expression of gratitude and reproach: 'In our language' – the language of his listeners and the mother tongue of the Romanian-born Jew whose mother had been killed by Germans – 'In our language the words "thinking" and "thanking" [denken, danken] have the same root. If we follow their meaning through, we enter the semantic field of "recollect" [gedenken], "bear in mind" [eingedenk sein], "remembrance" [Andenken] and "devotion" [Andacht]. Permit me, from this standpoint, to thank you.' Veiled references follow, notably to 'the thousand darknesses of murderous speech': compare 'Thousand-Year Reich'. As John Felstiner notes, the rude words, 'Jew' and 'Nazi' remain unspoken.

In 1960 the German Academy for Language and Literature awarded Celan the Georg Büchner Prize, and the speech he made on that occasion, 'The Meridian', must have left his listeners mystified, while no doubt impressed by the earnest obscurity of what they were hearing and the apposite if eccentric invocation of Büchner's works. The poem today 'clearly shows a strong tendency towards silence': here, Celan's most substantial, at any rate longest, piece of prose shows a strong tendency to say quite a lot but little or nothing clearly (he cites Pascal: 'Do not reproach us for lack of clarity, that's what we profess'), in a series of intimations and qualifications and a congeries of detours. ('But then,' he had remarked in the Bremen speech, 'is there such a thing as a detour?') He rehearses the opening of Büchner's 1836 novella, *Lenz*: On the 20th of January 1778, the mad poet Lenz 'was walking through the mountains... only it sometimes bothered him that he could not walk on his head'. (If you walk on your head, you have heaven as an abyss beneath you.) Celan comments: 'Perhaps we can say that every poem is marked by its own "20th of January"? Perhaps the newness of poems written today is that they try most plainly to be mindful of this kind of date?' Felstiner, wondering how many of the listeners would remember, reminds us that it was at Wannsee on the 20th of January 1942 that Nazi leaders decided on the 'Final Solution'. One thing stands out: the honorific incantation 'Meine Damen und Herren', which occurs fifteen times during the speech. A sign of unease (certainly), of excess politeness (better too much than none at all?), of ingratiation (hardly), of apology (for being so hard to follow), or (1942 wasn't so very long ago) of perceived incongruity?

Four pages of more or less cryptic aphorisms, under the heading 'Backlight' (in photography, illumination from behind), might seem to promise some slight relief. 'The hour jumped out of the clock, stood

146

facing it, and ordered it to work properly', 'Bury the flower and put a man on its grave'. But foreboding predominates. 'Do not be deceived: this last lamp does not give more light – the dark has only become more absorbed in itself.' Celan is no author for the faint-hearted; the idea that we forget because we must and not because we will is not entertained.

(1995; 2000)

'My Muse, Mnemosyne'

Czeslaw Milosz

Unity in a book is a comforting thing: we know where we are, whether or not we like where we find ourselves. In Czeslaw Milosz's *The Separate Notebooks*, made up of verse and prose written at various times between 1940 and 1980, the contents hang together precariously, but precariousness, the equal poise of some fell war, is the condition of the book. The author himself proves to stand more firmly than one could possibly have expected.

'Where is the truth of unremembered things?' The star called Wormwood has fallen, a third part of the rivers has become wormwood, and many have died of the bitter waters. Rather than crying 'Woe, woe, woe' like the angel, the Polish poet follows with acts of piety, an offering of memories, utterly unsentimental,

> stench, shit frozen into clods.
> And those centuries
> conceiving in the herring smell of the middle of night,

scenes from childhood, memories of ways of life, of ousted customs, of objects and incidents and persons, a pearl button on a glove, the burning of Giordano Bruno, a death in Auschwitz, someone lighting a pine chip soaked in resin, apples rolling across tables, the round bottom of a passing girl, a bird 'propped on your grey lizard legs, on cybernetic gloves'. And evocations of

> Ladies of 1920 who served us cocoa.
> Grow strong for the glory of Poland, our little knights, our
> eagles!...
> Ladies from the Polish Circle, ladies from the Auxiliary Corps,

of Aunt Florentyna, Lithuanian-born like Milosz, who, being a good Catholic and a landowner, had to accept a 'tacit change' in her habits, and of an anonymous woman in an undatable gown: 'By whom is she to be seen / If she is deprived even of her name?'

The narrator wonders at his 'reluctance to indulge in fiction, as if I believed that one could faithfully reconstruct what once was'. All those phenomena were prefaces, he had thought, temporary things, but no, they were prefaces to other prefaces, other temporary things. Wormwood has fallen, 'bitter rivers flowed', and 'no sign of divine care shone in the heavens'; the recollections and evocations are sometimes attended by icy comments from 'the Powers above the Earth', who know of human pain but feel no compassion: 'Why should we care about living and dying?' The creatures who 'traced their origin to the dinosaur / And took their deftness from the lemur's paw' are those who

> tied the hands of man with barbed wire.
> And dug shallow graves at the edge of the wood.
> There would be no truth in his last testament.
> They wanted him anonymous for good.

In 'Magpiety', a light-hearted piece in his *Selected Poems*, Milosz declares himself amazed that his Muse, Mnemosyne, has in no way diminished his amazement. Amazement is the enemy of anonymity. Rather than unacknowledged legislators of the world, poets are sometimes noticed memorialists. (A similar concern, equally reluctant to indulge in fiction though less grand than Milosz can be on occasion, is found in the poems of Piotr Sommer, another Pole, born in 1948 and Milosz's junior by thirty-seven years: 'that famous spinner Mnemosyne', 'the heart doesn't give up easily, and goes on knocking',

> Station lights connect with those above,
> the days of the week connect,
> the wind with the breath –
> nothing that doesn't.
>
> The broken heating plant in Zeran
> and my child, and the woman
> I picked out years ago because of
> her white kneesocks with blue stripes.
>
> Interesting, how the world
> connects tomorrow and the day after that...
>   – 'Stitch', *Things to Translate*

Not that there is any suggestion of 'I only am escaped alone to tell thee', of the messenger bringing evil tidings. Nor does Milosz work in the mode of the ornamental stonemason or the obituarist. He is more of an anecdotist or a one-act playwright; at times smilingly so, as in 'A Book in the Ruins', dated Warsaw 1941:

> You pick a fragment
> Of grenade which pierced the body of a song
> On Daphnis and Chloe. And you long,
> Ruefully, to have a talk with her,
> As if it were what life prepared you for.

The poem is a gloss on Blake's proverb, 'Eternity is in love with the productions of time', while adding that immortality is in love with the present, and 'is for its sake'. A short prose story, deriving from a family chronicle, tells of Pan Eugene, who lived in a castle at the turn of the nineteenth century and spent most of his time playing the piano. He continues to play after his death, besides walking abroad, and for a moment we might think we are in Dracula country. But his posthumous activities cease precisely when his brother dies in 1914: the concluding question is 'whether philosophy is really of any help against the passion of life?' What is wisdom worth, if petty feelings and family quarrels are so potent and durable that they force us to walk after our death?

The present is commemorated too, proleptically; future generations will stumble on our writings in some forgotten cave, and be amazed that 'we knew so many of their own joys, / Though our futile palace has come to mean so little'. But there is more to it than 'attempts at naming the world' or, in Macduff's words, remembering that such things were. There is also celebration, difficult as this must seem: 'How can laments and curses be turned into hymns?' Despite the speaker's bitter and confused life, despite his 'knowing better',

> the lips praised on their own, on their own the feet ran;
> The heart beat strongly; and the tongue proclaimed its adoration.

The following poem reinforces this celebration: the Earth is like no other place –

> What continents, what oceans, what a show it is!
> In the hall of pain, what abundance on the table.

It is, exactly, the life he has lived that makes him feel unable to write accusingly; 'joy would spurt in amid the lamentation'. No easy, sustained flow, but a 'spurt', by reason of the pressure of its opposite. (Milosz has observed, in an essay, that truly Christian writing comes from countries where Christians are persecuted.) The poem ends ambiguously:

> So what, if in a minute I must close the book:
> Life's sweet, but it might be pleasant not to have to look.

As regards the individual, death ends the succession of 'prefaces'; whether it is itself a preface – in which case what follows may quite possibly prove a disappointment compared with earthly life – is another matter, closed to the expectation which properly belongs to living.

Part of the ironic advice to a 'Child of Europe', in *Selected Poems*, runs:

> Love no country: countries soon disappear.
> Love no city: cities are soon rubble.
>
> Throw away keepsakes, or from your desk
> A choking, poisonous fume will exude....
>
> Do not gaze into the pools of the past.
> Their corroded surface will mirror
> A face different from the one you expected.

Elsewhere Milosz has stressed his distrust of ironic or sarcastic writing, which can speedily decline into nihilism and acquiescence, and his disapproval of sterile anger at the world, and of the 'mandatory style' of much modern literature, with its servile courting of the counterfeit 'demonic', cheap and shameful when set against the power of true evil as so many have experienced it.

Possibly the key poem – assuming that one has found the right lock – is 'Counsels', also in *Selected Poems*. If he were a young poet, says the speaker, he would prefer not to describe the earth as 'a madman's dream, a stupid tale full of sound and fury', though he grants that he didn't himself happen to see the triumph of justice. God appears to be strictly neutral, certainly not favouring the virtuous and innocent; or else, which comes to much the same, he is in hiding. 'And yet, the earth merits a bit, a tiny bit, of affection.' Not – he hastens to say – that he takes too seriously the consolations of nature, the moon, those clouds, the wild cherries on the banks of the Wilia … Indeed, one ought to keep well away from such 'persistent images of infinite space, of infinite time'. These things are not the proper study of mankind; maybe, like irony, they conduce to nihilism and acquiescence. In its unabstract manifestations, 'black earth and rye', nature is prominent here, part and parcel of what is to be praised and remembered. But nature is no loving mother. More to the point, as Donald Davie has proposed in *Czeslaw Milosz and the Insufficiency of Lyric*, is the poet's sympathy with Manichaean ways of thinking. In *The Land of Ulro* Milosz mentions how the obligations of a teacher brought him into conflict with his students in America: he 'openly acknowledged the existence of good and evil, a stance they dismissed as irredeemably reactionary'. The poem 'Counsels' ends with an unfinished sentence:

> There is so very much death, and that is why affection
> for pigtails, bright-coloured skirts in the wind,
> for paper boats no more durable than we are...

Milosz is more to be envied than mocked for his conviction that 'human reason is beautiful and invincible', 'an enemy of despair and a friend of hope', and that Philo-Sophia and poetry, 'her ally in the service of the good', will prevail over their foes. But perhaps it is a spurt of confidence, rather than a spate, as all poems are spurts: in some sense good will prevail, in some place, in some time, and for a time.

Milosz's hunger – though never a hunger for ease of mind – can sometimes look like Whitman, or like greed:

Every day and in every hour, hungry. A spasm in the throat, staring at the face of every woman passing in the street. Wanting not her but all the earth. Desiring, with dilated nostrils, the smells of the bakery, of roasting coffee, wet vegetables. In thought devouring every dish and drinking every drink. Preparing myself for absolute possession.

A kind of correction comes promptly, in a verse spoken by a woman and addressed to poets, philosophers, 'contrivers of romances', and other great talkers:

Not all creatures have your need for words.
Birds you killed, fish you tossed into your boat,
In what words will they find rest and in what heaven?

You received gifts from me: they were accepted.
But you don't understand how to think about the dead.
The scent of winter apples, of hoar-frost, and of linen:
There are nothing but gifts on this poor, poor earth.

To excerpt as I have done, perching here and there on what Davie calls 'particularities and angularities', may be – if not to force a false unity upon the compilation – at least to exaggerate here and under-state there: to be, as criticism can hardly help but be, more explicit than the text, cramped and contrived. What a reader manages to understand – and in this case, for me, what he manages to understand from a translation – is bound to carry most weight with him; and then, as the poet observes here in a rather different sense, 'What is pronounced strengthens itself.' But to be moved, again and again, is something.

(1984; 2001)

Did Nobody Teach You?

On Stevie Smith

The vivacious narrator of *Novel on Yellow Paper*, who claims to have written a long poem entitled 'La Fille de Minos et de Pasiphaë', declares a constitutional preference for Racine over Shakespeare. A French preference, obviously, and the reasons she gives are French (the admirer of Shakespeare will present much the same account as grounds for his admiration): Shakespeare's verse is 'conventional' whereas the feeling is 'so warm and so human and so disturbing', and for Pompey Casmilus this is an antithesis which makes her feel 'distraught and ill at ease'. Then there are too many complications in Shakespeare's plots, too many inessentials, too many (if beautiful) distractions. 'The plot of a tragedy must be bone-straight and simple.' Pompey has strong opinions about a number of serious matters, and distinct feelings (she is not unfeeling at all!), but she does not like a riot of emotion: 'I do not like it at all'. Thus she is at home with *Phèdre* because 'Racine is very serene, very severe, very austere and simple… And this tragedy is also very bracing…very strong and very inevitable and impersonal.'

These adjectives, or some of them, could be applied to Stevie Smith's own poetry. Severe, austere, simple, bracing, impersonal. If 'this is truly Greek, and what the Greek is', then Stevie Smith is somewhat Greek. If to be classical is not to be (in a number of senses of that peculiar adjective) romantic, then she is in some senses classical. Like these adjectives, she is equivocal, not half as simple as she seems. For instance, there is a sparsity of great expectations in her outlook, or so it would appear. The Frog Prince is 'fairly happy in a frog's doom':

> I have been a frog now
> For a hundred years
> And in all this time
> I have not shed many tears…

Why change? To have the *heavenly* time which the story promises once the princess has kissed him, he must free himself from his content-ment, for perhaps it is part of the spell 'to make much of being a frog', and open himself to disenchantment:

> Come, then, royal girl and royal times,
> Come quickly,
> I can be happy until you come
> But I cannot be heavenly,
> Only disenchanted people
> Can be heavenly.

The poem is not simple and straightforward, after all, because of that ambiguous word *heavenly*, which is both flapper-talk and terribly eschatological (or something else very serious), and here, it seems, modulates from one sense into the other, so that finally it is the 'romance' of living under a spell, in a frog's paradise as it were, that is to be exposed, not the romance which the fairy story holds out as the palace-living princess-loving future. Finally, to stand a chance of being 'heavenly', you must be undeluded.

If in the upshot this poem doesn't have much to say one way or the other about great expectations, it is an apt illustration of something else: that (as no doubt in Racine and in the Greeks) 'bone-straight and simple' doesn't necessarily mean shallow or obvious, and while you can usually dart through Miss Smith's poems with immediate enjoyment, some of them are deep and (though they make no overt demand in this direction) deserve and repay considerable thought. Among such substantial pieces are 'I had a dream…', 'The Last Turn of the Screw', 'The Airy Christ', 'Come on, Come back' and 'The Crown of Gold'.

If classicism is avoidance of the romantic, then one can adduce her best-known because most obvious attributes: the perverse off-rhyming (she goes out of her way to rhyme impurely, but at other times thumps down on the most obvious if pure rhyme), the inevitably comic and deflatory effect of rhyming English words with French, and the bathos which W. McGonagall achieved effortlessly but she had to work for. Thus 'Saffron' concludes on an inept rhyme, which reins in the reader abruptly, *and* with an austerely negative way-of-putting-it:

> Bice, Pale and Saffron but I love best
> Beautiful summer Saffron, running fast.
> Because this beautiful spirit should not be frozen
> And is furthest from it when she is saffron.

Lest 'Hymn to the Seal', in its celebration of 'God's creatures in their prime', should wax too grandiose, the middle stanza runs thus:

> When thou wast young thy coat
> Was pale with spots upon it,
> But now in single black it lies
> And thou, Seal, liest on it.

'The Small Lady', with her large washing machine, victim of a malicious witch, is shown as remonstrating in this way:

> 'Aroint thee, false witch!' cried the lady with a brave face,
> 'Human inventions help properly, magic is a disgrace.'

A good sentiment, surely, but somewhat reductively expressed. The philosophical dialogue between Eve and the Virgin Mary is left to continue, but the report on the proceedings terminates on a strong note of definitive inconclusiveness:

> And they talked until nightfall,
> But the difference between them was radical.

And in what is surely a very serious poem, 'A Man I am', with the reminiscence of Blake often remarked on in her work and a rather more pronounced flavour of the seventeenth century (particularly Herbert and Vaughan), the resonant lines

> But presently the spring broke in
> Upon the pastures of my sin

are followed by the deliberately flat

> My poor heart bled like anything,

and in turn this is succeeded by

> And falling ill, I soon grew worse.
> Until at last I cried on Him,
> Before whom angel faces dim,
> To take the burden of my sin
> And break my head beneath his wing.

Stevie Smith's Christianity – she described herself as an agnostic Anglican, and she seems to me to have known a lot about Christianity, what it was, or what it could be – was no Phantom Spiritual State, no theological preserve or Sunday subject, but very much part and parcel of everyday life. Perhaps the sensed kinship with George Herbert resides here.

'Unromantic' too are her reservations on the subject of Love. Or Love as it is generally written about. 'Anger's Freeing Power' tells of a raven who fancies himself a captive in a cell which has only three walls. The loving narrator cannot persuade the bird that in fact he is free to fly away, but then two other ravens come along and jeer at him in a nicely vulgar manner:

> You wretched bird, conceited lump
> You well deserve to pine and thump.

This treatment works wonders: 'Oh do I then? he says,' and off he flies to heaven's skies. The narrator is left to muse ruefully:

> Yet when I woke my eyes were wet
> To think Love had not freed my pet
>
> Anger it was that won him hence
> As only Anger taught him sense
>
> Often my tears fall in a shower
> Because of Anger's freeing power.

Here she is close to Blake, that unromantic romantic and angel-seeing realist: 'Damn braces. Bless relaxes', and 'The tygers of wrath are wiser than the horses of instruction'. Her Christ, too, is more tiger than lamb – 'He is Noble, he is not Mild.'

While part of her is in sympathy with dreamers, for to dream is human, part of her remains cool, sceptical and admonitory, and sometimes with an effect of what Derwent May has called 'comic, forthright, moral knockabout':

> I'm sorry to say my dear wife is a dreamer,
> And as she dreams she gets paler and leaner.
> 'Then be off to your Dream, with his fly-away hat,
> I'll stay with the girls who are happy and fat.'

'Accidie poisons the soul stream,' as Pompey reminds us. Life has to go on, despite dreams and dreamers, and if the dreamer can be shaken into sense, then he or she should be. We observe how the poet passes with relief from 'Dear Female Heart':

> Dear Female Heart, I am sorry for you,
> You must suffer, that is all that you can do.
> But if you like, in common with the rest of the human race,
> You may also look most absurd with a miserable face –

to 'Alfred the Great':

> Honour and magnify this man of men
> Who keeps a wife and seven children on £2 10

Paid weekly in an envelope
And yet he never has abandoned hope.

Miss Smith could be grim. The woman chatting harmlessly on the omnibus in 'Northumberland House', it transpires, is on her way to a lunatic asylum: the poet characteristically employs the old non-euphemism. And the gentleman uttering pious sentiments over a grave –

Farewell for ever, well for ever fare,
The soul whose body lies beneath this stone! –

is revealed as the murderer:

My hand brought *Filmer Smith* to this strait bed –
Well, fare his soul well, fear not I the dead.

She can be grim – but she won't stand for any nonsense about abandoning hope. That would be *ignoble*. In what looks like steps in a campaign against received 'enlightened' opinion, she shows something of the terrifying honesty which Eliot ascribed to Blake. On one plane she seeks to rescue and rehabilitate the word 'pretty'. On another plane, the poem which begins

A mother slew her unborn babe
In a day of recent date
Because she did not wish him to be born in a world
Of murder and war and hate
'Oh why should I bear a babe from my womb
To be broke in pieces by a hydrogen bomb?'

takes an unexpected, heterodox turn: we are not invited to sympathize with the mother and her 'tragic dilemma', but rather the opposite:

I say this woman deserves little pity
That she was a fool and a murderess
Is a child's destiny to be contained by a mind
That signals only a lady in distress?

And why should human infancy be so superior
As to be too good to be born in this world?
Did she think it was an angel or a baa-lamb
That lay in her belly furled?

At the very end there is, perhaps, another turn:

How foolish this poor mother to suppose
Her act told us aught that was not murderous

157

(As, item, That the arrogance of a half-baked mind
Breeds murder; makes us all unkind.)

Makes us *all* unkind – including the poet herself.

No, Miss Smith was not notably trusting. She didn't altogether trust the Muse. The Muse deserts you because you have complained that she doesn't speak loudly enough – and you hear her howling and muttering behind the door. Then you search for her by night and day, and you cry upon the Lord to give her back to you:

He did repent. I have her now again
Howling much worse, and oh the door is open.

The poet may be happy, healthy, in himself, but his poetry can be unhappy, distressing himself and others:

My heart leaps up with streams of joy,
My lips tell of drouth:
Why should my heart be full of joy
And not my mouth?

I fear the Word, to speak or write it down,
I fear all that is brought to birth and born:
This fear has turned my joy into a frown.

Not very trusting, but she was never cynical. And not hard so much as brisk, and especially brisk in situations which require briskness and a touch of bracing tartness. For all the dippiness, she was a moralist firm in degree and central in kind, and a moralist in the best sense, for she felt while she judged. The engaging combination of overt sternness with underlying gentleness is shiningly present in 'Valuable' ('After reading two paragraphs in a newspaper'), which I quote in full:

All these illegitimate babies…
Oh girls, girls,
Silly little cheap things,
Why do you not put some value on yourselves,
Learn to say, No?
Did nobody teach you?
Nobody teaches anybody to say No nowadays,
People should teach people to say No.

Oh poor panther,
Oh you poor black animal,
At large for a few moments in a school for young children in Paris,

Now in your cage again,
How your great eyes bulge with bewilderment,
There is something there that accuses us,
In your angry and innocent eyes,
Something that says:
I am too valuable to be kept in a cage.

Oh these illegitimate babies!
Oh girls, girls,
Silly little valuable things,
You should have said, No, I am valuable,
And again, It is because I am valuable
I say, No.

Nobody teaches anybody they are valuable nowadays.

Girls, you are valuable,
And you, Panther, you are valuable,
But the girls say: I shall be alone
If I say 'I am valuable' and other people do not say it of me,
I shall be alone, there is no comfort there.
No, it is not comfortable but it is valuable,
And if everybody says it in the end
It will be comforting. And for the panther too,
If everybody says he is valuable
It will be comforting for him.

Miss Smith wanted happiness to exist where it possibly could. Indeed, she would have liked to see Phèdre happily married to Hippolytus: 'I think it might have been a go…' But life, she knows, is a struggle, no matter what you might think you would like it to be instead:

> Ceux qui luttent ce sont ceux qui vivent.
> And down here they luttent a very great deal indeed.
> But if life be the desideratum, why grieve, ils vivent.

And though she has asked – more precisely, 'a little wind sneaking along That was older than all and infamously strong' has asked – 'Will Man ever face fact and not feel flat?', in practice man is often seen to rise superior to his myths. Even to the cruel story of Eve:

> …there is this to be said still:
> Life would be over long ago
> If men and women had not loved each other
> Naturally, naturally,
> Forgetting their mythology

They would have died of it else
Long ago, long ago,
And all would be emptiness now
And silence.

Man sometimes does contrive to face fact and not fall flat on his face, even to live not without honour, so that on balance

It is his virtue needs explaining,
Not his failing.

Away, melancholy,
Away with it, let it go.

As for eccentricity and quaintness, Miss Smith's themes are commonly the large ones, central to the human condition. Extremely interesting, and sufficient to dispose of any suggestion of her being a 'naïf', are her reflections on death and suicide. The possibility, or the availability, of suicide is a great strengthener, Pompey muses; every child should be told, 'Things may easily become more than I choose to bear' –

that 'choose' is a grand old burn-your-boats phrase that will put beef into the little one, and you see if it doesn't bring him to a ripe old age. If he doesn't in the end go off natural I shall be surprised… See what it's done for me. I'm twice the girl I was that lay crying and waiting for death to come at that convalescent home. No, when I sat up and said: Death has got to come if I call him, I never called him, and never have.

And so, in the terms of one simple little verse, you look at the bottle of aspirin when you feel mournful, you reflect that two hundred will free you from anxiety – but you don't do more than look. Death you should think of as a friend: though you can call upon a friend, you should not impose upon him – and moreover Death is also a 'great prince'. Miss Smith valued propriety and decorum. The argument is by no means unsubtle. On the one side,

a time may come when a poet or any person
Having a long life behind him, pleasure and sorrow,
But feeble now and expensive to his country
And on the point of no longer being able to make a decision
May fancy Life comes to him with love and says:
We are friends enough now for me to give you death;
Then he may commit suicide, then
He may go.

On the other side (as in 'Mr Over'), it may be a devil's voice that cries, 'Happy Happy the dead,' for God says this:

> In man is my life, and in man is my death,
> He is my hazard, my pride and my breath,
> I sought him, I wrought him, I pant on his worth,
> In him I experience indeterminate growth.
>
> Oh Man, Man, of all my animals dearest,
> Do not come till I call, though thou weariest first.

Neville Braybrooke recalls Stevie Smith having said to him towards the end of her life: 'People think because I never married, I know nothing about emotions. When I am dead you must put them right. I loved my aunt.' One could not for long suspect her of such ignorance. She was no cenobite – to use one of Pompey's favourite names for unfavourite things: 'two diseases we have right here that the modern world is suffering from – *dictators* like I said and *cenobites* like I said too…' In a short poem called 'Man is a Spirit' she points out snappishly that, even so, the spirit-guest oughtn't to wrinkle up his nose at the flesh-host who serves him well when the wind blows. And obviously she agrees with Ormerod when he maintains that he can have knowledge of God both before life and after death, but that here in temporal life, and only in temporal life, is permitted 'A place where man might impinge upon man, And be subject to a thousand and one idiotic distractions' –

> I knew, and shall know again, the name of God, closer than close;
> But now I know a stranger thing,
> That never can I study too closely, for never will it come again –
> Distractions and the human crowd.

There is a time and a place for everything. Ripeness is all, ripeness of time and rightness of place.

In its essence Stevie Smith's poetry is uncluttered, and hence must leave out, for instance, the reservations and modifications and clarifications which denser and slower-moving writing admits. But it leaves out what it could not accommodate and still be the kind of poetry it is: and that is all it leaves out. A reader may well prefer other kinds of poetry, of course, but he cannot make out that her poetry is one of those other kinds which has somehow 'gone wrong'. When it succeeds, it obeys its own laws, and they are not unduly restrictive. At moments she is like a lot of other poets – I would add Hardy, de la Mare, Ogden Nash, Edward Lear, the creators of ballads, of hymns, of nursery rhymes, to those already noted – but finally, in the totality of her work, she is simply like herself. At the worst her poems are rather dull, and one asks 'So what?': that is the way of failing of her kind of poetry. I think she fails surprisingly rarely, especially if we read the poems in bulk, when among themselves they provide their own qualifications and refine their arguments. To say this is to remind oneself that a part of her best work, at all events her most *own*, hasn't been touched on here. And simply because there seems to be nothing to say about it: children are likely to enjoy it unworryingly, it engages adults and yet leaves them baffled and a little uneasy. It is not amenable to interpretation or conducive to moralizing. And one thinks of Pompey's sharp remarks on clever talk about books and pictures and how 'you want to keep very mum-o, and you want to keep the smarties off, oh yes they can read now, and very cunning they are the way they pick things up, very quick and cunning, much fiercer about it they are…' Perhaps it is appropriate to end with one such poem, 'Voices about the Princess Anemone':

> Underneath the tangled tree
> Lies the pale Anemone.
>
> She was the first who ever wrote
> The word of fear, and tied it round her throat.
>
> She ran into the forest wild
> And there she lay and never smiled.
>
> Sighing, Oh my word of fear
> You shall be my only dear.
>
> They said she was a princess lost
> To an inheritance beyond all cost.
>
> She feared too much they said, but she says, No,
> My wealth is a golden reflection in the stream below.
>
> She bends her head, her hands dip in the water
> Fear is a band of gold on the King's daughter.

(1971)

III

The Tale of Genji; *and Japanese Women Diarists*

The Tale of Genji, the early eleventh-century Japanese classic, is a phenomenon which, in view of its originality and unprecedented scope, can only be likened to a combination of *Antony and Cleopatra*, *As You Like It* and *The Winter's Tale* (with a dash of *Love's Labour's Lost*) suddenly appearing in full flower against a backdrop of *Gammer Gurton's Needle* and *Gorboduc*. To review this new translation by Edward G. Seidensticker, in 1,100 closely set but handsome pages, is analogous to comparing the Revised Version with King James's – except that the general drift of the Bible is rather better known.

Since practically every reader is on occasion a common reader, perhaps the reviewer may venture upon a few common and possibly vulgar observations. The hero of Lady Murasaki's *Tale*, or of the larger part of it in that Genji dies two-thirds of the way through, is that not uncommon fictional character, the Great Lover – potent, gifted, irresistible, and nice with it. Genji *is* too good to be true, until sadness sets in. But that *The Tale of Genji* is not a 'romance' in the pejorative sense, that it is not simply a Heian fantasy of an earlier and better Heian world, a more sophisticated opposite number of England's Restoration comedy at its most sophisticated, can be seen by reference to other tenth- and eleventh-century Japanese women writers. In particular, Murasaki's contemporary, Sei Shōnagon, whose *Pillow Book* (a generic term, Ivan Morris suggests, describing an informal notebook kept in a drawer of its owner's wooden pillow) reveals her as an astringent, forthright and unromanticizing witness while also testifying to the general authenticity of Murasaki's more dreamlike impressions.

The impression of reality, as opposed to fantasy, is assisted in *Genji* by the author's periodical cool interventions; for instance, at the end of Chapter 4:

> I had hoped, out of deference to him, to conceal these difficult matters; but I have been accused of romancing, of pretending that because he was the son of an emperor he had no faults. Now, perhaps, I shall be accused of having revealed too much.

And more humorously: 'Though no one has asked me to do so, I should like to describe the surprise of the assistant viceroy's wife at this turn of events,' she writes in concluding Chapter 15, 'but it would be a bother and my head is aching.' In Chapter 25 there occurs a passage reminiscent of Jane Austen's spirited defence of novels in *Northanger Abbey* ('performances which have only genius, wit, and taste to recommend them'). After teasing Tamakazura about her fondness for romances – 'Women seem to have been born to be cheerfully deceived' – Genji changes tack:

> I have been rude and unfair to your romances, haven't I? They have set down and preserved happenings from the age of the gods to our own. *The Chronicles of Japan* and the rest are a mere fragment of the whole truth. It is your romances that fill in the details...to dismiss them as lies is itself to depart from the truth. Even in the writ which the Buddha drew from his noble heart are parables, devices for pointing obliquely at the truth.

No more than Jane Austen did Murasaki approve of running down the very activity she was engaged in.

Heian Japan was 'a man's world' – though apparently less overwhelmingly so than Japan (and the world at large) has been at much later dates – and it was left to the women to write about it. The men were busy with more pressing things, such as governing the country (or in the case of the *Genji* males serving at court), being accomplished and noble, writing 'seriously' or stodgily in Chinese – and seducing women. Women, it has been suggested, were less confined by convention than men, and had more time and licence for scribbling in their native tongue. Murasaki Shikibu was the most remarkable of a group of remarkable females: she has no male counterpart in her own country, indeed no male or female counterpart in any country. Proust is her nearest of literary kin.

None the less, her admiration for her hero is likely to stick n feminist gullets. One would say that she doted on Genji, were it not that such crude, barbarous emotions as that verb implies are never found in her. An attempt on the reader's part to enumerate Genji's love affairs would be incongruously loutish, and in any case frustrated by uncertainty in many cases as to whether the protagonists exchanged only poems or something more besides. Lack of privacy often seems to rule out the latter in these overcrowded compounds: people who live in paper houses should stay in their own rooms, especially when their silk robes rustle so loudly. (Though against this consideration one should perhaps set the Japanese ability to remain blind or deaf to those things it would be incorrect or inconvenient to see or hear.) Murasaki shows not the faintest interest in the physical act of sex. Desire or curiosity on the man's side is indicated, willingness (sometimes but by no means always) on the woman's, a relatively secret meeting has to be contrived, and there we leave them: 'let us not look in too closely upon their dalliance.' We take up the story again with the next morning's exchange of poem-notes or bed-and-butter letters. But Genji's affairs are indisputably many. 'He went on thinking about whatever woman he encountered. A perverse concomitant was that the women he went on thinking about went on thinking about him.'

Genji is not merely good at everything that counts, he is the best at everything that counts: poetry, painting, music, perfumes, dress, bearing, conversation, attentiveness…And of course he is the best-looking of all the good-looking nobles who throng the scene. The words of the imperial consort's attendant refer to more than the perfume he happens to be wearing: 'He brings everything all together in himself, like a willow that is all of a sudden blooming like a cherry. It sets a person to shivering.' For Murasaki, Genji is 'the shining one of whom the whole world talks'; and at times it strikes the reader that the whole of this world has precious little else to talk about, and precious little to do except talk. Admittedly Murasaki does chide the prince now and again, if fondly. 'It continues to be his great defect that his attention wanders.' We note with some amusement that when Genji becomes convinced that a current liaison is illicit, his attention at once wanders to a new liaison in which he anticipates unadulterated joy. Thus, when the fruits of his affair with his stepmother begin to show under her robe, his thoughts turn to a ten-year-old girl, although he knows he is taking risks: 'People would say that his appetites were altogether too varied.' But Murasaki insists, one of Genji's great qualities is that he never forgets his women, he does the right thing by them as far as is in his power. 'The result is, ' someone remarks, 'that he has a large collection.'

Not that the prince is a carefree Lothario. Oh no, he is Japanese after all, and a sense of the transitoriness of things is never far away, a tear never far from his eye. With a sensibility like his, a little suffering can go a long way: you barely need anything as uncouth as a reason. However, Genji does have his troubles. One unsuitable intrigue leads to his banishment for a period; the effect on his retinue reminds us of the defeated Antony's ability to make his followers weep. Another intrigue scars his soul permanently. Early on, he fell in love with the second wife of his father the Emperor, and the child he had by her is generally believed to be the Emperor's: his supposed brother is actually his son. A form of retribution arrives later, when Kashiwagi, son of Genji's closest friend, gets Genji's wife, the Third Princess (and Kashiwagi's sister-in-law incidentally) pregnant. When this comes to light, there is no duel, no recrimination, no overt recognition of the matter. Kashiwagi has been guilty of a lapse in taste, of bad manners, above all (the cynic might say) the bad manners to be found out. At least he has the good manners to die soon afterwards, just as Enobarbus dies after deserting his master Antony, and the Third Princess becomes a nun. This sequel, it may be felt, is necessary in Murasaki's eyes because it is the shining Genji who is the offended party: he himself didn't die when he got his father's wife with child.

What matters is manners rather than morals, or so it must seem to us, who distinguish more sharply between the two. The aesthetically pleasing way of doing a thing is of more consequence than the thing itself. And shame lies less in being naughty than in being so maladroit as to be discovered. Telling lies or inventing plausible stories in the cause of avoiding trouble and loss of face for either the offender or the offended is quite in order, even *de rigueur*. For worrying over 'what people will say' is almost incessant here: to be laughed at is a fate worse than death. Yet this delicacy of feeling is general, not solely self-directed. Having learnt that his elder brother Genji is really his father, the new emperor is fearful of embarrassing Genji by hinting at his knowledge. And when suffering from malaria, Genji takes care to consult a sage in secret – because, he explains, 'such is his reputation that I hated to risk marring it by failing to recover.'

The exquisiteness and precision of manners, broken on occasion by outbursts of animal spirits and a somewhat brutal disposing of other people's lives, intimates a social precariousness. Yet – and for all the rather mechanical readiness to shed *lacrimae rerum* – what does most to save *Genji* from brittleness and shallowness of soul is the pervasive sense of evanescence, of the fleeting insubstantiality of this world. If a child is intelligent and beautiful, everybody sighs: it cannot be expected to live long. That Genji lasted just into his fifties is a mark of the author's unwillingness to let go of him; even so his ladies muse, 'it is true – the cherry blossoms of spring are loved because they bloom so briefly.' Nor are thoughts of past or future particularly cheering. A 'stupid, senseless affair' is accounted for by 'a bond in some other life', and unsuccessful undertakings or actions injurious to others are put down to 'the disabilities we bring from other lives'. Karma can be thought a useful device for saving face or releasing from responsibility – or, more generously, a tactful and in some cases stoical admission of and allowance for human weakness. There is something of *Rasselas* here: 'Human life is everywhere a state in which much is to be endured, and little to be enjoyed.' Genji's philandering, like the conduct and attitudes of others in the story, can be traced without exercising undue charity to the hunger for human contact in a highly formalized society, for something beyond prescription and propriety, for love and companionship. This hunger is moving expressed in a poem alluded to in Chapter 47, 'Trefoil Knots', and given by Seidensticker in a footnote:

> A loose thread here to join to a loose thread there.
> If it cannot be so with us, what use is life?[1]

Truly speaking, it is futile to compare Seidensticker's *Tale of Genji* (1976) with Arthur Waley's translation (1925–33) since the two versions differ both in the material worked with and (more important) in their intentions. But it is also irresistible. We shall at times find it hard to believe they are concerned with the same original, even allowing for the work done on the Japanese text since Waley's day. For one thing, Seidensticker's version is complete, whereas Waley abridged, omitted a whole chapter, and frequently elaborated. The effect of his elaboration is generally to help the Western reader by weaving an element of explanation into the narrative. And when we come across a textual crux indicated by Seidensticker, and hence an annotation, the chances are that Waley has quietly skipped the passage – with no apparent loss, it must be said, as far as the general reader is concerned. Seidensticker is scholarly, enormously conscientious and (the lay reader feels confident) accurate. He is much brisker too (which in general is to be welcomed), as may be deduced from the fact that despite Waley's bold abridgements the new translation is actually shorter. This briskness, this economy in words, Seidensticker states, are characteristic of the original. At the same time he pays a handsome tribute to Waley when he tells us that the power of that pioneer version 'has continued to be so great that the process of preparing a new translation has felt like sacrilege'.

Much more than 'nuance' is involved. The difference between their priorities can be indicated, concisely, crudely, but without too much overstatement, by saying that Waley has the reader in mind whereas Seidensticker has Murasaki in mind. Where Seidensticker has the somewhat rebarbative 'Prajñapāramita Sutra', Waley softens with 'Spring Devotions', referring to the Buddhist nature of the ceremony in passing. Waley has 'Lady Murasaki' (the character, not the author) where Seidensticker more allusively and elusively gives 'the lady in the

---

1 The next step, the only further step, is withdrawal from the world into prayer and meditation – though hitherto one has considered it (as Donald Keene says) 'not in very good taste to show unusual piety'. Similarly, in Restoration comedy: 'What an odious thing it is to be thought to love a wife in good company.'

east wing'. The dramatis personae are many indeed, and Waley's habit of identifying them by name makes for smoother reading than Seidensticker's (no doubt literal) 'he' or 'she'. In Chapter 21 Sachūben, a master of poetry reading, is annotated by Seidensticker as 'otherwise unidentified'; Waley refers to him not by name but by office, 'the Under-secretary to the Council', a neat though perhaps unauthorized way of investing him with a little substance. A page later, however, the personage reappears as 'the Chief Secretary of Council'.

When a father is reflecting on his daughter's future, Seidensticker translates thus:

> If he is still interested when he is a little older, she would be better off in his hands than at court. I know his Lordship well. Once a woman has attracted his attention he never forgets her.

Waley's version is:

> There's this comfort about it, that if Prince Yūgiri is anything like his father he will continue to show an interest in her when he grows up. You know I have always told you that once Prince Genji takes a fancy to people, he never forgets them, come what may.

Waley has spelt out the pronouns and distinguished between the son and the father, thus assisting the reader to keep his bearings. Seidensticker writes elliptically, presumably in accord with the original, and in fewer words. Immediately afterwards he has the advantage in ready comprehensibility with 'I know that people are calling me the unpromoted marvel, and I don't enjoy going to court' over Waley's 'Why should I go to court if I do not choose to? As a matter of fact, it is very unpleasant to be only in the Sixth Rank. People notice it and make remarks.'

Very occasionally Seidensticker's expressions strike one as obtrusively slangy where Waley's language is bland and timeless, though it may be that some readers will welcome little modern jolts. 'When they are side by side, my husband seems rather short on good looks' comes jarringly from the second daughter of the Eighth Prince: Waley has 'When they are together I sometimes think that Niou comes out of it none too well.' And surely Seidensticker's sentence 'He sought to dismiss it as an ordinary marital spat' offends by mixing two quite contrary modes. When young men are discussing the wiles of women and one remarks that 'The fact is not up to the advance notices', the anachronism shocks more than it enlivens; at the same place Waley gives 'But when we take steps to test their statements we are invariably disappointed', which is long-winded and a shade pompous for the gilded youth who is speaking.

In making these spot-checks, much of the time one is conscious less of inferiority or superiority than of difference, and more to the point would be to suggest that the average reader (who is unlikely to be all that dumb) might still welcome a résumé offering a ready reminder of the story's tangled relationships and its more important events. This is scarcely a book to be knocked off in a couple of winter evenings and the list of 'Principal Characters', though helpful, doesn't go far enough.

Just as Proust is the only Western writer I can think of as bearing any resemblance in manner or preoccupations to Murasaki Shikibu, so the comparison of Waley's *Genji* with Scott Moncrieff's *Remembrance of Things Past* (before Terence Kilmartin's revision) is the only possible one – in respect of inaccuracies and liberties taken, and of triumphs scored – although it would need someone of surpassing scholarship and literary sensibility to assess the implications. At all events, the reader coming fresh to the Japanese novel will meet with very few obstacles in Seidensticker's version that Seidensticker himself can be held responsible for. The reader acquainted with Waley's version will do well to banish it to the back of his mind while engaged on Seidensticker. My guess is that the two translations are going to coexist peacefully, neither ousting the other.

Heian Jane

People who complain that Jane Austen's books have little to do with 'life' ought to be made to study the literature of the Heian period, of the aristocratic world of tenth-century Japan. Admittedly Heian society, as we know of it through the prose writings of its ladies, did go in for sex, but rather as an exquisite exercise in social manners than as anything spiritually more momentous for better or worse. To a large extent, it seems to have been a question of skilfully calculated risk, of knowing how much to let other people know about and how much not to. The 'next-morning letter' which the lover was obliged to send his mistress appears to have loomed larger than whatever happened the night before. The Japanese were – are? – an incorrigibly literary people.

Miss Austen admits farmers to the human race. On her way to the Kamo Shrines one day, Miss Shōnagon[2] observes some oddly dressed women moving backwards across a field, bending down and then

2 *The Pillow Book of Sei Shōnagon*, translated and edited by Ivan Morris.

straightening up again – 'for what purpose I cannot imagine'. Ivan Morris comments that the occupation of planting rice, a common sight, was 'one that no elegant Court Lady would admit to recognizing' – just as once our ladies could not admit to recognizing certain words used by our gentlemen. Moreover, Shōnagon disapproves of these particular peasants because they are singing a disrespectful song about the *hototogisu*, a poetic bird and hence the property of the upper classes. No nonsense about folk culture here. We notice, however, that a little later on Shōnagon is less coy when it comes to recognizing the operation of harvesting the rice. But perhaps consistency was regarded as boring and vulgar. Among 'Things That People Despise' she includes 'Someone with an excessive reputation for goodness'.

The common people are referred to here by such polite circumlocutions – though this one may be literally true – as 'the people of whom one does not know how to speak'. And in a list of 'Unsuitable Things' Shōnagon mentions 'Snow on the houses of common people', adding that 'This is especially regrettable when the moonlight shines down on it.' And probably, in our day, we do need Professor Morris's gloss: 'Because such beauty is wasted on *hoi polloi* and inappropriate to their gross nature'. There were no working-class poets at that time, no scholarship-boy scholars.

Shōnagon herself was quite a poet, though Professor Morris remarks that her poems are often more ingenious than poetic – an observation which, I would think, applies to a lot of Japanese poetry of whatever date. She is sensitive in all the proper respects and insensitive in the proper respects too. Thus she finds the 'parasite tree' moving or pathetic because it is dependent for its existence on other trees. But when a rather common fellow whose house is burnt down in a fire originating in the Imperial Stables comes to the palace hoping for alms, Shōnagon presents him with a peculiarly obscure and unfeeling poem, thus winning the admiring laughter of her companions, including the Empress. The scheme of priorities and compartmentation of the sensibility seem, if I may say so, not un-Japanese.

Of course it would be useless to reproach Shōnagon for her undemocratic attitudes. It is equally silly to admire her for them, since they were merely inherited. The highly ritualistic Heian civilization represented in Shōnagon's journals and (more romantically, Arthur Waley has suggested, and less accurately) in Lady Murasaki's novel, *The Tale of Genji*, will have a special appeal for the modern reader – how Shōnagon would hate to think she was read by us common readers! – and is likely to be over-estimated. Though not, it would seem, by the more sceptical scholars. Professor Morris's comments are sometimes quite tart, albeit expressed in rather gingerly fashion, as if he feared Shōnagon might materialize in his study and stab him with a double-edged quotation, while Waley (who translated about a quarter of *The Pillow Book*, interspersing it with his own commentary) remarked that the 'figures and appurtenances' of the period sometimes seem to us 'to be cut out of thin, transparent paper'. Stretches of *The Pillow Book* are plain boring, and could have been composed by some lady-in-waiting of our own day or yesterday – 'everything about well-born people delights me' – though she would need to be a lady with a sharp visual sense besides a gift for writing fashion notes.

But neither is this the whole story. Shōnagon was not herself of especially elevated birth (though a distinguished poet, her father was also a provincial governor, a class of people not highly regarded at court), and it seems probable that she was not a beauty either. To keep her end up, she was dependent on her learning (or her reputation for learning), her ready wit and her ready tongue. 'In this palace one is always sorry when one has made some inadvertent remark,' whines the Captain First Secretary, who has just been smartly put down by Shōnagon in the matter of an inapt poetic allusion. One likes to think of this sharp-tongued lady keeping the under-employed and over-dressed courtiers on their toes. It says something for Heian civilization that Shōnagon was not rudely silenced! Within the limits firmly imposed by social assumptions which apparently no one questioned seriously, she was truly what in a hardly covert self-reference she described herself as – 'a woman who has quick wits and a mind of her own'.

Her shrewdness, among other qualities, comes out in one of the liveliest sections of *The Pillow Book*, on 'Hateful Things', where, as in most of her catalogues, sentiments to which every bosom returns an echo rub shoulders with feelings which strike us as arbitrary and esoteric. On the one hand,

> One is telling a story about old times when someone breaks in with a little detail that he happens to know, implying that one's own version is inaccurate – disgusting behaviour!

On the other,

> An elderly person warms the palms of his hands over a brazier and stretches out the wrinkles. No young man would dream of behaving in such a fashion; old people can really be quite shameless.

Then we have this:

> A man with whom one is having an affair keeps singing the praises
> of some woman he used to know. Even if it is a thing of the past,
> this can be very annoying. How much more so if he is still seeing
> the woman! (Yet sometimes I find that it is not as unpleasant as all
> that.)

Fleas too, we hear, are very hateful – we are reminded of Pope's incongruous juxtapositions in *The Rape of the Lock* ('Or stain her honour or
her new brocade') – 'When they dance about under someone's
clothes, they really seem to be lifting them up.' A little later one is told
how 'sometimes one greatly dislikes a person for no particular reason
– and then that person goes and does something hateful'. Though not
exactly a pleasant one, Shōnagon was certainly a rare character, and
cut out of something much tougher than paper.

Two Women Diarists

Sarashina Nikki? *Sarashina no Nikki*? The Sarashina Notebooks? Lady
Sarashina's Diary? Sarashina is a mountainous district in central Japan,
the word doesn't appear in the book, and no one seems to know why
it was picked on. But 'Takasue's Daughter', as she is usually called, is
an unilluminating and lowering designation for the author – as if, says
Ivan Morris, George Eliot's sole appellation were 'Evans's Daughter'.
The phrase 'bridge of dreams' doesn't appear either, but dreams do
(in some abundance) and the whole thing is distinctly (or indistinctly)
dreamlike, and so Ivan Morris's title, *As I Crossed a Bridge of Dreams*, is
as good as any other, if not better. 'Dreamlike' is exactly what the
earlier woman diarist, Sei Shōnagon, was not; and here we must not
expect the varied pleasures of *The Pillow Book*, nor the presence of so
vivacious, witty and acerbic a female.

Born in 1008 into the Heian administrative middle classes, Lady
Sarashina was the daughter of an assistant provincial governor, wife to
a provincial governor (she married at the age of thirty-six), and mother
of a provincial provincial governor. No wonder that she was addicted
to 'Tales' – *The Song of Everlasting Regret* and *The Princess Who Sought a
Corpse* are mentioned here besides her favourite *Genji* – and later in life
to pilgrimages to celebrated temples. Her husband died or 'faded away
like a dream' when she was fifty, and towards the end of her little book,
having mentioned his cremation ('he vanished with the smoke'), she
writes: 'If only I had not given myself to Tales and poems since my
young days but had spent my time in religious devotions, I should have

been spared this misery.' That is, or so she seems to mean, she should have gone on some other pilgrimage earlier and then might have become an Imperial nurse in the Imperial Palace. Another dream!

Ivan Morris's substantial introduction and notes occupy virtually the same space as the insubstantial text. The text does often need the explanation it receives, without the explanation rendering it notably more fascinating. He tells us of the Japanese literary women of the tenth and eleventh centuries that 'they reveal themselves to us in all their nakedness': a misleading phrase, particularly so in the case of Lady Sarashina, whose kimono doesn't slip an inch. Her sensibility may be said to be naked, but it is disembodied, and again one has the sense of human wastage, of a quick, feeling and intelligent woman trapped (however, 'naturally') in the cocoon of convention, of 'expected behaviour'. Lady Murasaki was immensely talented, of course, an unstoppable scribbler – but even the characterful Sei Shōnagon, for all she gave, doubtfully gave as good as she got. Lady Sarashina is very much the woman of sensibility: apart from what Morris calls her 'remarkably low tolerance for bereavement', she is forever yielding to fits of weeping. Up is the heartening and the strong reply (as Eastern Empson puts it) that we often want to make to her, poor thing.

Poems loom quite as large (or as small) as reality in these pages. 'I enjoyed seeing the Ford of Shikasuga between the provinces of Mikawa and Owari and was truly worried about whether or not to cross.' A necessary note refers us to a poem by Lady Nakatsukasa conveying the depressing message that whether you cross the troublous Ford of Shikasuga or you don't, trouble lies ahead – and informs us that Lady Sarashina was mistaken, it couldn't have been Shikasuga Ford she was looking at. She needn't have worried – but reason not the need. Arthur Waley may have been right when he described her book as 'a much worked-up and highly literary production'. Her own poems, with a few bright exceptions, provoke the response, 'So what?' Ivan Morris takes the blame upon his translations, on those of other people, on the sheer impossibility of translating Japanese poems to any effect. But one wonders... To know the conventions that govern them is to guess how conventional they are.

He does succeed, however, in transmitting the delicacy of spirit, the muted charm of Lady Sarashina's prose, in her mild self-punishing romanticism and, above all, in her unfussy, strong and exact descriptions of the natural scene. For example, of Mount Fuji: 'Its thick cover of unmelting snow gives the impression that the mountain is wearing a white jacket over a dress of deep violet.' It may be thought that the Japanese have always used their eyes to better effect than their other senses, and these Heian ladies had especially keen eyes.

The Confessions of Lady Nijō is a serious book, and one should start by saying what it is not. It is not an oriental *Fanny Hill* or a medieval *Histoire d'O*. It is not even comparable to Saikaku's writings and the gamy Japanese accounts of life in the floating world and the gay quarters of the turn of the seventeenth century. It belongs to the tradition of women diarists represented by such impeccable dames as Murasaki Shikibu, Sei Shōnagon, Izumi Shikibu and 'Lady Sarashina', and is a worthy later addition to this distinguished if not invariably enthralling line. The original title, it seems, means 'unrequested tale', or something you can't hold in any longer. 'Confessions' is not the aptest of substitutes, given its present associations, and though Lady Nijō served at court and slept with some of the very best people, the jacket reference to her as a 'famous courtesan' (though one sees the point) builds up improper expectations.

For not an improper word is spoken in this narrative, not an improper scene depicted. 'All' is not told; or if it is, then it is told discreetly and obliquely, by way of poems and literary allusions. One advantage of a literary heritage is that the most intimately personal feelings and happenings can be gracefully intimated through a swift, casual-seeming reference to a verse, a legend or a figure in some novel of the past. This may not be seen as an advantage nowadays, when readers have grown used to having the whole thing explicitly in front of them – the blood, the bed, the members of the party in full fig – as if nothing remotely comparable had ever happened before.

The law of diminishing returns having worked its slow but ineluctable effects, the result here is that some of Lady Nijō's 'revelations', couched in a quotation or in her own sparse words, carry quite a charge. The Retired Emperor proposes to her father that the latter's fourteen-year-old daughter should become his concubine simply by mentioning 'the wild goose of the fields', an allusion to the tenth-century *Tales of Ise*. Nijō is confused and distressed (her mother was dead, but why couldn't her father have told her what was in store?), and the first encounter ends with His Majesty (only twenty-nine, by the way) leaving at dawn, disgruntled: 'Now to go back pretending something happened!'; the second ends with Nijō's thin gown getting badly ripped. Not long afterwards, 'I discovered that my condition was not normal': she is pregnant.

Later in the story she is uncouthly grabbed by Ariake, a Buddhist priest (also half-brother to the Retired Emperor), who tells her (or himself) that 'Even when we walk in paths of darkness, we are guided by the Lord Buddha.' She whispers back ('but my words were wasted'),

'Some things are embarrassing even to Buddha.' Before long she records, 'he did have an undeniable way about him, a manner that was both pathetic and appealing': we gather she has ceased to resist. She has remarked, in connection with an earlier suitor, that her heart is 'far from adamantine'. By means of an allusion to *The Tale of Genji* the Emperor indicates that he knows Nijō is pregnant again, this time by Ariake, but accepts the situation.

Lady Nijō's memoirs span the years 1271–1306, more than two and a half centuries after the Heian women diarists. The Heian aristocracy or cultivated middle classes were given to literary allusion, and Nijō has them to allude to as well. Her society was heavily retrospective in its cultural habits and ceremonial activities; she recounts the enactment at a palace party of an episode from *Genji*: the novel had become in effect a combination of Shakespeare, the Book of Common Prayer and Emily Post. The vast number of source-references provided by the stalwart translator, Karen Brazell, inclines one to ask whether Nijō's contemporaries ever said anything in their own words –except, in some small degree, when composing short verses for later generations to invoke.

The complaint may be made that, in journals of this kind, we don't know what the lady *really* felt. Though it is hard to know what *really* really means, I think we do. In outline, the circumstances of these court ladies were determined by uncontested conventions, and they made what they could of life within those conventions. Murasaki and Sei Shōnagon made of themselves very considerable writers, infinitely more memorable as writers and personalities than their male contemporaries – and the thought comes to mind that possibly a 'free life', like free verse, either doesn't exist or is boring, or at any rate does not lend itself to the purposes of literary composition. If when reading these diarists we are conscious of human wastage – and we are – then we have to ask ourselves whether matters are arranged more fruitfully today. If the rather insistent aestheticism of these ladies, their too conscious sensitivity, makes us want to shake them, yet we note the glint behind the tear, and we admire them still. Mrs Brazell comments that 'sleeves damp from weeping soon become soppy'. Certainly melancholy was 'an acceptable tone' in Nijō's day ('Life is more fleeting than a dream within a dream'), and women were expected then (and later) to weep, but Nijō is much less damp than Lady Sarashina.

She is also less sharp and lively and entertaining than Sei Shōnagon, but her life was differently disposed – and she does have a story to tell, however obliquely she tells it. Ingenious and disingenuous she clearly was, and she needed to be, given her independence of mind.

When she is pregnant by Akebono, another of her lovers, the Retired Emperor supposes himself to be the father-to-be on this occasion. Unfortunately there is a discrepancy of two months. The Emperor is told that Nijō is ill and an abortion has proved medically necessary: the baby is carried away by Akebono and brought up by his wife as her own. It is not that the Emperor would have sought revenge on the lovers, for Nijō's behaviour was not altogether 'unexpected' in view of her circumstances and, as for Akebono, men will be men: the concern was to spare feelings and save faces as far as possible. The Emperor had his own fun, sometimes enlisting Nijō's assistance in it, and he displays a commendable suavity in the matter of her affair with his half-brother the priest. 'After thinking about the subject at great length,' he tells her, 'I have concluded that there is nothing sinful in the relationships between men and women inasmuch as they are usually caused by bonds from former lives and thus defy our resistance.'

The last part of the narrative, beginning in 1289, records Nijō's travels as a Buddhist nun. Her expectations at court have been thwarted and now, she says, she is 'suppressing my emotions by lecturing my heart'. She comes on an island community of nuns who were formerly prostitutes, and their ex-madam tells her, 'I was over fifty when some karmic effect suddenly enabled me to shake off the sleep of illusion'; she makes friends with the Shinto priests at the Ise shrine ('We are usually reluctant about allowing people in Buddhist orders to visit the shrine,' one says, 'but you look so tired I am sure the gods would understand'); and she has a touching last meeting with the Emperor. In a dream her father appears to her, reminds her of the many generations of poets in the family, and recites a poem:

> Sow all the words you can
> For in a better age
> Men shall judge the harvest
> By its intrinsic worth.

It was up to her and her journal, undiscovered till 1940 – and with the help of Karen Brazell's excellent translation – to keep the family reputation alive.

(1976; 1968; 1975)

Chinese Fictions – At Home and Abroad

The Golden Lotus

Legend has it that the anonymous author of the sixteenth-century novel, *Chin P'ing Mei*, impregnated the corners of the manuscript with poison and sent it the Prime Minister, an enemy of his, in the expectation that the recipient, licking his fingers avidly to turn the pages, would meet an interesting death. Colonel Clement Egerton's translation, *The Golden Lotus*, appeared in four volumes in 1939, with the naughty bits rendered into Latin: he apologized for any exasperation thus caused, 'but there was nothing else to do'. These passages have now been turned into (somewhat ornate) English – except for two lines on p. 213 of Volume 2 which escaped the notice of the counter-censor – and can easily be located since the inking tends to be fainter. They look as if they have been well licked.

Having admitted that such passages seemed more exciting in Latin, when the linguistic skills acquired at school from the study of Caesar's *De Bello Civili* were applied to them, I shall not need to dwell long on the novel's famous eroticism. The descriptions are – or sound – rather more sophisticated or arcane than those found in modern permissive writing, covering most of the exercises known to readers of fiction today and contributing at least two extra gimmicks. Since these are unlikely to find favour in a society where women incline to be low on docility, I shall not report them. (Not that the women swarming here are shrinking violets: 'Soon she whispered, "My darling, my dearest, would you like to enjoy the flower of my bottom?"') The sexual encounters are generally grotesque in that oriental manner to be observed in male-glorifying Japanese erotic prints. Yet such grotesqueness is equally Western, for no pornographer can afford a sense of humour.

Indeed, oriental fantasists are in a sense more modest than occidentals: their sexual champions have open and unashamed recourse not merely to 'interesting pictures' but to unlisted drugs, magic powders, bamboo splints, gold and silver bells, improbable surgical transplants (see the decidedly brisker seventeenth-century novel, *The Before Midnight Scholar*, or 'Prayer Mat of Flesh', which introduces canine reinforcement, hot from the dog) and other aids not yet on sale in our sex-supermarkets. Our native champions generally reckon to stand on their own feet, going naked into the bedchamber, and thus

179

laying themselves open to a degree of scepticism.

Some Western scholars – Chinese scholars have shown less concern for this side of their literary heritage, novels being thought a vulgar pursuit – have managed to identify a working moral in *The Golden Lotus*. It relates the history of the prosperous family of Hsi-men Ch'ing and its ruination through strenuous concupiscence, worldly ambition, vanity, greed, corruption and diverse malpractice and mayhem. 'There is no escape from the fatal circle of Wine and Women, Wealth and Ambition' – or, as the concluding verses have it:

> The record of this house must make us sad.
> Who can deny that Heaven's principle
> Goes on unceasingly?

This admonition, lurking underneath 1,500 action-filled pages, is about as forceful as that delivered in *Fanny Hill*: 'Truth! stark, naked truth, is the word...' Other and more prudent scholars have prized the novel ('the translation of such a book would render superfluous any other book upon the manners of the Chinese': Henri Cordier) for its elaborate accounts of domestic life, ceremonial junketings and business deals, and its meticulous descriptions of buildings, furnishings and clothing. True, it is interesting to hear that ginger-broth was given to women who had tried to hang themselves, and to gather that in these polygamous households (Hsi-men had the run of six wives, their maids, and singing girls *ad lib.*) much more fuss was made over a missing shoe or wine-jar than over murder, torture or sexual practices so extreme as to cause the less-than-fragile Plum Blossom to complain, 'You mustn't do this again. It is not simply fun. My head and eyes swim so that I hardly know where I am.'

For the literary-minded the most engaging aspect of the book may well be the idiomatic. Aside from sexual euphemisms – 'Striking the Silver Swan with a Golden Ball' sounds to be in a different class from Tossing Cream Puffs – there are some fine (if occasionally cryptic) expressions. 'He is one of those men who can see a bee piddling forty miles away, but not an elephant outside their very own doors'; 'Strike the gong for a day, and be a priest for a day'; 'If a bitch will not have it, the dog cannot get his way'; 'She is talking out of her queynt'; 'When the butcher is dead, you must eat your pork with the bristles on it'; 'If the only poker you have is a wooden spoon, and a short one at that, it is still better than using the fingers'; and 'The stream of matter from his nostrils looked like chopsticks of jade.' That last euphuism, it should be explained, refers to a holy man, the Indian Monk who supplies Hsi-men with the medicines which 'give ease to men' – before finishing them off.

Some readers may doubt the trustworthiness of social and cultural history which is so thickly interspersed with gobbets of unrealistic sex. Yet we should not disallow the possible coexistence of highly dissimilar genres, and it may be a sign of the book's exhaustiveness as history that at the end of it the reader feels quite old and tired. As the author remarks in the course of Volume 4: 'Heaven abhors extremes.'

The Yellow Peril

William F. Wu's all too well attested thesis is that the Yellow Peril (to wit, the real or supposed threat to the United States posed by Asians and more particularly Chinese) is 'the overwhelmingly dominant theme in American fiction about Chinese Americans' between 1850 and 1940. It was in the late 1870s, on the West Coast, that the fictional stereotypes hardened – in such novels as *Almond-Eyed: The Great Agitator* ('A Story of the Day') by Atwell Whitney and Robert Woltor's *A Short and Truthful History of the Taking of Oregon and California by the Chinese in the Year A.D. 1899*. Prince Tsa Fungyan, the leader of the invasion in the latter pseudo-history, is said to bear less resemblance to a human being than to Milton's Satan (perhaps the first appearance of that piece of stereotyping); while a story called 'The Battle of Wabash' (1880) by one Lorelle depicts an America with three Chinese to every white, the decapitation of a chicken replacing a hand on the Bible in oath-taking, and a Chinese billionaire running for President in 2080, followed by the eponymous battle ending with five million Chinese casualties and virtually no whites left at all.

The social factors behind what was to be a long succession of less than truthful fictions are believed to be the fear, particularly pronounced among Irish immigrants, of a flood of cheap labour from war-torn China, and the radical difference between the Chinese and other immigrant groups such as the Poles, or the Irish. The Chinese were unChristian, unmonogamous, given to strange foods and (if the need arose) infanticide, and hideboundly unassimilable – especially when given precious little chance to assimilate. Much of this instant characterization derived from disappointed missionaries and frustrated diplomats. Chinese immigrants were for long disqualified from testifying in courts of law and therefore unable to defend themselves: fairly naturally, this accounts for the growth of traditional-style benevolent associations and the rise of the less traditional and less benevolent tongs or 'secret societies'.

For writers, the Chinese became the new and local exotic, throwing

Shylock's ménage into the shade, even surpassing in its attractions the Italian dukedoms (poison, adultery, incest, corruption notwithstanding) so dear to our Jacobean horror-dramatists, and reducing the indigenous Red Indians and blacks to fodder for the kiddies. In what seems no time a notably industrious and long-suffering people (miners, railroad labourers, servants, launderers), civil, respectable and if not exactly God- then ancestor-fearing – the people who in a recent British sociological study were termed 'the invisible Chinese' – were transported into Chinatowns reeking with slave-prostitutes, murder, treachery, opium-smoking, and pervasive degeneracy, including gambling and inscrutability. It was *The Golden Lotus* all over again, less the more recherché frills.

In the early years of this century Jack London wrote about unsavoury Chinese shrimp catchers around San Francisco Bay and also about China, in the shape of 'a flood of yellow life', invading the rest of the world in 1976: 'his socialism is not evident here,' comments Dr Wu. The world is saved only when an American scientist comes up with a device for dropping the germs of every known form of plague on the Chinese, who are then completely eliminated. London can scarcely be said to have rectified the balance in two stories involving Chinese immigrants in Hawaii – not quite the US of A? – amiable though these are. One of his heroes, Chun Ah Chun, works hard, amasses a fortune, is barred from a fancy hotel in Macao on the grounds of race, buys the hotel and sacks the management, produces (quite monogamously) fifteen children who are half-Chinese, one-sixteenth Italian, one-sixteenth Portuguese, one-thirtysecond Polynesian and eleven-thirtyseconds Anglo-Saxon, and finally retires to live in solitary peace and quiet in his native Amoy.

An exceptionally mean sub-category of stories would seem to be directed against the theory that, say whatever else you might, the Chinese make good domestic servants. An author called C.E.B. (1884) has a launderer who spits water on the clothes when ironing them and Mary T. Mott (1882) features servants who variously wash their feet in the dishpan, spoil flannels by boiling them, and use the oven to cremate polecats whose ashes then go into native medicines. Even worse, sometimes they get fresh with white women by kissing their hands – this is pardonable, one tale implies, if the woman is Italian – though such misconduct may occasionally be offset by saving white females from earthquakes, fires and other domestic calamities. Loyalty is a well-known Chinese characteristic; as is also treachery.

No doubt, where there's smoke, there's fire (or, give a dog a bad name and soon he will be eating puppies as well as rats), but popular fiction has rarely succeeded in producing so much smoke out of one minor industry. Sometimes, however, it was a different story. Thus, in his tales of western frontier life, Bret Harte showed himself sympathetic towards the Chinese: at the worst, as in 'See Yup' (1898), his orientals are smarter at cheating than the whites who set out to cheat them; while Ambrose Bierce, though he never presented the Chinese positively, made what Dr Wu calls 'negative efforts' on their behalf: that is, he was less for the Chinese than against their persecutors. Then there were the missionary authors, much agitated over the buying and selling of young women and the use of opium, that notorious religion of the poor, but eager to show the salvatory effects of conversion on their erstwhile heathen characters. In this mode, Nellie Blessing Eyster's *A Chinese Quaker: An Unfictitious Novel* (1902) describes both the evil aspects of San Francisco's Chinatown and the good that, with the help of Christianity, can come out of it. For once we hear of a complexion blending the rose with the olive, a skin not pock-marked but as smooth as ivory, and large, soft and dark eyes: '"A Chinese Adonis!" she mentally exclaimed.' Even so, Dr Wu is obliged to reproach the author for asserting that the Chinese eat rats and are deficient in family affection.

More accurate in their details were the occasional stories written by American Chinese or half-Chinese, like Edith Eaton ('Sui Sin Far'), who was born in England in 1867 to a Chinese mother and an English father but moved to the United States as a child, thus acquiring 'a clear understanding of bicultural pressures'; and likewise H.T. Tsiang, the titles of whose novels of the 1930s indicate his sympathies with the Communist Revolution in his native land: *China Red* and *And China Has Hands*. The realism stemming from actual knowledge of the situations portrayed ('a rare and valuable contribution to the fiction on this subject,' Dr Wu remarks coolly) is also seen in *Lim Yik Choy* (1932), the fictional biography of an orphaned immigrant who turns Christian, tangles with Irish Americans (the natural enemy, it appears), proves a fine football-player despite racist opposition, befriends a black shoeshine, and goes to Canton to run an orphanage. The worthy author, Charles R. Shepherd, was himself superintendent of a home for orphaned Chinese American boys in California.

Some incidental entertainment is provided by Dr Wu's complaints about minor inaccuracies in his chosen field, or swamp. In 'Behind the Devil Screen', an 'action-packed melodrama' of 1921, James Hanson commits the solecism of giving a Manchu a Cantonese name and dresses tong killers in tweeds, silk shirts, striped socks and fedoras *à la* Mafia. In C.W. Doyle's series of stories, *The Shadow of Quong Lung*

(1900) – by way of introduction the author proposes that San Francisco's Chinatown ought really to be burnt down, 'but the scheme is too Utopian to be discussed in a mere preface' – one of the plots hinges on a scribe who writes people's letters for them because they use a different dialect from the recipients. Alas, dialects exist only in speech and do not affect the written language. Incidentally, the villain of the title, who is a graduate of Yale and a barrister of the Inner Temple (London), and also a tong leader, could well be an ancestor of the great Fu Manchu. He comes to grief when accidentally falling against an electric chair intended for somebody else. Dr Wu does show qualified admiration for Mary E. Bamford's well-researched novel, *Ti: A Story of San Francisco's Chinatown* (1899), in which the evangelizing author explains knowingly that Chinese gamblers, being superstitious, will never read any book, including the Bible, because 'shü' ('book') is a homonym for the word meaning 'to lose'. Unhappily she 'fails to relate gambling and opium-smoking to social and environmental pressures'.

Dr Wu's book bears traces of its origin as a doctoral dissertation, albeit one of uncommon enterprise and liveliness. Despite the admirable dispatch and even lucidity with which the plots are potted, the reader begins to feel he is suffocating under a yellow flood of homogeneous pulp. Luckily, just in the nick of time, along come the two great figures of this curious genre, the fine flowers of popular orientalism. Between them they sum up the whole proceedings, one standing at each pole: the evil Dr Fu Manchu (the name alone makes you shudder), created by our very own cheese-and-beer-loving Sax Rohmer (for further details of his colourless life, see *Master of Villainy* by Cay Van Ash and Elizabeth Sax Rohmer, 1972); and the good, equally well-named Charlie Chan, brain-child of Earl Derr Biggers.

Fu Manchu (*fl.* 1913–59), that grander ancestor of the neurotic Dr No, was of British provenance, neighbourhood of Gerrard Street; he emigrated to the United States and rose to be the hero/villain of books sold in millions, films, radio and TV adaptations and comic strips. Described by his creator as possessing 'a brow like Shakespeare and a face like Satan', 'the yellow peril incarnate in one man', he was a large-scale international adventurer and mischief-maker (busy in one novel engineering the election of one of his white servant-stooges to the Presidency), specializing in ingenious (and, one might think, chancy) assassination by means of animals (scorpions, adders, baboons, mice), and giving offence – in reality, this – to the humourless government of China... Moreover, he fathered Fah Lo Suee, prettier but morally no superior, owner of 'an unforgettable hand, delicious yet repellent, with pointed, varnished nails', 'a long oval contour' and 'slight, curving hips' etc., sexually available (in this doing the image of Asian womanhood no good at all) and treacherous in the extreme.

While he too appeared in serial and feature films, Charlie Chan (*fl.* 1925–32) was Fu Manchu's opposite in practically every respect: to begin with, a Chinese Hawaiian (sharing the relative innocuousness of, say, a Channel-Islands Frenchman) and, as a police detective in Honolulu and San Francisco, supporting white law and order and white supremacy. A white man's Chink, in short. If Fu Manchu, tall and lean, resembles Satan, Charlie Chan is closer to Mr Pickwick: short, fat and pink (not yellow), with cheeks 'chubby as a baby's', affable, mild, calm, very much a family man. He has a disarming propensity to aphoristic utterance in the style of 'Confucius say' and to flowery language: 'Relinquish the firearms, Mr Jennison, or I am forced to make fatal insertion in vital organ belonging to you.' Fu Manchu of course speaks impeccable English, altogether superior to that of the wretched whites who litter his path. What the two great Chinamen have in common is an egregious share of cleverness.

To quote that no doubt oriental proverb, Where there is opium smoke there is conflagration. And the sinister stereotype of the Chinese was confirmed by the treacherous attack on Pearl Harbour in 1941 (Japanese, Chinese, what's the difference?) and again by the Korean and Vietnam wars. What is now needed, Dr Wu says in winding up, is that serious attention should be paid to fiction written by the Chinese Americans themselves, 'the source material that can best counter the racist presentations of characters such as Fu Manchu and Charlie Chan.' By all means – but he doesn't actually mention any names. One springs to mind: the semi-fictitious Maxine Hong Kingston.

History has a habit of transferring the boot to the other foot – though usually after the original kicker and the originally kicked have departed the scene. I remember how, some forty years ago on the (ethnically) Chinese island of Singapore, Han Suyin (half-Belgian, please note) was in disgrace with the authorities for promulgating 'yellow culture', as it was officially known, through such sexful fiction and non-fiction as *A Many Splendoured Thing*. Concurrently I was myself in trouble for semi-facetiously protesting against the ban on juke-boxes (well, there was more to it than that) and teaching Wordsworth and Milton. The term 'yellow culture' embraced any form or channel of foreign influence or foreign values deemed likely to imperil the correct development of a brand-new pure-minded (also single-minded) nation. Han Suyin was teaching at the Chinese-medium

Nanyang University, and I at the older, colonially established University of Singapore. Between us, you would have thought, we had contrived to turn two respectable educational institutions into veritable Chinatowns, with all that that dread name implies. Like Fu Manchu, we were yellow perils incarnate! As Confucius says, More different, more same.

The Woman Warrior and China Men

The subtitle of Maxine Hong Kingston's first book, *The Woman Warrior*, embodies a pun: 'Memoirs of a Girlhood among Ghosts', that is to say, among Chinese story-ghosts and also among non-Chinese, who by definition are ghosts if not demons. 'Those of us in the first American generations have had to figure out how the invisible world the emigrants built around our childhoods fits in solid America.' In her books Mrs Kingston comes near to suggesting that it is America which is invisible – populated by the Mail Ghost, the Newsboy Ghost, the Garbage Ghost – while China, the China of her parents, or the China her parents told her about, is the solid world.

This raises a question which, though it sounds prissy, is legitimate: how much of this 'China' is true, how much is tale-telling or, as Mrs Kingston puts it, talking-story. For the insider, whatever country he is inside, there is no settled boundary between actuality and myth: all is part and parcel of life as it is lived. While realizing this – for we all have our legends – the outsider still likes to know, of a country he is outside, which is which. We are sufficiently able to distinguish (say) between Hans Andersen and the real, geographical country of Denmark: we have heard tell of both of them ore or less concurrently since we were children. But China is a different kettle of mysteries.

Just as the last English gentleman is reckoned to be, if not an Indian, then an Englishman living in India, so Mrs Kingston, born in Stockton, California, in 1940, is possibly more Chinese than the Chinese in China. There is nothing like emigration and expatriation, especially when it shows in the face, for bringing out one's nativeness; 'characteristics' are accentuated in a way they never were at home. 'What is Chinese tradition and what is the movies?' One is moved to reply that one Chinese tradition is never to explain Chinese traditions to benighted foreign barbarians. Such refusal or reluctance can evince itself as arrogance. Or, in a politer person, as modesty. Outsiders won't be able to understand: or, outsiders surely won't want to be bothered with understanding. Being a true writer, Maxine Hong Kingston has no truck with either of these considerations.

One way for Chinese girls to escape being merely wives or slaves was for them to be swordswomen. Mrs Kingston weaves a story about herself as heroine, based on the tales her mother told of Fa Mu Lan. In a small epic along the lines of *The Water Margin*, she is a version of Maid Marian as Robin Hood ('My army did not rape, only taking food where there was an abundance. We brought order wherever we went'), or a female avenger, at times a Bruce Lee in drag. She defeats a giant who then changes into his true shape, a snake, whereupon his disgusted soldiers pledge their loyalty to her. Her followers, she remarks in a nice aside, never knew she was a woman: 'Chinese executed women who disguised themselves as soldiers or students, no matter how bravely they fought or how high they scored on the examinations.' Finally she overthrows the emperor and beheads him, then inaugurates the peasant 'who would begin the new order'.

The 'new order' sounds rather like Communism. Under it a male chauvinist baron loses his head too, exploiters of the people are tried, and ancestral tablets are torn down. 'We'll use this great hall for village meetings... Here we'll put on operas... we'll sing together and talk-story... This is a new year, the year one.' No wonder, as she says when the tale ends, that 'my American life has been such a disappointment'; if she tells her mother she has got straight A's at school, her mother replies, 'Let me tell you a true story about the girl who saved her village.' To make matters worse, news comes from the old country that the revolutionaries have taken an uncle's store away from him and killed him, along with other members of the family, for the crime of selfishness. 'It is confusing that my family was not the poor to be championed. They were executed like the barons in the stories, when they were not barons.' In her role as female warrior, 'we would always win,' she had declared: 'Kuan Kung, the god of war and literature, riding before me.' Now, it appears, war and literature have gone their separate ways.

From time to time there comes a thin mosquito-like sound of feminist grievance. No husband of hers – the author announces – will say that he gave up his cherished career for the sake of the wife and kids. No one will have to support *her* 'at the expense of his own adventure'. But 'then I get bitter: no one supports me; I am not loved enough to be supported.' Even now her feet are bound, figuratively speaking. Just to get dates she has to 'turn myself American-feminine'. So she refuses to cook, or if she has to wash the dishes, she contrives to break them. Chinese women have more cause than most to complain of their status and treatment. It took a whole revolution to nurture a Chiang Ch'ing. (It must have taken all hellishness to breed a Chinese revolution.) Mrs Kingston dwells on those hurtful old expressions like 'Better to raise geese than girls', 'When fishing for treasure in the flood, be careful not to pull in girls' and 'Girls are maggots in the rice'. In *The Gate of Heavenly Peace* Jonathan D. Spence mentions the young revolutionary poetess, Qiu Jin (Ch'iu Chin), who wrote in 1904:

> We, the two hundred million women of China, are the most unfairly treated objects on this earth. If we have a decent father, then we will be all right at the time of our birth; but if he is crude by nature, or an unreasonable man, he will immediately start spewing out phrases like 'Oh what an ill-omened day, here's another useless one.' If only he could, he would dash us to the ground.

Three years later she was captured by government troops, tortured and beheaded. In the case of the young Maxine, one feels sorry for her mother; and not merely because she was closer to such events. Mothers tend to experience the dirty end of both sticks, masculism and feminism alike.

Brave Orchid, the mother, is a great character, a teller of myths but herself no myth. She had been a doctor before coming to America, the Gold Mountain, in the winter of 1939–40 to join her husband in running a laundry. On receiving her diploma from the To Keung School of Midwifery, she went to market to buy herself a slave. The parents who were selling their children liked to talk with buyers. 'If they could just hear from the buyer's own mouth about a chair in the kitchen, they could tell each other in years to come that their daughter was even now resting in the kitchen chair. It was merciful to give these parents a few details about the garden, a sweet feeble grandmother, food.' The little girls who were being sold by a professional dealer might stand in a line, bowing together, while the older ones chorused, 'Let a little slave do your shopping for you', or singing 'a happy song about flowers'. Brave Orchid picked a healthy girl with a strong heartbeat, who pretended to be less than wholly competent in order to bring the dealer's price down. The slave cost her the equivalent of $50, and she found her a husband before leaving for America. The author cost her mother $200 in hospital bills at birth.

Here is a subject for someone to study: the ways whereby Eastern people have managed to clothe their fearful hardships and humiliations in something approaching dignity, in ritual, in the necessary and sometimes almost elegant *euphemism*, when nothing else remained to them. No doubt what discourages any such study (cf. the stridency of affluent reformers and educated revolutionaries) is the fear of seeming to condone the conditions which bred this precarious civility. But there is quite enough unpalliated horror in the chapter about the Lady Doctor: we hear of a baby without an anus, left in an outhouse (euphemism for latrine) to die, and the box of clean ashes placed beside the birth bed in case the baby was a girl – suffocation by the midwife or a relative was 'very easy'.

The account of Brave Orchid's sister promises to be rather more jolly, chiefly because it shows first-generation Chinese Americans as viewed through Chinese eyes. In her late sixties, Moon Orchid arrives from Hong Kong in search of her errant husband whom she hasn't seen for thirty years. He is suitably terrified, having married again and being a citizen of a country where bigamy is frowned upon. Moon Orchid is useless in the laundry, and upsets the children by trying to smooth their hair or leaning over them when they are studying. 'They're so clever,' she exclaims: 'They're so smart. Isn't it wonderful they know things that can't be said in Chinese?' But then the story turns sad. Moon Orchid imagines that Mexican 'ghosts' are plotting against her life, and has to be put away. She was too old to move; her spirit, her 'attention', was scattered all over the world, her sister explains. 'Brave Orchid's daughters decided fiercely that they would never let men be unfaithful to them.'

Mrs Kingston's second book, *China Men*, in which (the blurb announces) she 'turns her attention to her patriarchal forebears', starts off menacingly with a fable about a man who is looking for the Gold Mountain but finds himself in the Land of Women, where he is forcibly rendered female: holes bored in his ear lobes, his feet broken and bound, his womb improved by vinegar soup. There follows a short anecdote telling how the narrator and her brothers and sisters mistake a stranger for their father, whereas (we take the implication to be) they would never confuse their mother with another woman.

The suspicion or expectation that men are about to get it in the neck is strengthened by the beginning of the next chapter. The narrator's father swears a lot, in the (not exclusively) Chinese manner: 'bag cunt', 'your mother's smelly cunt'... The narrator wants him to tell her 'that those curses are only common Chinese sayings, that you did not mean to make me sicken at being female', that he was not referring to her or her mother or her sisters or grandmothers or women in general. The narrator herself is no sensitive plant, and this doesn't ring altogether true. If it isn't ritual sensibility or a sign of acquired American delicacy, it may be an excuse for what follows. Since BaBa is given to silence or to few words (and those, apparently, obscene), she will have to tell his story for him. 'You'll just have to speak up with the real stories if I've got them wrong.' In the event she does men no wrong at all.

BaBa – the story goes – passed the last Imperial Examination to be held, turned to village teaching, married, got fed up with his pupils, listened to yarns about the streets that were paved with gold, emigrated (legally or otherwise: the narrator gives alternative versions), was detained at the Immigration Station outside San Francisco, started a laundry in New York, was joined by his wife fifteen years later, then was cheated out of the laundry by his partners and left for California, 'which some say is the real Gold Mountain anyway'. If women have a right to complain, it looks as if men have a right to curse. Except that later, mind you, the author says her father was born in San Francisco in 1903. Then what was all that about the Imperial Examination? Just a good story? And what about the two children, brother and sister of the author, who (we were told) died back in China? Dream children are one thing; dream children killed off as testimony to historical hard times are another.

I do not think it was solely because I read it immediately after *The Woman Warrior* that *China Men* struck me as the less fresh and persuasive of the two. One item here is a Crusoe-like story which adds little to Defoe and looks rather like padding. Another, 'The Ghostmate', takes a theme common in old Chinese stories, a love-affair between a young man and a beautiful woman who turns out to have been dead for centuries, and treats it conventionally, except perhaps for the mention of a song we would like to have in full – 'What Does the Scholar Do with His Bagful of Books After Failing?' – and a concluding comment which blends Chinese realism with the author's modernity: 'Fancy lovers never last.'

But Mrs Kingston gets into her stride when she moves to her great-grandfather's adventures while clearing forests in Hawaii, the Sandalwood Mountains. The chapter contains an authentic description of the state of mind induced by opium-smoking, the only dubious touch being that Great-Grandfather experienced these effects after his very first (and last) session. Even stronger is the story of the grandfather Ah Goong, who worked on the construction of the Central Pacific Railroad in the Sierras during the 1860s. It was the time when dynamite had been invented, and was being tested by or on the railroad workers: 'chinamen had a natural talent for explosions.'

'Stupid man to hurt yourself,' they bawled out the sick and wounded. How their wives would scold if they brought back deadmen's bones. 'Aiya. To be buried here, nowhere.' 'But this is somewhere,' Ah Goong promised. 'This is Gold Mountain. We're marking the land now. The track sections are numbered, and your family will know where we leave you.'

Ah Goong lost his citizenship papers in the San Francisco fire of 1906, returned to China and lived to be bayoneted in the head by a Japanese soldier. This left him a bit queer – not surprisingly; since he must have been a hundred years old by then.

The author was a small child during World War Two but remembers how her father was exempted from service – the draft, she says, was one reason for leaving China in the first place, the other was having to pay taxes with grain – because he was too skinny. She also remembers when the AJAs, Americans of Japanese Ancestry, were released from the relocation camps at the end of the war. One such family lived on her block:

> We had not broken into their house; it had stood shut for years... They gave us their used comic books, and were the only adults who gave us toys instead of clothes for Christmas. We kids, who had peasant minds, suspected their generosity; they were bribing us not to lynch them. The friendlier they were, the more hideous the crimes and desires they must have been covering up. My parents gave them vegetables; we would want them to be nice to us when the time came for us Chinese to be the ones in camp.

Yet the finest chapter, a noble conclusion to the book, concerns her brother, a high-school teacher who was drafted into the Vietnam War and resolved to 'follow orders up to a point short of a direct kill', on the grounds that it was better to be a pacifist in the Navy than a pacifist in jail. As his ship nears Asia he has dreadful dreams in which he is unable to distinguish between villains and victims: they all have 'Chinese faces, Chinese eyes, noses, and cheekbones'. He visits the Philippines and Korea, and also Taiwan, 'a decoy China, a facsimile', where nevertheless he meets apparently real Chinese who tell him how lucky he is to be an American. Planes from his aircraft-carrier bomb Hanoi, but he can't see the bombs falling. Then he is promoted and transferred to Taipei: he has been cleared by Security, which in turn implies that the whole family is truly, securely, American, despite all the black marks (real or imagined) in its history. Mustered out, he returns to Stockton. 'He had survived the Vietnam war. He had not gotten killed, and he had not killed anyone.'

Here, in Keats's words, there is no 'irritable reaching after fact and reason', for fact and reason are safely within the reader's reach.

Elsewhere, it is because Mrs Kingston's subject is real men and women, a real and long immigration, and a real nation or indeed two nations, that one feels some uncertainty and hence some irritation. Her mother once told her: 'You can't even tell real from false' – and if she cannot, then how can we? At other times, and much of the time, poetry doesn't smudge truth, and we rest content in the spirit of another of Keats's sayings: 'What the imagination seizes as Beauty must be truth –whether it existed before or not.'

(1972; 1982; 1981)

Flaubert: His Letters and Ladies

Flaubert and an English Governess

The English governess in question in Hermia Oliver's book – very much in question – was Juliet Herbert, governess at the Flaubert home in Croisset to Flaubert's much-loved niece, Caroline, between 1854–5 and 1857. Her acquaintance with the novelist lasted till his death in 1880, which suggests it was far from casual, but the nature of the acquaintanceship is in dispute. The most tender of Flaubert's affairs? Or a non-affair? Miss Oliver believes that Juliet was 'almost certainly' Flaubert's mistress, but her book, a record of indefatigable research and rather meagre revelations, is stuffed with 'probably's', 'may's', 'if's' and 'just possible's', a case of seeking hopefully rather than arriving.

Born in 1829 as the daughter of a London builder, Juliet came from 'the artisan rather than the professional classes,' remarks Miss Oliver, who is faintly surprised that Flaubert should have been devoted (if devoted is what he was) to so humble a being. 'It seemed far more probable that the father of a woman who held Flaubert's interest for so long a period would have been more highly educated, like Mr Brontë.' That is grossly unfair to governesses! – and, I would think, to Flaubert too. However, all is well on that front, for Mr Herbert was a master builder (if a small one) and even, in 1831, enjoyed the professional cachet of bankruptcy. Who could better sympathize with Flaubert, Miss Oliver asks, after his niece's husband's financial collapse? Though that happened in the mid-1870s.

The sad fact, or the fact, is that there are very few references to Juliet in Flaubert's letters and no letters at all between the two putative lovers. Three possible reasons are advanced for this: Caroline resented the closeness of the relationship which she discovered on sorting her uncle's letters after his death, and so destroyed those from Juliet; she suppressed the letters in order to spare the feelings of Juliet and surviving members of the Herbert family; or, an explanation Miss Oliver favours, Flaubert himself burnt the letters in the course of an eight-hour bonfire, at which Maupassant assisted, in the year before his death. (This last being an act which, like any decent biographical writer, Miss Oliver both understands and regrets.) As for the letters written by Flaubert, it is 'almost certain' that Juliet, who died in 1909, destroyed them.

It is known that after Juliet left Croisset in 1857 she paid summer visits there in succeeding years, and also that Flaubert came to England in 1865, 1866 and 1871 and met Juliet then. It is possible, too, that the couple met during short holidays which Juliet took in France at intervals between 1872 and 1878; references in Flaubert's letters to Caroline prove that they met in 1872 and 1874; at any rate. It is the case that during her stint as governess at Croisset Juliet read *Macbeth* with Flaubert and translated *Madame Bovary* into English, though – which was probably just as well for her reputation – the translation was never published. And in 1856 Flaubert wrote to his friend and confidant Louis Bouilhet that 'the governess excites me immeasurably; I hold myself back on the stairs so as not to grab her behind' – by the standards of his correspondence with Bouilhet this is a mild enough confession, or boast – although the first mention of Juliet by name occurred only the following year, in a letter from Flaubert to his niece.

In the accounts of the novelist's visits to England, instead of amorous encounters the reader must rest content with a listing of the pictures he saw at Bridgewater House, Grosvenor House, the National Gallery (South Kensington) and Hampton Court. Flaubert's travel diary is otherwise uncommunicative, but on 6 July 1865 he recorded dining at a restaurant and thereafter a '*retour délicieux*' – to which Miss Oliver appends, 'possible in a cab'. If Juliet was with him at the time, the reference 'can surely only indicate a relationship that was something other than friendship'. It could merely signify that Flaubert was glad to get back to his lodgings after a hot, stormy day spent touring the Crystal Palace.

Similarly, it may have been Juliet who in 1869 sent the novelist some translated information about the Calves' Head Club which he wanted for *L'Éducation sentimentale*: whoever it was addressed him in a gloss by the intimate form, '*tu*'. 'If it can indeed be proved that it was Juliet who wrote the covering letter, the use of "*tu*" is itself highly indicative.' There are certainly some similarities between the handwriting of the translation and Juliet's inscription in a copy of Hans Andersen which she gave to Caroline, and 'it may or may not be considered' that the resemblances outweigh the differences. But, as Miss Oliver allows, there can be no proof unless the covering letter can be traced: it 'may be' still in private ownership 'if' it was not lost during World War II.

'It is by now impossible,' Miss Oliver declares, 'to doubt the emotional nature of their relationship.' What does the latter phrase mean? We cannot know what Juliet's feelings for Flaubert were, but 'that she must have suffered anguish, "the torment of love unsatisfied", seems undeniable…' Miss Oliver continues: 'We can only hope and suspect that she too received the kind of letter' – then quoted – 'that in 1858 he had written to another woman whose beauty moved him.' Yes, Flaubert was a great letter-writer, and (within limits) a great admirer of women, and the thought is a nice one – but it looks as if research is now aspiring towards the condition of romantic fiction. Miss Oliver's intention is a worthy one: she is, I take it, seeking to do Juliet a posthumous good turn, she would like to prove that this English woman, this mere governess, actually slept with a celebrated foreign novelist…in somewhat the same spirit in which not so very long ago she would have been concerned to prove that Juliet had done no such improper thing. Other times, other pieties… One must respect the scrupulousness shown in these investigations, for it is not all that common, and the total absence of anything approaching prurience. Even so – and while no one would grudge those involved what happiness they could snatch, from a perhaps constricted life, from a life certainly made over to art – one has to ask: is all this labour in a worthwhile cause? *Flaubert and an English Governess* seems to me an instance of book-making, however superior. But then, ours is an age when books are increasingly made rather than born.

The Letters of Gustave Flaubert 1830–1857

That Flaubert, as a writer and as the kind of writer he was, was born rather than made is plainly indicated by the opening letters in Francis Steegmuller's excellent selection, the first of two volumes. The very first item, addressed to a schoolfriend and written on the eve of 1831, when Flaubert was nine, includes these sentences: 'I'll also send you some of my comedies. If you'd like us to work together at writing, I'll write comedies and you can write your dreams, and since there's a lady who comes to see papa and always says stupid things I'll write them too.' At the age of ten, Flaubert signs off, 'Your dauntless dirty-minded friend till death'. At thirteen he is attacking theatre censorship and restrictions on press freedom: the representatives of the people 'are depriving the man of letters of his conscience, his artist's conscience', and what matters more than people, crowns and kings is 'the god of Art, who is ever-present, wearing his diadem, his divine frenzy merely in abeyance'. Two years later, writing to the same friend, Flaubert displays a peculiarly clear recognition of what was to be more than an adolescent conflict:

…for the most beautiful woman is scarcely beautiful on the table of a dissecting-room, with her bowels draped over her nose, one leg minus its skin and half a burn-out cigar on her foot. Oh no, it's a sad thing, criticism, study, plumbing the depths of knowledge to find only vanity, analysing the human heart to find only egoism, and understanding the world only to find in it nothing but misery. Oh how much more I love pure poetry, cries from the soul, sudden transports and then deep sighs, the voices of the soul, the thoughts of the heart.

Ex ungue leonem... All Flaubert is in these first five pages of letters, in embryo. In 1846 he wrote to Louise Colet: 'I am ripe. Early ripe, it's true, because I have lived in a hothouse.' His hothouse – while it embraces the family apartment in the Rouen hospital where his father was director and chief surgeon – was very largely him.

Among these letters, which the editor has knit together with an intelligent and succinct narrative-cum-commentary, the three big constituents are the correspondence with Louise Colet (less love letters than love-and-literature or even love-versus-literature), the travelogue (or brothelogue) addressed to Louis Bouilhet from the Orient, and the letters relating to the trial of *Madame Bovary* for outrages against public morals and religion.

Steegmuller's earlier book, *Flaubert in Egypt*, has treated us to the distinctly alarming blend of the sumptuous and the squalid, the romantic and the clinical, found in Flaubert's account of his travels in Egypt and the Middle East with Maxime Du Camp between 1849 and 1851. He wrote from Constantinople towards the end of 1850 that 'There's nothing like travel for the health': this was after his umpteenth venereal chancre. Incidentally, the apparently total frankness with which he communicated his sexual activities to his male friends makes it seem odd that, if he slept with Juliet Herbert, he should never have mentioned it to them. It could be, I suppose, that he held *les Anglaises* in greater awe than the famous courtesan Kuchuk Hanem and her ilk.

Notwithstanding Flaubert's obvious contempt for the Establishment, the case against *Madame Bovary* in early 1857 was dismissed, though without costs awarded. His counsel made effective play with the distinguished medical careers of the accused's father and also his brother Achille, and Achille saw to it that the Ministry of Justice was fully aware of the importance of the Flaubert family, 'whom it might be dangerous to attack because of the approaching elections'. It sometimes helps to have bourgeois connections. Not that Flaubert was wholly placated: the trial had 'deflected attention from the novel's artistic success,' he complained, quite genuinely, 'and I dislike Art to be associated with things alien to it.'

Most profoundly interesting of all are the letters to Louise Colet. Flaubert met her in 1846 (she was eleven years his senior) and their increasingly troubled liaison ran out in 1855. Passionate, sensual, even violent as these letters are, they are marked by chilling phrases right from the start:

> Ever since we said we loved each other, you have wondered why I have never added the words 'for ever'. Why? Because I always sense the future, the antithesis of everything is always before my eyes. I have never seen a child without thinking that it would grow old, nor a cradle without thinking of a grave. The sight of a naked woman makes me imagine her skeleton. As a result, joyful spectacles sadden me and sad ones affect me but little. I do too much inward weeping to shed outward tears – something read in a book moves me more than a real misfortune… Forgive me, forgive me in the name of all the rapture you have given me.

During the first eighteen months of their relationship Flaubert wrote some hundred letters to Louise, but saw her only six times. As Steegmuller observes, we cannot altogether blame her for her growing bitterness and her expostulations. Art, Flaubert told her, was greater than earthly love, he had never sacrificed anything to passion and never would; and the concentration of thoughts about literature and the artist ('Come now, smile, kiss me. Stop being hurt because I speak to you about Shakespeare rather than myself') will commend these letters more readily to the later reader than to the fretful recipient.

In his third letter, Flaubert exhorts her: 'You speak of work. Yes, you must work; love art.' (She was a poet, a journalist, in the way many people are poets, journalists, not in the way that Flaubert was a literary artist.) 'Of all lies, art is the least untrue. Try to love it with a love that is exclusive, ardent, devoted. It will not fail you.' A plain enough intimation of priorities, one would say. And it was to Louise that, in 1852, he delivered this splendid manifesto:

> I like clear, sharp sentences, sentences which stand erect, erect while running – almost an impossibility. The ideal of prose has reached an unheard-of degree of difficulty: there must be no more archaisms, clichés; contemporary ideas must be expressed using the appropriate crude terms; everything must be as clear as Voltaire, as abrim with substance as Montaigne, as vigorous as La Bruyère, and always streaming with colour.

'If I weren't so weary, I would develop my ideas at greater length,' he told her in 1853 after a brisk lecture on *Hamlet*. 'It is so easy to chatter about the Beautiful. But it takes more genius to say, in proper style: "close the door", or "he wanted to sleep", than to give all the literature courses in the world.' And, the same year:

> The day before yesterday, in the woods near Touques, in a charming spot beside a spring, I found old cigar butts and scraps of pâté. People had been picnicking. I described such a scene in *Novembre*, eleven years ago: there it was entirely imagined, and the other day it was experienced. Everything one invents is true, you may be sure. Poetry is as precise as geometry... My poor Bovary, without a doubt, is suffering and weeping at this very hour in twenty villages of France.

At the same time his letters do convey passion, tenderness, concern, much gratitude, and indeed riches of other sorts. Including some common earthiness. 'Blessed be the Redcoats' (as the euphemism has it) – from time to time there is anxiety over the failure of '*les Anglais*' to disembark, and Louise thinks of visiting an abortionist (or '*faiseur d'anges*', as another euphemism goes), while Flaubert is horrified by the idea of bringing someone into the world. Occasionally the personal and the professional come together – 'Then, after ten more pages... I'll have finished the first section of my Part Two. My lovers are ready for adultery: soon they will be committing it. (I too, I hope.)' – though not always in a manner wholly gratifying to Louise. 'Yes, for me you are a diversion,' he informs her in 1852, 'but one of the best, the most complete kind.' And late the following year he speaks even more plainly, and serviceably:

> ...in fact everything is bound up together, and what distorts your life is also distorting your style. For you continually alloy your concepts with your passions, and this weakens the first and prevents you from enjoying the second... You are a poet shackled to a woman, just as Hugo is a poet shackled to an orator... Do not imagine you can exorcize what oppresses you in life by giving vent to it in art. No. The heart's dross does not find its way on to paper: all you pour out there is ink, and no sooner do you voice your sorrows than they return to the soul through the ear, louder, reaching deeper than ever.

The letter ends: 'Do not be upset. The sweet things I might have written you instead of this would have carried less affection.' Louise would no doubt have preferred those sweet things. No one likes to take second place, not even to Art. No one likes to think that the pleasure he or she can give falls short of the delight the other person knows in writing, in creating – in being both lover and mistress, and the horses on which they ride, and the wind and the sun. Flaubert's mother must have echoed Louise's sentiments (and those of the parents, spouses, friends and well-wishers of many another writer) when she told her son: 'Your mania for sentences has dried up your heart.' (He quoted this remark admiringly to Bouilhet, adding that its sublimity was 'enough to make the Muse hang herself out of jealousy at not having thought of it herself': 'the Muse' was the name they used between themselves for Louise.) But the final remark quoted here should be one of Flaubert's, for it demonstrates both his utter devotion to his art and also a sense of balance, of proportion, something not always allowed him. *Madame Bovary* first appeared in the *Revue de Paris*, edited by Flaubert's friends, Du Camp and Laurent-Pichat, who cut the first instalment for (as they saw it) artistic reasons. Flaubert resented this deeply, and was aghast to discover that in a later instalment the editors had none the less made a further cut, this time (vainly, as it turned out) for reasons of prudence. He sent a firm, dignified protest to Laurent-Pichat, addressing not his 'dear friend' but the *Revue de Paris*, 'an abstract personality, whose interests you represent'. 'You are objecting to details,' he wrote, 'whereas actually you should object to the whole...you cannot change the *blood* of a book. All you can do is to weaken it.' And he ended the letter by declaring that while he might break with the *Revue* he would still remain a friend of its editors. 'I know how to distinguish between literature and literary business.'

Flaubert – Sand: The Correspondence
translated by Francis Steegmuller and Barbara Bray

Flaubert and Sand? The one an austere, dedicated artist, the other a copious scribbler; the one a reclusive old bachelor of 45, his wild oats apparently all sown, the other a youthful granny of 62, her man-eating days behind her. On the face of it a most unlikely friendship. But then, it seems unlikely that a man who spent two days casting and recasting a single paragraph of a novel without getting it to his satisfaction could have written such a mass of fluent, sparkling letters.

In 1843 Flaubert had referred scathingly to George Sand as an author read by schoolchildren and seamstresses, and in a letter of 1852 to Louise Colet in terms far more distasteful. Yet, after reading this volume, one believes his sincerity when he wrote to Sand in the year of her death, 'You have never done me anything but good, and I love you tenderly.' It was shortly after she died that he said he had begun *Un Coeur simple* 'solely to please her'; and that he was addressing her son Maurice is no reason to dismiss the assertion. Perhaps his savoury comparison, 'For me, you are like good bread', *bon comme du bon pain*, is the strongest evidence of all.

The friendship began in the way that literary friendships often do, with Sand, who had defended *Madame Bovary* in 1857, praising *Salammbô* enthusiastically in the Paris press. At that stage Flaubert remained suspicious of the tenor of her writings, but a thank-you letter elicited a reply dated 28 January 1863, headed *Mon cher frère* and inviting him to visit her when he had time: 'But I'm an old woman – don't wait till I'm in my second childhood.' They met several times at the 'Magny dinners', held at a restaurant of that name in the Latin Quarter, and presided over by Sainte-Beuve and the Goncourt brothers. (Sand was the only woman ever to attend as a member of the circle.) From then on their relationship ripened swiftly. Sand described her family life, and herself picking flowers, making dresses for her daughter-in-law and costumes for puppets, and playing with her grandchildren. Poor Flaubert had only his mother to talk about. From time to time he visited Sand at Nohant, or she would come to stay at Croisset with him and his mother. Perhaps the latter, observing this curious attachment, wondered if she shouldn't modify what she had said about her son's mania for sentences drying up his heart.

Flaubert's manner is invariably courteous, using the feminine adjective before the masculine noun in *chère maître* and, though Sand came to *tutoyer* him, always addressing her more formally as *vous*. Not that their interchanges were formal; far from it. Neither was averse to colloquialisms, mimicry, and racy language. In the fourth of Flaubert's letters printed here he says, 'You are right to love me: it's only a fair exchange.' Physical passion, while it was a perfectly proper topic for discussion, was over for both of them. Difference of sex no more they knew, you might say, than our guardian angels do; indeed, in a sense each of them became the other's guardian angel. In large part the friendship was a success because it was one of maturity. 'During the phase of power and personality you test a friend, as you might test the ground, for reciprocity,' Sand wrote,

> But when you feel your own 'self' getting less intense, you love people and things for what they are in themselves, what they represent in the eyes of your soul, and not at all for what they will contribute to your own destiny.

Like a picture you love but cannot own, it won't be modified by contact with you, and you can truly say that you won't merely be loving yourself when you profess to love it.

At the very beginning Sand asked Flaubert to write down criticism of her work:

> People ought to do this service for another... It doesn't mean you change one another – on the contrary, it usually makes one cling more firmly to one's own point of view. But in so doing one supplements it, makes it clearer, develops it more fully, and that's why friendship is a good thing even in literature, where the first and foremost condition for having any sort of worth is to be oneself.

Each expressed admiration for and envy of the other's writings and way of writing. 'You don't know what it is to spend an entire day with one's head in one's hands, taxing one's poor brain in search of a word,' Flaubert told Sand. 'With you, the flow of ideas is broad, continuous, like a river. With me it's a tiny trickle... I know them well, the Pangs of Style!' Sand, esteeming style far less highly, answered, 'I *have* got a flaw. I like classification: I have a touch of the teacher. I like sewing and wiping babies' bottoms: I have a touch of the servant... And lastly, I wouldn't like perfection.' They laid their cards on the table, but neither set out to score off the other. The years bring a degree of tolerance; good bread comes to take precedence over doctrine.

There may be a tinge of *politesse* about, perhaps even of soft soap; one feels at times that Flaubert is pulling his punches while Sand is putting on the old home-loving granny act (and the next minute quite likely rushing off to the theatre to see about a play of hers). Flaubert to Sand, of the novel *Cadio*: 'You've gone and written a masterpiece!'; Sand to Flaubert, of *L'Éducation sentimentale*, in advance: 'You're so good you're incapable of being cruel.' The letters lack the edge and shock effect of Flaubert's earlier correspondence – the youthfully excited letters to Louis Bouilhet, the mixture of sensuality and clinical coolness in those to Louise Colet – but they have their own very considerable attractions. The correspondents rattle on, comically or earnestly, whether like two old dears, enquiring solicitously after each other's health, condoling on the deaths of friends, offering each other loans, or waxing indignant over literary wickednesses and lamenting the distresses of the Franco-Prussian war.

Sand claimed to have given up indignation, exchanging it for the order, consistency and placidity she found in 'real Nature'. Flaubert admitted that he was given to useless rages ('and I love you the more for loving me on that account'), though a little later, apropos of his treatment in *L'Éducation sentimentale* of the reactionaries and *arrivistes* of the Second Republic, he wrote that he wanted to have 'neither love nor hate, pity nor anger'; his creed of impersonality ruled that a novelist should not state his opinions on worldly matters (though he might be allowed to communicate them indirectly). Not for the only time, Sand is the wiser, older and wiser, in lecturing him tactfully on how he should look after his health since the physical being is 'a necessary adjunct' to the moral being:

> I don't go along with you about the need to flatten the breast in order to draw the bow… I think an artist ought to live as much as possible in accordance with his own nature. Let those who like fighting have war; those who like women, love; let old stagers like me who like nature and travel and flowers have rocks, great landscapes, children, a family, everything that militates against moral anaemia,

adding, as if she suspected he would find this somewhat cloying, 'But perhaps all this doesn't apply to a mind like yours, which has acquired much and merely needs to digest.'

Again and again she recurred to his rages and the ill effect they must have on his constitution, trying sensibly but largely in vain to calm down his obsessive fury against Michel Lévy, his publisher and hers. 'What does it matter if one has a hundred thousand enemies if one is loved by two or three good people?' Though he couldn't quite admire her 'childish, innocent principles' (her words), he prized her 'contagious' serenity, just as for her, she said, his letters came 'like a good shower of rain, making all the seeds in the ground start to sprout'. The closest she came to overstepping the mark was when she asked him why he didn't get married: 'Living for oneself is a bad thing… You're trying to turn a kind and tender heart into a jaundiced misanthropist.' To Princesse Mathilde he confided that Mme Sand's 'perpetual pious optimism' sometimes set his teeth on edge, but to her he replied temperately that 'the feminine existence has never fitted in with mine', that he wasn't rich enough to marry, he was too old, and he wouldn't care to inflict himself on anyone else. In the past he had *loved*, as much and as stormily as the next man, or more so, but 'Deep down, there's something of the priest in me that no one suspects.'

There is a sense that as the years passed Sand began to get the upper hand. Flaubert 'shows his age much more than I do,' she noted in her diary in 1873, during a visit from him; he only wanted to talk about literature, whereas Turgenev, also present, was simple, cheerful and charming, 'a good and convivial genius'. And in December 1875 she tackled him head-on:

I know you disapprove of personal attitudes entering into litera-ture. But are you right? Isn't your stand due to lack of conviction rather than aesthetic principle? It seems to me that your school of writers fails to concern itself with the depths, and tends too much to stay on the surface. By dint of striving after form it underrates content. It addresses itself to a literary audience. But that audience doesn't really exist, as such. We are human beings before we are anything else.

Flaubert responded firmly but amicably: he didn't go in for desolation wantonly, he just couldn't change his eyes, and 'alas! I'm only too full of convictions. I'm constantly bursting with suppressed anger and indignation. But my ideal of Art demands that the artist reveal none of this, and that he appear in his work no more than God in nature.' He has avoided both monsters and heroes, and as for having 'a school', he is wrecking his health trying not to have one.

Sand returned to the charge in January 1876 with a long and weighty disquisition on the theme of 'mere *words*', virtually repeating his mother's diagnosis of the dried-up heart – 'You regard form as an end when it is only an effect. The best visible effects emerge only from emotion, and emotion comes only from conviction' – and remarking sharply that his contention that one wrote only for twenty intelligent people hadn't stopped him agitating over his lack of success. She consoled him with the thought that he would soon be entering old age, 'the happiest and most propitious part of life', when art, which in youth had taken the form of anguish, 'reveals itself in all its sweetness'.

Flaubert's reaction was singularly mild; the very length of her letter was a proof that 'you do love me!', and he even managed to speak well of two new books of hers, though in private he found them poor. He may have felt content to recall what she had said three years earlier: 'You want to write for all time; I think *I* shall be completely forgotten, perhaps severely denigrated, in fifty years' time. That's the natural fate of things that are not of the highest order.'

The reflections on life can be quite up to date, as on the topic of 'hysteria', when Sand asked,

Isn't it a discontent, an anguish, caused by desire for something or other that's unattainable? In that case all of us who have any imag-ination suffer from that strange malady; why should it be attributed to only one sex?... Men and women are so much alike it's hard to understand all the subtle distinctions and theories on the subject that have coloured our various human societies. I myself have observed the childhood and subsequent development of my son and daughter. My son was the image of me, and so more a woman than my daughter; she was a failed man.

And the passages on literature are more profound, more vivacious, and often more generous than those we are accustomed to meet in our contemporary market-place of letters. In some ways things haven't changed. So-called enlightened people, Flaubert grumbled, are becoming more and more inept about art. 'How rare a true feeling for literature is! A knowledge of languages, archaeology, history, etc. – all that should help. But not at all! ... Glosses are more important for them than the text. They value crutches more highly than legs.'

George Sand died on 8 June 1876. Though indignant that her daughter should have arranged for a Catholic funeral, Flaubert journeyed again to Nohant, subsequently writing to Turgenev in Russia that 'The good country people wept copiously around the grave... Her funeral was like a chapter in one of her books.' To her son he wrote, 'It seemed to me that I was burying my mother a second time.'

(1980; 1980; 1993)

IV

What Happened to the Devil?

In *Lucifer: The Devil in the Middle Ages* Jeffrey Burton Russell considers it strange that, 'at a time when evil threatens to engulf us totally, when evil has already claimed more victims in this century than in all previous centuries combined', one should hear less and less on the subject from theologians. 'Why is there a tendency to reject belief in the Devil today?' When reviewing his book, I offered the facetious answer that while churchmen appear on television, the Devil doesn't; and then needed to add that the Devil did so appear, in light disguise. When the Witch addressed Goethe's Mephistopheles as the *Junker Satan*, he ticked her off:

> The name has been a myth too long.
> Not that man's any better off – the Evil One
> They're rid of, evil is still going strong.[1]

If churchmen seem barely to believe in God (a sometimes bearded, patriarchal Being, otherwise a dispersed Presence unamenable to visualization) we cannot expect them to believe in the Devil (a goat-like figure, with dirty habits and a nastier sort of beard, and horns and talons). Like most of us, they still believe in Good, but rarely in Evil, a word which even sounds like Devil. Evil – a term which indeed most people would go far to avoid using [2] – is simply the absence of Good, and often accounted for by the absence of such self-evidently good things as a decent, loving childhood, a stable marriage or family background, regular employment, or cash. The view of crime as a result of being underprivileged has taken a beating of late; in especial, not too many of us are able to perceive exactly what those privileges can be

---

1 *Faust Part One*, translated by David Luke.
2 'But how to be morally severe in the late twentieth century?' asks Susan Sontag, in *Illness as Metaphor*. 'How, when there is so much to be severe about; how, when we have a sense of evil but no longer the religious or philosophical language to talk intelligently about evil. Trying to comprehend "radical" or "absolute" evil, we search for adequate metaphors. But the modern disease metaphors are all cheap shots.' She is objecting to the crass and impermissible use of the 'cancer metaphor' in polemics of all kinds, notably political, and adds that those who have the real disease are not helped by hearing its name 'constantly being dropped as the epitome of evil'.

whose lack, whether early in life or later, leads to the rape and murder of children.[3]

Russell opines that some modern theologians have been motivated by the thought that the subtraction of Devil/Evil from Christianity would 'remove barriers' and 'be ecumenical'. Yet it is barely credible that theologians could soft-pedal Devil/Evil purely as a tactical, popularizing measure: their personal belief in him/it would surely need to have waned already. (Otherwise, one takes it, they would scarcely leave moral damnation to Chief Constables.) To get rid of God will remove barriers, too, and prove even more ecumenical, for it admits convinced atheists into the Church. Why nibble away at such marginal matters as the Immaculate Conception, the Virgin Birth, the loaves and fishes, the Resurrection? As for the Crucifixion, it was all so very long ago, as they say, that by the grace of God it may not be true.

Among the scribes and Pharisees swallowing camels is still accompanied by straining at gnats. The Bishop of London declared that if female ordination was permitted, he would have no choice but to transfer to Rome. The only argument against women as priests is that they are women, whereas Christ appeared in this world in the form of a man. But he had to assume one gender or the other: God would hardly have dispatched us a hermaphrodite. The implication that priests somehow identify themselves with Christ on the grounds of adventitiously shared gender is staggering. For this might be supposed a circumstance in which

> Difference of sex no more we knew,
> Than our guardian angels do.

Surely a little effort on the part of theologians, once a nimble enough race, ought to open the way to women. After all, these women positively *want* to be priests.

What is pathetic is the lack of genuine conviction, not among the sheep, whether hungry or lost or otherwise, but among those who make a living as shepherds. A.W. Schlegel sketched out the inevitable sequel to the revisionism touched on by Jeffrey Burton Russell: first

---

3   It appears that some observers regard the 'normal' family – that's to say, not a family in marked financial or other distress – as a primary source of domestic violence ranging from wife-battering to child abuse. I had noticed myself that poorer families often boast (not that they would boast) the best parents. Q.D. Leavis once told me, when I had mumbled a complaint about college dinners, that had I been one of those unfortunates with experience of public schools (as the English call them) behind me, I would have appreciated what I was now being given.

the Devil is attacked, then the Holy Spirit, next Christ, and finally God. (No mention here of attacking the male monopoly of ordination.) You will end up, in Heine's comparison, with what some people quite like: turtle soup without turtle.

What could more understandably afflict modern theologians are the embarrassments surrounding that ancient crux: how on earth to reconcile evil, man-made or natural, with a merciful, loving God? Over the centuries innumerable explanations have been advanced for the permitted existence of Evil and the Devil, some of them less far-fetched than others. Churchmen ought to hammer away at the problem even so, and even though they are unlikely to come up with anything more cogent than the theory that God elected to limit his omnipotence in order to favour man with free will, freedom to choose virtue or vice. Or of course the argument, misused, distasteful, but irrefutable, that we cannot understand the ways of God and no amount of sublunary enquiry will enable us to. In *Religio Laici* Dryden hints a threat: 'For what could fathom God were *more* than He', but Hardy's Lord, in 'A Dream Question', remains bland or offhand:

> A fourth dimension, say the guides,
> To matter is conceivable.
> Think some such mystery resides
> Within the ethic of my will.

Otherwise, if ecumenism can extend itself so far, we are left with the Manichaean struggle, unending, between the two great and inde-pendent antagonistic powers of light and darkness. While obviously curtailing the Almighty's almightiness, in another respect this dualism saves his face; it brings the Father closer to the Son, making that rela-tionship more credible, and it might actually persuade us, through a sense of fellowship, to side with the light.

Many will rate all such speculations as sterile and pigheaded, yet it would be rash to dismiss them as 'irrelevant', and on the theoretical side no patently better justification of the cloth is to be seen. However, in a recent paper in the *Journal of Literature and Theology* Margarita Stocker points out that since the problem of evil arises precisely in the context of belief in a beneficent Creation, God's goodness is a logical pre-condition of the argument, whereas literature caters for those who are not necessarily theists, and 'literary theodicies are therefore (in our time at least) problematically detached from proper theological discourse'. So perhaps it is a subject best left to amateurs after all. And notably to literary people, for 'If evil does not exist, what is going to happen to literature?', a character asks slyly in V.S. Pritchett's comic (and more than comical) novel, *Mr Beluncle*, alluding to a sect which ascribes all set-backs to sensory illusion.

In the meanwhile we are driven back on the sayings of Adrian Leverkühn's polymorphous visitor in *Doctor Faustus*. 'But I hope you do not marvel that "the Great Adversary" speaks to you of religion. Gog's nails! Who else, I should like to know, is to speak of it today? Surely not the liberal theologian! After all I am by now its sole custodian! In whom will you recognize theological existence if not in me?'

Earlier I was thinking of the everyday evil that television news assiduously brings to our attention. But the entertainment side of television has been enriched – oddly, that seems the right word – by the myth-like stories of Dracula and Frankenstein and the questions they raise. Can these, often inane in treatment and incidentals, compete as regards power and persuasiveness with the highbrow dramas we are offered? The answer is: without difficulty.

Dr Frankenstein at least has respectable origins, being the creation of the wife of a famous poet. And the novel carries a reputable Miltonic epigraph on its title-page:

> Did I request thee, Maker, from my clay
> To mould me man, did I solicit thee
> From darkness to promote me?

The story has obvious similarities with that of Faust. 'It was the secrets of heaven and earth that I desired to learn,' says Victor Frankenstein of his younger self. Like Marlowe's Faustus, he has studied Albertus Magnus and Cornelius Agrippa. After years of 'incredible labour and fatigue' he discovers 'the cause of generation and life', and is able to bestow animation on lifeless matter: a new species is at hand, whose 'happy and excellent' members will bless him as their source. Wagner, the erstwhile famulus of Goethe's Faust, contrived to create Homunculus – a sharp, energetic, and endearing little spirit, safely confined within a test-tube – probably after the recipe given by Paracelsus, another author studied by the young Victor. Such homunculi, Paracelsus declared, were wondrous wise in that they had acquired their life through art, and hence art was incorporate and innate in them.

But something went wrong with Frankenstein's art. Wagner's ingredients all seem to have been inorganic ('everything depends on the mixing'), whereas Frankenstein not only collected bones from charnel-houses but also tortured living animals, a means bound to taint the end. The dreary November night on which his creature opens a dull yellow eye is very different from the scene in Wagner's comical medieval laboratory, where the project was to find a mode of reproduction more befitting man's present dignity, the atmosphere further lightened by Mephistopheles' naughty jokes. Homunculus's first words to his creator were 'Well, Daddy, how's things? That was no joke!', followed by an invitation to press him to his breast, but not too ardently because of the glass.

The monster, as we have to call him since Frankenstein omitted to give him a name, is far from brutish. Greeted by his creator, 'Begone, vile insect!', he replies urbanely, 'I expected this reception.' He ought to be Frankenstein's Adam, he observes, but he is 'rather the fallen angel'. He has been reading *Paradise Lost*, in French translation, along with *The Sorrows of Werther*, whose 'lofty sentiments' and account of domestic manners have impressed him, and also Plutarch's *Lives*, among whom, in harmony with Shelleyan principles, he admired 'peaceable law-givers' rather than famous warriors.

'I was benevolent and good; misery made me a fiend. Make me happy, and I shall again be virtuous.' This is the defence offered by criminals, we note, or more often by their solicitors and caseworkers, though here couched in more resonant terms. Villagers attack him with stones; when he saves a girl from drowning, her companion shoots and wounds him; every man's hand is against him, and in turn he declares everlasting war 'against the species'. A species not his own: he was created by an experimental scientist, not by God, as Adam was, and so is closer to Satan, concerning whose provenance we are less sure. Yet he returns to the comparison with Adam, having derived from Milton the picture of 'an omnipotent God warring with his creatures': Adam, even so, was provided with a companion, whereas the monster has no friends, no relatives, no Eve to soothe his sorrows, and hence – 'What was I?' – no identity. Created desolate, by killing Frankenstein's younger brother in whom, an innocent and unprejudiced child, he had hoped vainly to find a friend, he proves that he too can create desolation.

And so, he tells Frankenstein, passing from the Byronic mode to the Shelleyan, he must be given a female with whom he can live 'in the interchange of those sympathies necessary for my being'. Reasonably enough, this female should have the same defects: neither miscegenation nor hypergamy is in the monster's mind. What he wants is something approaching normal human life, *mutatis mutandis*. (Homunculus, more overtly allegorical, flings himself into the ocean, where life as we know it began; by due evolutionary process he is to escape from his test-tube existence into something putatively richer.) Again and again the hunger for companionship is expressed; if one sole being would show benevolence towards him, he would make his peace with the whole race: this is a more generous offer than Jehovah's, who finally agreed to spare Sodom could ten righteous citizens be found there.

Given that, as Adam admitted to Raphael,

> For man to tell how human life began
> Is hard; for who himself beginning knew?

the monster's account of the growth of consciousness is discreetly and movingly done. His memories are 'confused and indistinct'; 'a strange multiplicity of sensations seized me, and I saw, felt, heard, and smelt', seemingly all at the same time, without differentiation between the senses. He discovered the moon, with wonder, and birds, and fire, left by wandering beggars; observing the cottagers from hiding, he learned such basic words as 'milk', 'bread', 'wood'. He is a vegetarian, living on acorns and berries. In the Notes on *Queen Mab* the young Shelley held that the allegory of Adam and Eve and how they ate of 'the tree of evil', thus bringing down God's wrath on their posterity, admitted of no other explanation than that disease and crime have come from 'unnatural diet', the eating of *meat*.

God told Adam that it was not good for man to be alone, but Frankenstein rejects the view that a change in family environment will reclaim his creature, asserting that one of the first results of 'those sympathies for which the daemon thirsted' – thirst suggests lust, which is not what we have perceived in the monster – would be offspring, a race of devils bound to endanger the existence of mankind. He is of the opinion that the female of the species, in this instance, might well be more deadly than the male, perhaps ten thousand times more malignant; she could even desert her mate for the 'superior beauty of man'. Mary Shelley has told us of the villagers' cruel treatment of the then innocent and well-intentioned monster, but it is improbable that she was being ironical about the beauty of man; and what she intended by Frankenstein's notion of the greater malevolence and capacity for evil of the female can only be guessed at. And yet her subtitle cannot well be other than ironic: 'The Modern Prometheus'. Much in the novel is plainly in tune with the romantic movement, but essentially it is unromantic, chastened, even-handed in its sympathies, turning the romantic, humanist Greek hero ('Forethought') on his head. This nineteen-year-old girl seems much older, not to say wiser, than her excitable male colleagues and comrades.

Frankenstein destroys the Eve he has been working on, and is appositely warned (despite the words sounding like those of a jilted lover in a different sort of tale): 'Remember, I shall be with you on your wedding-night.' Having murdered Frankenstein's bride, the monster avers, 'Evil thenceforth became my good', almost literally the words of Milton's Satan as he approached Eden and prepared the downfall of man.

Yet the monster's agony is 'superior' to his creator's, in that he feels the bitter sting of remorse. And he makes, one would say, a good end, sailing northwards to build his funeral pyre. 'My spirit will sleep in peace; or if it thinks, it will not surely think thus.' The equipoise of the phraseology, and its restrained pathos, recur in Wilfred Owen's 'Strange Meeting': 'And if it grieves, grieves richlier than here.'

It is a nobler epitaph than mankind is likely to pronounce on itself. We may have thought of Mary Shelley as an enlightened free-thinker and a relatively simple soul, yet in her pleading of the abandoned creature's case against the creator she too is of the Devil's party without knowing it: simultaneously a 'liberal' thinker and a 'devilish' theologian. Milton at least nominally justified God's ways – God gave his creatures freedom of choice, he 'formed them free', whereas Frankenstein's creature hasn't heard of such delights – but Mary Shelley had no intention of doing so. Her husband maintained that the great secret of morals was love, a going out of one's own nature to identify with others – a truth indistinctly but profoundly sensed by the monster – and that 'the great instrument of moral good is the imagination'. Frankenstein is deficient in imagination, an incompetent father; and God is less than adept at putting himself in the place of another. Or he does so only belatedly: 'Account me man,' says Milton's Son of God, as if to warn men that they can always be crucified.

Mary Shelley is a theologian after the Great Adversary's heart, it being conceded that since he has no heart he will esteem her liberal compassion towards man only as it reflects discredit on the other great adversary.

But the story and the suppositions on which it rests, it may be objected, are plain nonsense. And the same will be said, more emphatically and more contemptuously, of vampire tales. The sad thing is not that we don't believe in the factuality of such stories, but that we cannot accept them as fiction, as products of the incited imagination. (If we accept the visitation in Mann, then it is because Leverkühn is insane, prone to hallucinations; or, just possibly, in retrospect, because the author is so persuasive.) Heaven knows, we are prepared to swallow no end of fancy nonsense, and loads of grinding banality, in the name of fiction. What we recognize, and resent, I think, is the presence of myth. Myths are old bullies, still throwing their weight about, what weight they retain, and we would prefer something new, something that is 'ours', never mind if its grip on us lasts no longer than the time it takes for our eyes to pass over the print or the pictures.

Equally old as classical legend and European folklore, in English writing the vampire story began at the same time as *Frankenstein*, and in the same place: in Switzerland, during the wet summer of 1816, when, in competition with Mary Shelley, Byron drafted a tale which his physician, John Polidori, later published as *The Vampyre*.

The idea of the vampire, Clive Leatherdale states in *Dracula: The Novel and the Legend*, is founded on two concepts, 'the belief in life after death, and the magical power of blood'. Other factors could easily be added: the destructive power of sexual desire; parasitism in diverse forms; the fear of sickness, often mysterious in its causes (*Nosferatu*, the title of F.W. Murnau's 1922 cult film, based on Bram Stoker's *Dracula*, indicates 'disease carrier'). By its openness, and because of its abiding fascination, the theme has lent itself to strange applications and accretions, some of them nervously humorous. A Hammer film featured lesbian vampires (nothing new there); Roman Polanski's comedy, *Dance of the Vampires*, included a homosexual male vampire, given to coffin-hopping, and a Jewish one, gleefully immune to the crucifix; *Blacula* was black throughout. Lusty though dead lady lovers glide through old Chinese and Japanese tales, and Malay legend has the *pontianak*, the ghost of a woman who died in childbirth and returns at night to attack men; I have heard talk of them hailing taxis and vanishing without paying the fare. Practically every ethnic group has been accommodated. On film, where his blend of pathos and rage made Boris Karloff the only possible Frankenstein's monster, Bela Lugosi (said to have been buried in his black cloak lined in blood-red) was the best Count Dracula because he combined piggishness with arrogance, while Christopher Lee has excelled in home-grown libidinous gentlemanliness.

So much is obvious in the story and its various versions and reworkings that there is small need to import significances. This hasn't deterred the exegetes. Leatherdale mentions someone's discovery that the name of the hero of Stoker's *Dracula* (1897), Professor Van Helsing, approximates to 'Hell Singer', and points out that Mina (Harker) spelt backwards is very nearly *anima*, soul. Dracula's 'orality' is illustrative of regressive infantilism (as long as we ignore the fact that drinking blood is the quickest way of absorbing it, and vampires cannot be expected to carry transfusion equipment around); and of course the vampire's teeth are phallic symbols, and likewise – the punishment fitting the crime? – the wooden stake that destroys him. How endearing, compared with these crude formulations, is the discourse of the old-fashioned, old fictional characters themselves. When Carmilla, in Sheridan Le Fanu's story of that name (1872), embraces the innocent young lady, Laura, and kisses her ardently: 'You are mine, you *shall* be mine, and you and I are one for ever', the bewildered Laura asks, 'Are we related?', and 'What can you mean by all this?'

Latter-day political interpretations have run the gamut. *Dracula* represents the eventual victory of the middle classes over the blood-sucking aristocracy. The novel is racist in that the villain is made a foreigner, and said to smell bad. Dracula is a capitalist since he accumulates blood. He is a bloodthirsty Nazi (it appears that copies of the book were supplied gratis to American forces fighting overseas in the Second World War). He is a Communist, hailing from behind the Iron Curtain, an expansionist who subverts others to his way of life (or death). A man for all fearful seasons!

Other commentators have gone so far, such is modern niceness, as to insist on the unethical conduct of the 'good' characters in failing to allow Dracula an opportunity to explain his actions, and in openly admitting that they are responsible for the deaths of a number of alleged vampires. But this is the standard perversity of modern exegesis: Claudius is a pretty stout fellow, really, the stuff of which rulers are made, whereas Hamlet is a pain in everybody's neck. Apropos of those ill-done-by and alleged vampires, someone has pointed out that their bodies have dissolved into dust and hence (habeas corpus?) their killers run little risk of prosecution. More interestingly, Clive Leatherdale intimates that, left to themselves, vampires' bodies do not decay – in this resembling the bodies of saints.

The potency of the legend is commensurate with its ability to elicit multifarious interpretations of itself.[4] The sexual charge of the vampire legend is undeniable, though the ingenious Mr Leatherdale probably exaggerates when he claims that a careful search of Stoker's

---

4 Praise of another and contradictory nature, negative yet heartfelt, has been accorded films on the subject, which not fairmindedness alone moves me to record. A letter in a recent *Radio Times* quoted Christopher Lee on old Hammer films – they afford 'terror without risk' – and added: 'When you see a Hammer vampire or zombie you know that when the film ends you're safe because such things don't exist, unlike many of today's horror films which feature things that do exist, like madmen armed with dozens of nasty-looking weapons.'

novel unearths 'seduction, rape, necrophilia, paedophilia, incest, adultery, oral sex, group sex, menstruation, venereal disease, voyeurism'. Enough, as he concludes, to titillate the most avid sexual appetite. Yet there is no evidence, as far as I know, of anyone reading that very Victorian novel specifically for the sake of sexual titillation, albeit *Dracula* has been said, correctly or otherwise, to be the second-best-selling book of all time. The same statistician has the Bible standing at number one in the charts.

Goethe's Mephistopheles admits, quite cheerfully, that

> Devils and spirits have a law, as you may know:
> They must use the same route to come and go.
> We enter as we please; leaving, we have no choice

– to which Faust replies pertly: 'So even hell has laws?' Indeed its agents are of necessity subject to conventions, rules of conduct, circumscriptions, and vulnerabilities. No more than Mephistopheles, no more than Mary Shelley's monster, is the vampire a mere *lusus naturae*. He is preternaturally cunning, and as strong as twenty men, he can transform himself into a wolf or a bat, he can see in the dark, he can change his size, he can vanish altogether. 'He can do all these things, yet he is not free,' Van Helsing, the authority, comforts his unnerved confederates. 'He who is not of nature has yet to obey some of nature's laws.'

Given that everyone who succumbs to a vampire's attentions becomes a vampire in turn, obviously some limitations and restraints have to be built in. To begin with, the vampire's potential victim must evince a degree of complicity, at least to the extent of inviting it (here we can easily avoid gender embarrassment) into the house on the first occasion. It doesn't have to be asked twice. Coleridge's Geraldine and Le Fanu's Carmilla appear as damsels in distress, to whom help and hospitality are naturally extended. Mephistopheles, although taken home in the shape of a frisky poodle, tells Faust that he must leave and then be invited back three times before they get down to serious business. Heathcliff in *Wuthering Heights* – 'Is he a ghoul or a vampire?' Nelly Dean asks herself – has been adopted by Mr Earnshaw, a starving orphan picked up on the streets of Liverpool: '...a gift of God; though it's as dark almost as if it came from the devil'. This is the obverse of entertaining angels unaware.

Then, according to some versions, in its various enterprises the vampire is obliged to use names that are anagrams of one another: Carmilla, Millarca, Mircalla. Less troubled by this formality, when negotiating a lease in Piccadilly Dracula introduces himself to the house-agents as Count de Ville, thus echoing Jonson, whose Pug, a junior demon, is given in polite London society the prettier name of De-vile, which 'sounds as it came in with the Conqueror'. Unsubtle slapstick of this sort, though it won't do in serious television drama, is common in mankind's central myths.

The vampire's ascendancy ceases with the coming of day, it is devitalized by the 'Sun of righteousness', and must retreat to its coffin, lined with earth from the creature's native place. That a cross made of the thorns of wild roses will detain it in its grave is a Christian touch, as is its fear of the crucifix. And that it is averse to garlic appears to be an old Transylvanian belief; garlic is a preventive against disease, and it might be that one bad smell is thought to drive out another. Some say that it cannot endure fire, others that it can pass over running water only at the slack or the flood of the tide. Another penalty laid on the vampire is that, if it is so forgetful as to pass in front of a mirror, it can be identified by the absence of a reflection: it can have no reflection because it has no soul; its immortality is a soulless one, at best only of the body, which still requires nourishment and sleep.

There are several set ways of dispatching a vampire; the favourite, after the manner of St George impaling the dragon, is to thrust a stake through the heart, ideally a stake made of the wood used for the Cross, and in one blow, as if to prove conviction, or prevent resistance. In the struggle between good (no matter how inept) and evil (however tawdry) there must be a minimum of observed conventions, conventions more binding than the laws pertaining to secular warfare.

Julian Birkett has remarked of *Frankenstein* that 'the novel's passionately religious and metaphysical themes are even more out of favour today than the rhetoric that Mary Shelley employs to deal with them'. Nevertheless, having noted that the novel's concern is with the purpose of creation, he opines that the many popular spin-offs – he cites thirty-five films and some 2,500 plays, musicals, stories, comics, etc. – might paradoxically be said to flourish 'precisely because they touch secretly upon metaphysical anxieties'. The paradox stems from the simple truth that what is out of public favour can always be present in the private mind.

What this phenomenon, this secret perturbation, has to do with *belief*, to what extent believing is involved, is hard to say. The postulation of a half-way house between belief and disbelief is the best we can manage; that famous 'willing suspension of disbelief for the moment' doesn't fill the bill, nor does the 'hoping' (or fearing) 'it might be so' of Hardy's poem, 'The Oxen'. We can agree with William James that what keeps religion going is 'something else than abstract definitions and systems of concatenated adjectives, and something different from faculties of theology and their professors'. And we shall probably find it easier to assent to Octavio Paz's summing-up: 'Although religions belong to history and perish, in all of them a non-religious seed survives: poetic imagination.' Yet the relationship between imagination and belief remains an indecipherable mystery.

Despite lacking an author as well connected as that of *Frankenstein*, the vampire stories too are highly theological. Here the concern is with eternal life, but an eternity passed on earth, a shameful immortality thrust on the vampire's victims. Love will have its sacrifices, and 'No sacrifice without blood,' Carmilla pronounces. 'Whoso drinketh my blood hath eternal life' is the Christian promise. The vampire could say, widdershins, he whose blood I drink dwelleth in me, and I in him. When describing one of Dracula's victims, Lucy Westenra, as she was before and as she is after her release at the hands of her lover, Van Helsing invokes a pair of related opposites: 'the devil's Un-Dead' and 'God's true dead'.

Dracula, we understand, chose to be a vampire; like a suicide – primal vampires were believed to be people who had killed themselves – he took matters into his own hands, he was not infected by others. Those he has bled to death, to untrue death, are to be pitied – especially when they haven't as yet brought further vampires into the world – and delivered, though by the same grisly means, from their miserable travesty of a life after death. The distinction between hunter and prey parallels that between Satan and his victims, in whose exclusion from Eden he found solace for his exclusion from heaven. Stoker may merely have set out to write a hair-raising story, but he ended by doing much more. In his introduction to the World's Classics edition of the novel, A.N. Wilson makes the excellent observation that Stoker's 'classic distinction is not artistic, but mythopoeic':

> He reflects the very bewildered sense, still potent in a world which was (even in 1897) preparing to do without religion, that mysteries can only be fought by mysteries, and that the power of evil in human life is too strong to be defeated by repression, violence, or good behaviour. Virtue avails the characters in *Dracula* nothing. It is the old magic – wood, garlic, and a crucifix – which are the only effective weapons against the Count's appalling power.

In part, he adds, posterity will be able to judge us by our continuing interest in the book.

Bram Stoker shows little pity for his Dracula, and endows him with little that could arouse compassion in us. And yet, as Jonathan Harker administers the *coup de grâce*, Mina sees on the vampire's face 'a look of peace, such as I never could have imagined might have rested there'. Slightly more of Satan's equivocal dignity, and of the fleeting compunctions inspired by the sight of Eve, whose innocence

> overawed
> His malice, and with rapine sweet bereaved
> His fierceness of the fierce intent it brought,

is briefly visible in *Varney the Vampyre*, published in 1847, fifty years before Stoker's novel, and attributed variously to James Malcolm Rymer and Thomas Peckett Prest, both of them diligent churners-out of penny dreadfuls. Sir Francis Varney explains that he is subject to laws, like any other being. He did not choose to be what he is; he must endure a fate laid on him as a punishment for accidentally killing his young son in a fit of anger.

> Flora Bannerworth, you are persecuted – persecuted by me, the vampyre. It is my fate to persecute you; for there are laws to the invisible as well as the visible creation that force even such a being as I am to play my part in the great drama of existence. I am a vampyre; the sustenance that supports this frame must be drawn from the life-blood of others.

He brings to mind Frankenstein's monster when he declares: 'Even at the moment when the reviving fluid from the gushing fountain of your veins was warming at my heart, I pitied and I loved you. Oh, Flora! even I can now feel the pang of being what I am!' And similarly when he tells her that it is a condition of his 'hateful race' that 'if we can find one human heart to love us, we are free'. Flora can give him pity, but love is out of the question. 'I am answered,' he says, for once laconically. 'It was a bad proposal. I am a vampyre still.'

While this turgid, rambling and interminable novel (876 double-columned pages) doesn't have much to recommend it, Varney comes out well in comparison with most modern fictional villains and their declarations, indeed with many modern heroes. 'Even I can now feel the pang of being what I am!' If a participant in a talk show or an 'intimate' interview so far departed from the contemporary brand of rhetoric as to voice a half-way noble sentiment, the cameras would crack from side to side.

Reverting to Jeffrey Burton Russell's question, we ask ourselves whether a belief in evil might not reduce the amount of what looks like evil active in the world, for at least it would endow our behaviour with some sense of seriousness. The 'dedemonization' of life has clearly failed to do what it professes. But we see only the outward face of things, the official side, and the media, like governmental departments, are predominantly secular. We really don't know very much about private states of mind, despite the current outpourings and public baring of tailored breasts. We have become a society of actors, yet the majority of us, I think, would still rather play the clown, or keep our mouths shut, than pretend to some petty, partial Hamlet, stripping off selected veils.

A thought from George Steiner's book, *In Bluebeard's Castle*, provides a felicitous if grim conclusion.

> Much has been said of man's bewilderment and solitude after the disappearance of Heaven from active belief... But it may be that the loss of Hell is the more severe dislocation... The absence of the familiar damned opened a vortex which the modern totalitarian state filled. To have neither Heaven nor Hell is to be intolerably deprived and alone in a world gone flat. Of the two, Hell proved the easier to re-create.

There *may* be heaven, one of Browning's characters conjectured, but there *must* be hell. And in that case, we had better re-create it, such snatches of it as we decently can, in our arts and even our entertainments. Vulgarities and absurdities, frequently found in the most elevated company, are a small price to pay for the release from triviality.

(1988)

Hell's Angels

Stefan Heym's The Wandering Jew

The authorized version has it that Lucifer fell through pride, having set himself up as the equal of the Almighty, and thereafter sought revenge by seducing God's newly created favourites, mankind. In *The Wandering Jew* (1981) Stefan Heym has come up with an alternative reading, according to which Lucifer and his associates, among them the archangel Ahasuerus or Ahasverus, whose name means Beloved by God, were expelled because they refused to bow down before man, that curiously arbitrary invention. Lucifer declined on the not unreasonable grounds of superior birth (created on the first day, not the sixth) and superior qualities, and Ahasverus out of pity for man. For both of them saw how man would turn out. 'It was such a great hope,' sighs Ahasverus as they fall, seemingly without the hideous ruin and combustion reported by Milton, towards the depths. 'Such a beautiful world! And such a beautiful man!'

What is made of dust, Lucifer points out, must return to dust; and so they bide their time, Ahasverus fretted by his 'Jewish impatience'. A 'little angel', Lucifer calls him, 'a regular saviour of mankind', unrest personified, driven by the desire to change things. Whereas he, Lucifer, insists – as would any expert in dialectical thinking – that every thesis carries within itself its antithesis, and one simply has to wait for things to change in their own time, 'their own, God-given time', as he expresses it.

In time, and in accordance with the medieval legend, Jesus, bearing the cross, pauses wearily outside the house of the cobbler Ahasverus. Heym's Ahasverus, eager to redeem the world through action, tells Jesus that he possesses a sword of God, whereby the guards can be put to flight and Christ lead the people of Israel to victory, 'as is written in the book'. But Christ will not listen: his kingdom is not of this world, and the meek shall inherit the earth. In anger and despair, Ahasverus, although he loves Reb Joshua, as he calls him, drives Christ from his doorstep: 'Get going, you idiot!' Christ then speaks the words which initiate the legend of the Wandering Jew: 'You shall remain here and tarry till I come.'

In Heym's brilliant theological fantasy, at once profound and farcical, spiritual and fleshly, we meet Ahasverus in different guises, at various times and in various places, including the Warsaw ghetto, where he suffers death without dying. For the greater part the

221

narrative shifts back and forth between the sixteenth century and the present. As is generally the case, the devil has the best tunes, and the liveliest passages concern a mysterious, scruffy, but powerful club-footed hunchback named Leuchtentrager, which translates into Latin as 'Lucifer'. He takes under his wing a dim but zealously self-seeking young cleric, Eitzen, whose career, by virtue of his knowledge of the future, he promotes with outstanding success. Eitzen can never tell whether his friend is being serious or not when he advances unorthodox opinions. Thus,

> But I have a liking for the snake. The snake saw that God had equipped man with two hands to work and a head to think with, and to what good purpose might man have used those in paradise? In the end they might have withered like anything not being used, and what, my dear *Studiosus*, would under these circumstances have become of the likeness of God?

But Eitzen knows which side his bread is buttered. By means of magic, Leuchtentrager sees to it that he passes the examination in divinity. Having managed a question about *angeli boni*, he finds himself (or is it someone else?) discoursing eloquently on *angeli mali*:

> And behold, the power of the bad angels is greater than any which humans possess, for it derives from divine force, and is but a whit less than the power of God. And their lord is the angel Lucifer… and another of them is Ahasverus who wants to change the world as he believes it can be changed, and man along with it. And no one knows how many of them there might be and what shape they will take.

The gentlemen from the city council like the sound of this, in so far as they understand it: it lets them off the hook. The chief examiner, Doctor Luther, is uneasy but impressed. This young fellow, he thinks, is worth watching.

We are on familiar (and fertile) German ground. Eitzen rises to fame and fortune as Luther's leading apostle and Superintendent of the Duchy of Sleswick. In the latter capacity he has the Jew Ahasverus seemingly whipped to death. In due course, in return for services rendered him, his miserable little soul is forfeit to Leuchtentrager, and he is discovered with his head twisted backwards, his tongue hanging out of his mouth, and his eyes staring in horror. In one of the early Faustbooks, Faust's head is twisted back to front. Moreover, Heym has introduced a female demon to stir but not assuage Eitzen's lust: Margriet is ostensibly Leuchtentrager's housemaid, and she much prefers a young Jew, calling himself Ahab, whose hands wander all over her body. Rude knockabout comedy emits theological overtones: souls are made fun of, but souls are in peril.

Finally Margriet turns into a scarecrow made of a bundle of straw and a feather duster. A similar demon appears in the Faustbooks and, in Marlowe's play, as a devil dressed like a woman, bearing fireworks about her: that is, 'a hot whore'. Margriet is no sort of Gretchen, but another source of inspiration (not that Heym stands in much need of it) may have been Goethe's 'Prologue in Heaven', where Mephistopheles jokingly bemoans the sorry condition of mankind and swears to reduce Faust to eating dust 'like my cousin, the well-known snake'.

As if this were not riches enough, Heym interlards the story with letters from an ongoing correspondence, dated 1979–80, between a Professor Siegfried Beifuss of the Institute for Scientific Atheism in East Berlin and a Professor Jochanaan Leuchtentrager of the Hebrew University in Jerusalem, both of them in their different styles specialists in the legend of the Wandering Jew. The Israeli professor is actually acquainted with a Mr Ahasverus, and sends Beifuss snapshots of him outside his shoe shop on the Via Dolorosa: 'the person portrayed indubitably is a man of character, intelligent, and – if you will look at his mouth and eyes – with a good sense of humour.' 'On principle,' the German professor replies, 'I should like to state that we in the German Democratic Republic do not believe in any kind of miracles, just as we do not believe in spirits, ghosts, angels, or devils.' To accept the longevity of Mr Ahasverus would be tantamount to believing in Christ knows what. In a fit of donnish jocularity, Beifuss permits himself a smile at the idea of almost two thousand years of business carried on by the same proprietor at the same address. 'What capitalist enterprise could claim for itself a record even approximating this one!'

The correspondence preserves the civility of tone ('dear Colleague') we would expect from scholars of integrity and international standing, but the watch-dog at the GDR's Ministry of Higher Education advises Beifuss to concentrate on 'the close interaction of religion and imperialist expansionism, particularly in relation to Israel', and later warns him (an instance of Heym's unobtrusive, effective interlocking) that he had better steer clear of the Lutheran connection in view of the approaching Luther anniversary of 1983, sponsored by the highest representatives of the State and the Party. Beifuss confides to his Israeli confrère that his Institute has promised a paper, to mark May Day, on an allied topic, 'the reactionary character of the myth of the transmigration of the soul'. The soul itself is a myth, of course, unlike the psyche, which is a function of the nervous system and something we are intimately acquainted with through the labours of psychologists, psychiatrists, psychoanalysts, and psychotherapists.

The Israeli academic informs his opposite number in Berlin that Mr Ahasverus has recently encountered Reb Joshua, the alleged messiah, dragging himself along the Via Dolorosa – whereupon he invited the man into his house for a drink of water and to have the wounds on his head cleaned. Professor Beifuss will appreciate his correspondent's happiness at having 'just such a Marxist sceptic as yourself as the first person to be informed by me of so astonishing and cataclysmic an occurrence as the second coming of Christ', even though for the moment only one source vouches for it. Professor Leuchtentrager promises that Mr Ahasverus and he will shortly be visiting East Berlin for a fruitful exchange of views, and Beifuss intimates tactfully that while Leuchtentrager, to all appearances a champion of law and order, might conceivably be allowed in, there is no chance of his friend qualifying for an entry permit. Somehow the fellow makes him think of Trotsky.

Despite which – I am running impatiently ahead – the two of them, later identified as Israeli secret agents specializing in 'ideological penetration', show up on New Year's Eve and make off with Beifuss through a hole inexplicably blown in the wall of his eighth-floor apartment. Two policemen, subsequently disciplined for drinking while on duty, claim to have seen three shapes in the sky, two of them with fiery tails (jet-engine exhausts?) and the third, in the middle, hauled along by the other two. So that was the fruitful exchange of views.

The highest fantasy always has its roots in reality, like some dreams, or some nightmares, but to modulate from fantasy into reality is always a dodgy proposition. Ha, we think, now we are being got at! We think this when we hear of Mr Ahasverus's conversation with Rabbi Joshua in 1980 and the Rabbi's account of Armageddon in terms of nuclear submarines and intercontinental missiles, the 'entire hellish force' in the hands of a few men of limited intelligence:

> In his lust for power, paired with fear of his own kind, man had made a grab for the forces of the universe, but without being able to control or regulate these; thus Adam himself, once made in the image of God, had turned into the beast with the seven heads and the ten horns, the all-destroyer, the antichrist.

There needs no ghost, holy or otherwise, come from the tomb to tell us this. Still, it is not something that considerations of literary refinement should forbid us to retell.

And Heym is as artful as the subjects he has set himself are tricky. He ends his book with a touching coda, though for us mere mortals an ambiguously consoling one. Armageddon is fought, and the old earth destroyed. Following Ahasverus's earlier advice to take to the sword, the Rabbi ousts his fainéant father, old and feeble, and announces the imminent creation of a new heaven and a new earth where love and justice rule and the wolf shall lie down with the lamb. As he raises his sword against his father, the old man grows to giant size, reminding the Rabbi that 'your image is also my image because you cannot be seen separate from me, as no man can'. To the echoing laughter of the angel Lucifer, the great champion of law and order, and in a reprise of the fall with which the book began, Ahasverus and the Rabbi merge lovingly into one and then, becoming one with God, into 'one image, one great thought, one dream'.

Beer and onions, bums and breasts, slapstick and horror, metaphysics and damnation… This is the composite matter in which the German literary genius is most at home and at its best. Stefan Heym has surpassed himself here, sustaining his imagination and maintaining our engagement in it; and by force of wit holding in check what might be thought – or is it that we are jealous of the love that exists between angels? – a drift towards sentimentality. Heym spent some twenty years in America and writes English with panache and apparent ease; he has a weakness for the progressive form – 'I am still seeing the Rabbi's face growing pale' – though such minor eccentricities may be deemed appropriate to the story's time or timelessness.

A character in his previous novel, *Collin*, a writer, gave as his reason for staying in East Germany the opportunities provided for observing so much that was contradictory. And Heym has said *in propria persona* that East Berlin is a fascinating place for a writer to live in because there are so many contradictions. It is perhaps by no contradiction that *The Wandering Jew* is unpublishable in its author's country. Its meaning, or part at least of the fable's meaning, as manifest in Ahasverus's conviction that man is free to make changes and redemption requires revolution, might hold some historic charm for the authorities. But, even if the story's Manichaean implications were glossed over, Heym's metaphors could only appal them. He has arrived at what might just be considered sound doctrine by a distinctly unscientific route. And, what is worse, while his writing is full of vigorous *disputatio*, its deployment of dialectics smacks of the disapproved device, sterile and formalistic, known as parody. It may occur to us that the Devil cited a modern scripture when, in tempting the composer Leverkühn, he dismissed parody as a melancholy form of aristocratic nihilism generating little profit. If you want to be enraptured, impassioned, ravished, then the Devil's your man.

(1984)

Master of Horror

Karl Kraus

Apart from a vague impression that some people think Karl Kraus a guardian of language and morals of super-Confucian proportions while others consider him an intemperate destroyer of reputations by means as foul as fair, all that most of us anglophones know about the Viennese satirist (1874–1936) is that his writings are unamenable to translation. Erich Heller, whose essay on him in *In the Age of Prose* is a capital introduction, has declared that Kraus's peculiar way with the German language simply isn't reproducible outside that language, while Harry Zohn, although the editor of the Kraus reader *In These Great Times*, concludes by modestly exhorting us to learn German. The translator's task is certainly more than commonly hazardous in the case of an author who maintained that after his death he would worry more about a misplaced comma than about the actual dissemination of his works. For much of the time Kraus was dealing in the German language, idiosyncratically, with usages and perversions of the German language. In translating, we are told, what gets lost is the poetry. But in not translating even more can get lost. And it is true that, for much of the time, Kraus's concerns, like those of any satirist or polemicist worth his salt, are universal and timeless in their nature.

Kraus's conception of the direct relation between language and behaviour is unique only in its unyielding intensity, its thrusting to extremes. 'Psychopathologists now concern themselves with poets who arrive for their check-up after they are dead. It serves the poets right. They should have raised mankind to a level where there could have been no psychopathologists.' Nothing is seen as fortuitous or free from consequences, not even a printing error. He was remote from those of our contemporaries who regard words as workaday signs of no greater inner consequence than the painted arrow directing us to an exit. For Kraus, corruption of language entailed corruption of thought, and hence of action, public and private. His habit of establishing guilt by induction and association has naturally drawn obloquy – 'When a man makes personal polemics into a way of life,' Idris Parry has commented, 'he runs a serious risk of error' – but there is a curious logic to it. You can tell a man by the words he uses, so you can tell the words by the man (assuming you know him) who uses them – and there's an end to it.

Getting style and tone right or wrong doesn't much affect Kraus's reflections on contraceptive advertisements in the daily press: the only decent, sensible, and tasteful contributions consistently found there, their propriety marred solely by the highly moral front pages disavowing gratis what is presented, against payment, on the back pages – and by the accompanying picture of an officer 'who, in order to make things more palatable, strokes his moustache'. On a similar theme, 'The World of Posters' starts with the straight-faced proposition that art and intellect have been removed, much to their advantage, to the realm of advertising, and cultural ideals now manifest themselves in the wrappings of a patent clothes-hanger.

The piece grows increasingly phantasmagoric. 'Is there life beyond the posters?' We lie there helplessly and suffer the torments of Macbeth – 'What, will the line stretch out to the crack of doom? Another yet?' – as they pass before us: the Button King, the Soap King, the Carpet King, the Cognac King, the Rubber King (whose eyes 'remind us of our sins, but his features bespeak the untearability of human trust'). William Tell enters as the trade mark of a chocolate firm; a snatch of song approximating to a line of Heine's as set by Schumann – *ich liebe alleine / Die Kleine, die Feine, die Reine, die Eine* – heralds a brand of lozenge… We might recall the more explicit judgment of Robert Musil, Kraus's fellow Austrian and contemporary: 'What this age demonstrates when it talks of the genius of a racehorse or a tennis-player is probably less its conception of genius than its mistrust of the whole higher sphere.' Nothing of this is outdated; rather the opposite, in view of the more sophisticated television commercials of our day.

Translation doesn't fatally harm the elaborate and more bitter comedy of 'The Discovery of the North Pole'. This was the great American event of 1909 (the glory shared by Germany since the discoverer was Frederick A. Cook, formerly Koch), all the greater in that it compensated for the miscegenetic scandals arising in New York's Chinatown that same year (the shame also shared by Germany since a murdered white woman bore the name Elsie Siegl). The great dream of Christian civilization was to conquer the Pole, virgin nature. But when the dreamer realizes his dream he behaves like a suitor to whose advances a virgin has at last surrendered. 'I was disappointed,' said Mr Cook. Kraus interjects: 'for the only valuable thing about the North Pole was that it had not been reached.' The argument grows more complex when he comes to the rival claims of Commander Peary and the question, 'What is truth?' Certainly 'it is not the midnight sun which brings it to light'.

And what does the Zeppelin bring to light? The newspapers gaily print the headline 'Conquest of the Air' alongside other headlines announcing the deaths of hundreds of thousands in earthquakes, typhoons, and floods. 'What good is speed if the brain has oozed out on the way?' The ice-fields of the abused intellect have gradually killed reason and imagination, and the piece ends: 'We who thought, died.' Harry Zohn duly notes the parallel with the 'conquest' of the moon and with other developments in the ice-fields of applied science.

Irony cannot save the fighting satirist and moralist, with his sense of being a voice in the wilderness, from sounding much like a prig at times. Despite its celebrated opening, in which the inaugural cliché is elegantly whittled at from all angles, and despite its expressing Kraus's central beliefs at their keenest and most persuasive, the essay 'In These Great Times' (late 1914) is repetitious and uneven in force, omitting to differentiate between sins and peccadilloes, and treating honest disagreement and inveterate viciousness with equal contempt: those who were not a hundred per cent with him were a hundred per cent against him. (In this we may be reminded of the later writings of F.R. Leavis, a figure Kraus resembles in other ways as well.) Rilke remarked that he distilled a very pure poison; he could also lay about him with a rather blunt instrument.

A common misfortune of cultural historians, scholars who offer to supply the background to the work of writers, is that the writers have already supplied not only a foreground but, by implication, a background as well, a peculiarly intimate one. We know medieval England through Chaucer, and Victorian London through Dickens; we know Habsburg Austria because of *The Man Without Qualities*, and because of Karl Kraus.

Kraus's magazine, *Die Fackel* ('The Torch'), ran for thirty-seven years and 922 numbers, and more than the writers mentioned above, possibly more than any other writer, he occupied himself with the minutiae of the local life of his time, the personalities and practices of what Schoenberg called 'our beloved and hated Vienna'. Edward Timms's task in *Karl Kraus: Apocalyptic Satirist* – to trace his subject's literary career and personal life up till the founding of the Austrian Republic in 1919 – would seem to be more supererogatory than usual. Except that Kraus is little known to the larger English-speaking public: interest in him has been mounting for some time now, and hence Timms's book arrives opportunely. It is no great matter that it makes heavy weather of describing the fragmented condition, ethnic, social, political, and religious, of Austria-Hungary and especially of Vienna. More could have been left to the reader's imagination, itself capable of feeding on Kraus's imagination. But we should be grateful for the lively illustrations: a literary coffee-house; the Kaiser kitted out in medieval armour, fearing God but nobody else; a repulsive grinning male advertising the virtues of something called Lysoform, 'the most perfect disinfectant. Indispensable for ladies.' And for such insights as the quotation from Arthur Schnitzler, to the effect that before one joined a cycling club one would need to ascertain whether it was a Progressive, or Christian Social, or German Nationalist, or anti-Semitic organization.

Erich Heller wrote on Kraus in *The Disinherited Mind* (1952), and honour should also be accorded Frank Field's early study, *The Last Days of Mankind: Karl Kraus and his Vienna* (1967), and Thomas Szasz's *Karl Kraus and the Soul-Doctors* (1977). The latter deals entertainingly with Kraus's attitude towards Freud and his followers, though Timms insists that Kraus's strictures were directed against the followers rather than Freud himself. Szasz cited not only the famous epigram, 'Psychoanalysis is the disease of which it claims to be the cure', but also Kraus's fundamental principle, 'Language is the mother, not the maid, of thought', as well as that useful distinction, 'The agitator seizes the word. The artist is seized by it.'

The greatest step forward was Harry Zohn's selection, *In These Great Times*, published in Canada in 1976 and in Britain in 1984. Untranslatable – that high yet equivocal accolade – often means that the right translator hasn't come along, or that for one reason or another few people desire a translation and hence publishers evince no interest. In Kraus's case the situation seems to have been aggravated by the discomfort felt among German-speaking critics: he doesn't fit into any 'school', any of the prime, well-founded, well-thought-of categories – and that, where taxonomy has ruled so long, is a sin. English-speaking Germanists have tended to follow suit, or else, as with J.P. Stern, their thoughts have been chiefly confined to academic circles, where popularization or vulgarization (which includes translation) is itself a solecism. An exception is an essay by Stern, printed in *Encounter* in 1975, in which he mentions a professor of German literature at an Austrian university who knew of Kraus only as 'one of those typical querulous coffee-house literati, who is said to have waged a peculiarly quixotic linguistic campaign lasting more than forty years against his fellow journalists'.

Paradoxes are fairly easily come by; we can pluck them out of the air once we have the knack. They are virtually bound to surface where people commit themselves to opinions and causes, and they serve the critic and the commentator as faithful stand-bys. Paradoxes and contradictions flourish in Timms's commentary. Kraus attacked ideological thinking in all its shapes: while his campaign for reforms could only be implemented with political support, 'his intransigence towards organized factions effectively precluded it'. Politics is said to be the art of the possible; Kraus's art was that of the truth as he saw it, and we cannot honestly regret that he forfeited the power which political affiliation would in theory have supplied. Had he enrolled in a party, it would have been the end of him, or more likely of the party. In a breezy piece calling for the demotion of tourism in Vienna, he mentioned a female tourist who asked if what she had heard was true and he was incapable of being constructive. After some hesitation he admitted it, 'but not without at the same time boasting of a positive ability: that I am capable of being destructive'.

Timms quotes Kraus's remark that if scoundrels cannot be improved then it is still an ethical aim to vex them, and juxtaposes it with Swift's objective: 'to vex rogues though it will not amend them', adding truly if tritely, 'Both formulations reflect the difficulties inherent in any attempt to set the world to rights by means of the pen.' Not even the consciousness that no one is going to read him can stop a writer writing; Günter Grass will be busy at his desk while the debris from the Big Bang is falling about him. Related is 'a paradox which runs right through Kraus's writing': that's to say, he desired to raise the standards of Austrian journalism, and yet he proclaimed that the press was irretrievably corrupt. The theory that the satirist must be optimistic (or at any rate not pessimistic), since otherwise he wouldn't go to the trouble of mounting his assaults, has never convinced me. One could as well maintain that no optimist would ever bother himself with satire since he knows that time or some other benign agency will rectify whatever is amiss.

Brechtian *avant la lettre*, Kraus asserted that he did not want 'performance' to overpower the intellectual understanding of the text. 'When I give public readings, I am not making literature into a performance.' Yet contemporary reports of his recitations – there were some seven hundred of them, from Shakespeare, Goethe, Offenbach's librettos, Johann Nestroy, and (mostly) his own work – dwell on his declamatory and histrionic style. This paradox, Timms says, 'can only be resolved by seeing his public role as a quest for authentic identity'. It could be that, to Kraus's way of thinking, when he did it, it was right, and when others did it, it was wrong. But that, too, might be taken as questing for identity.

A more engaging paradox emerges from Kraus's dealings with women, or with women and Woman. His public emphasis was on women as the brainless but bountiful vehicles or vessels of sensuality, in contrast with men, whose strength and purpose lie in ideas. 'The sensuality of woman,' he wrote, 'is the primal spring at which the intellectuality of man finds renewal.' In private, however, his taste was for intelligent women, such as the actresses he loved, and the blue-blooded and cultivated Sidonie Nadherny. A man may well apotheosize the pure (in one sense, at least) and elemental *Weib* or Earth Mother, while in personal matters preferring a woman, a lady even, whom he can converse with as well as embrace in bed. Intelligence, it might be reckoned, is more likely to stimulate or enhance sensuality than to deter it. Not infrequently one is oneself the great exception to the rule one is promulgating, possibly the exception that proves it.

There is no compelling reason for surprise when we hear that, according to his acquaintances, in private life the fierce and unforgiving battler was sociable, charming, relaxed, and kindly. But George Steiner touched on another oddity when reviewing Kraus's letters to Sidonie Nadherny (*Encounter*, 1975), though he was too wily to invoke the word 'paradox':

> One may, in one's public writings and utterances, be a ferocious rationalist, contemptuous of human lies and illusions. But one is privately, and almost obsessively, involved with a graphologist and clairvoyant whose interpretations of Sidonie's handwriting and of the handwriting and horoscopes of her friends seem 'miraculously accurate' and fill numerous letters.

The best comment on the phenomenon occurs in Johnson's *Rasselas*, when Imlac, asked why his father desired to increase his wealth when he already had more money than he could enjoy, answers: 'Inconsistencies cannot both be right, but, imputed to man, they may both be true.' This isn't much of an explanation, but some things can only be described. The rationalist tells you that the reason he doesn't walk under ladders is purely because a brick or a pot of paint might fall on him. Instead, he steps off the pavement and risks being run down.

So marked were Kraus's attempts to discard his Jewish identity that he has been associated with the notion of 'Jewish self-hatred'. He no more wanted to be categorized as a Jew than Heine did. Jews were prominent in commercial, financial, and journalistic spheres, and hence among the enemy, but when Kraus described himself as 'Aryan' he set the word inside inverted commas: 'arisch'. He meant he was unaligned, and therefore uncompromised; or, *tout court*, 'ethical'. He embraced Catholicism in 1911, seemingly without much passion, and remained within that faith for twelve years, though always silently; 'baptized Jews' was another category to be avoided. There was little trace of Christianity in his writing. Perhaps the point was not so much entering one religion or community as extricating himself from another. (There is a faint suggestion of leaning over backwards in these 'liberating' manœuvres.) As Timms notes, it is not the redeeming Christ who informs his satire, but rather the retributive and Judaic Jehovah.

'If the roles of satirist and Christian are incompatible, what of those of satirist and lover?' Incompatibles, or what look like them, are a more extreme form of paradox, equally handy as a trellis on which critics and biographers weave their deliberations. To understand a love-affair from inside is hard enough; to assess it from outside can be impossible. Timms is properly circumspect. Kraus fell in love with Sidonie Nadherny, a Catholic and an aristocrat, in 1913; between that date and his death in 1936, although the decisive break came in 1918, he addressed nearly eleven hundred letters, postcards, and telegrams to her. Their love was clandestine, less because satirists are forbidden love than because Sidonie needed to make a socially acceptable match. Kraus was well off: he had inherited an income from his father, a paper manufacturer, and – another paradox here? – *Die Fackel* prospered, its first number, published on 1 April 1899, having sold around 30,000 copies. But affluence alone wasn't sufficient qualification. In 1914 Sidonie wrote in her diary, 'He is the only man living… K.K. shall always remain the *glory & crown* of my life!', yet apparently she felt she couldn't stay faithful to one man, even the only man living, and an entry of 1918 reads, 'the greater his love grows, the less I can return'. The relationship made little impression on his published writings; disguised, his love for Sidonie evinces itself in his poetry, in poems that are elegiac in mood. In this respect love resembled religion: satire seems to rule out, as themes, the very matters you would expect to inspire it. But then, inspiration can work in roundabout ways.

Apropos of Kraus's 'mythopoeic imagination', Timms points out that you don't need to know anything about the Viennese journalist, Felix Salten, to appreciate the authority of Kraus's portrait of him. Historically accurate though the portrait is, the individual has become a type. Kraus has moved from the particular to the general while retaining all the cogency that the particular carries. 'Am I to blame,' he asks, 'if hallucinations and visions are alive and have names and permanent residences?' Every great satirist must be a great creator, a myth-maker as well as a realist. The proponent of Swift's *Modest Proposal* takes on mythic stature as we listen to him. He is a counsel

SIGNS AND WONDERS

we would eagerly hire for our defence were we guilty as charged; he is politically sophisticated; as an economist he cannot be faulted; he is a skilled demographer, a sound psychologist (his plan will secure pregnant wives from being kicked by their husbands), and not a bad butcher (he knows about salting meat). A veritable Nestor, a Daniel come to judgment! If there is nothing in Kraus that reaches this level of reasoned insanity, then it is not to be wondered at.

Kraus is a superb aphorist. 'A school without grades must have been concocted by someone who was drunk on non-alcoholic wine.' Very timely; my local school has banned competitive sports such as running because someone might win, ergo others might lose, and this would offend the golden rule of equality. 'Sex education is legitimate in that girls cannot be taught soon enough how children don't come into the world': that's up to the minute too. And pertinent in an age of revisionist bishops is this: 'It is a mystery to me how a theologian can be praised for having brought himself to disbelieve dogmas. I've always thought that those who have brought themselves to *believe* in dogmas merit the true recognition owing a heroic deed.' There hasn't been so much change since Old Vienna: 'If something is stolen from you, don't go to the police. They're not interested. Don't go to a psychologist either, because he's interested in only one thing: that it was really *you* who did the stealing.'[1]

An example of Kraus's rather fearsome extrapolation, his turning of individual offence into universal disgrace, was prompted by the case of a young man who had been acquitted of a *crime passionnel* – murdering his wife because she sought a divorce – and was seen some months later dancing in public. (He had shot himself too, but clearly without doing much damage.) Writing about the affair in a poem, *Tod und Tango*, Kraus deduces from it the moral bankruptcy, indeed the living death, of the world at large. 'Guilty is the age, not to perish at such sport!' In defence of the poem, the feminist point has been urged that it exposes the double standard of Austrian justice: coming from a 'good family', the man got off whereas, Kraus notes, a woman who killed her husband during her menopause was condemned to death. So much is valid. Only a cad would bring up Kraus's aphorism, 'I am not for women but against men.'

Kraus runs the risk of being branded an aesthete. In the piece 'Interview with a Dying Child' we may think him more angry about

1 These examples come from the excellent selection, *Half-Truths & One-and-a-Half Truths*, edited and translated by Harry Zohn. As is, of course, 'An aphorism never coincides with the truth: it is either a half-truth or one-and-a-half truths.'

callous and exploitative journalism than pitiful towards the victim, and, when he is contemplating the war, on occasion more indignant about the crass or disgusting reporting of the slaughter than on the subject of the slaughter itself. He was too ready to equate a badly written sentence with moral degeneracy, and a good literary style with truth and moral virtue – even reasoning (though we should allow for coat-trailing) in the reverse direction: 'A poem is good until one knows by whom it is.' A tendency to take short cuts is understandable in one who was always on the go. But it is central to Kraus's mode of operation that, as Timms puts it, apocalyptic conclusions are drawn from apparently commonplace and trivial symptoms. Heller's gloss is apposite here: 'It was Karl Kraus who discovered to what satanic heights inferiority may rise.'

Two essays in Elias Canetti's *The Conscience of Words* are very much to the purpose. In the second of them, a lecture given in Berlin in 1974, Canetti asserts that

> what annoys today's reader of the *Fackel*, what makes it unbearable for him over long stretches, is the evenness of assault. Everything happens with the same strength, everything is drawn as equally important into one and the same language. One senses that the attack is an end in itself, a superior strength is demonstrated where absolutely no strength would be necessary; the victim vanishes under the incessant blows, he is long since gone, and the fight continues.

None the less Canetti insists on Kraus's place as the greatest German satirist, largely by reason of the vast drama, *The Last Days of Mankind*, a war against war, against World War I, conducted by one man, the most belligerent of pacifists, concurrently with World War I, without the benefit of hindsight.[2]

In the earlier and more personal essay, dated 1965, Canetti tells of the first time he heard Kraus lecture, in 1924. Kraus's law was certain and inviolable, it '*glowed*: it radiated, it scorched and destroyed'.

---

2 Kraus's views at the time may not have been as simple and unqualified as this suggests. Another paradox detected by Timms is that of 'the loyal satirist': Kraus was on fairly good terms with the Austrian authorities and with the censorship during the war, though decreasingly so as time went by. He was (a self-description) 'a word-fetishist'; it was the press, the propagandists, the profiteers, and the armchair warriors whom *Die Fackel* attacked, rather than the military men, some of whom had a respectable literary style. *The Last Days of Mankind*, begun in 1915, was not published in its final, book form until 1922, and not produced on the stage before 1962.

These sentences, built like cyclopean fortresses and always carefully dovetailing, shot out sudden flashes of lightning, not harmless, not illuminating, not even theatrical flashes, but deadly lightning. And this process of annihilatory punishment, occurring in public and in all ears at once, was so fearful and dreadful that no one could resist it.

Canetti became a devoted and passionate follower of Kraus's dictatorship, for a while. Gradually he rebelled against it, against the ever-extending Chinese Wall of relentless judgments, against 'the general shrinkage of the desire to do your own judging' which set in after a brief exposure to *Die Fackel*. A man so rigorously and comprehensively 'responsible' left little responsibility to his followers. Yet Canetti acknowledges his indebtedness – Kraus opened his ear to a new dimension of language – and his account of 'the master of horror', the man's energy, his gift for condemning people out of their own mouths, his courage and relish, the sheer necessity of him, is eloquent.

A deft breaking of a butterfly happens in a short item inspired by the announcement in a St Gallen newspaper of 1912 of a forthcoming performance at the municipal theatre of what must have been a hitherto unknown tragedy by Shakespeare – *King Lehar*. The printer wasn't trying to make a joke. 'The word that he was not supposed to set, the association that got into his work, is the measure of our time. By their misprints shall ye know them.' Nearer the knuckle is an advertisement spotted in the *Neue Freie Presse* in 1900: 'Travelling companion sought, young, congenial, Christian, independent. Replies to "Invert 69" poste restante Habsburgergasse.' Again Kraus's design was to bring out the discrepancy between the paid ads and the Pharisaical editorials.

A more sustained, and quite irresistible, instance of his humour and light-heartedness is the story of his beaver coat. It has been stolen, the whole of Vienna knows about his loss, people pity him, they forgive him, they admire him, they stop him in the street to condole with him. 'I wrote books, but people understood only the coat.' His life has been transformed; the solitary and estranged satirist is suddenly 'in the thick of it, the earth has me again'. (*Die Erde hat mich wieder*: the words come towards the end of the first scene of Goethe's drama, when Faust's superhuman aspirations have been knocked on the head and only the sound of the Easter bells dissuades him from drinking poison.) But all this solicitude, this unwonted solidarity, is too much for him. Next thing, the tax collectors will realize he was rich enough to own a fur coat. 'But I still had one hope left: by publishing a new book I might manage to make the Viennese forget me.'

Harry Zohn's selection also demonstrates the grimmer side of Kraus, where the indignation and the punishment truly fit the provocation and the crime. As in parts of *The Last Days of Mankind*, which (its prologue admits) would take ten evenings of earthly time to perform and was meant for a theatre on Mars. In it news reports are seen to 'stand up as people, and people wither into editorials', phrases walk on two legs while men make do with one. The villains of the piece are what we would expect: demagogues and militarists, arms manufacturers and other profiteers, fire-breathing churchmen ('the miracle of the U-boats', etc.), propagandists and culture-mongers (freely adapted: 'They call us Huns and Krauts, and killers – / Where are their Goethes and their Schillers?'), and of course the ladies and gentlemen of the press. Fury conduces to frenzy, and at times it is hard to disentangle the anti-rant from the rant, but Kraus's alertness to linguistic mayhem provides light relief from the glut of denunciations. Some patriots persuade the owner to change the name of the Café Westminster to Westmünster (it means the same, 'and it's German. Perfect'), but on parting so far forget themselves as to wish one another *adieu* and *addio* and *au revoir*. In another scene the waiter in a restaurant needs to identify the dish 'Fatherland mutton with Valhalla nectar' as the pre-war English mutton with Worcestershire sauce; in the original, the waiter explains that *Butterteighohlpastete* is what used to be known as a *Volavan*.

The Last Days of Mankind ends with the Voice of God echoing the words attributed to the dying Austrian Emperor in 1916, *Ich habe es nicht gewollt*: he did not will it. Some late words of Kraus were *Mir fällt zu Hitler nichts ein*: on Hitler he found nothing to say. The disclaimer is ambiguous, in the manner of irony, but hardly affects one as a confession of feebleness. Words, as the saying goes, did fail him.

On the subject of the press – and, now, on television – the key text is the essay or oration, 'In These Great Times'. Progress, with the brand of logic at its disposal, claims that the press serves an existing need: in short , it is nothing other than 'an imprint of life'. In reality it is increasingly the case that life is only an imprint of the press. 'Is the press a messenger? No, it is the event itself… Once again the instrument has got the better of us.' (Marshall McLuhan anticipated.) If we had any sense, then – like Cleopatra – we would beat the messenger. It's too late for that, however: through decades of practising his trade the reporter has 'produced in mankind that degree of unimaginativeness which enables it to wage a war of extermination against itself'.

Perhaps most forceful – and nearest to Swift's *Modest Proposal* – is an extract from *The Third Walpurgis Night* (the first two came in *Faust*), written in 1933 but not published until 1952. In neighbouring Germany, according to press reports, unusual events are happening. Despite efforts to save them, people taken into protective custody are dying, because – the doctors say – they have lost the will to live. Others are so perverse as to inflict wounds on themselves while in transit to a camp. (A camp of the kind defined in the press as 'a temporary curtailment of liberty with an educational aim'.) A Polish workman 'died of heart failure; in any case, he was stateless'. Many of these people are sickly, no doubt as a result of regrettable habits, and liable to have fainting-fits while standing near open windows on upper floors. Nevertheless great things are expected, and indeed claimed, in the way of spiritual rehabilitation, but unfortunately – Kraus interjects – the patients themselves cannot testify to this because their astonishment leads to speech disorders, or because 'the spiritual transformation which often occurs at a stroke not infrequently results in unconsciousness or at least an impaired memory'. Here the subject-matter is heavy, the writer's hand light. Fortunately for him, Kraus's heart failed three years later.

As for paradoxes, Kraus provided one for himself, along with an explication, in a poem entitled *Mein Widerspruch* ('My Ambivalence'):

> Where lives were subjugated by lies
> I was a revolutionary –
> where norms against nature they sought to devise
> I was a revolutionary…
>
> Where freedom became a meaningless phrase
> I was a reactionary –
> where art they besmirched by their arty ways
> I was a reactionary…

(1986)

The Executioner Himself

Elias Canetti

Our attitude towards the great European thinkers and writers of the late nineteenth and early twentieth centuries can be a distinctly mixed one. In their high seriousness and sombre admonition they seem to have said virtually everything of importance there was to say, charting the disintegration of values and prophesying the doom that promptly followed. History set its seal on them. Indeed, so thorough and authoritative were their diagnoses and prognoses that we begin to wonder whether in some way they weren't partly responsible for what they described and foretold.

Having this shameful thought in mind, I should have been gratified rather than disconcerted by what Elias Canetti says on the first page of *The Play of the Eyes*, his third volume of memoirs, relating to the years from 1931 to 1937. In his novel, finished during that time, and later known in English as *Auto da Fé*, he had burned the books before Hitler got to work on them. His hero's library, which contained everything of account to the world, had gone up in flames. 'All that had burned, I had let it happen, I had made no attempt to save any part of it; what remained was a desert, and I myself was to blame.' He continues, not in self-aggrandizement but in tribute to the power of words:

> For what happens in that kind of book is not just a game, it is reality; one has to justify it, not only against criticism from outside but in one's own eyes as well. Even if an immense fear has compelled one to write such things, one must still ask oneself whether in so doing one has not helped to bring about what one so vastly fears.

Such is human perversity that one wishes to console him: no, sir, please don't take on so! *Auto da Fé* is only a book, no matter how chilling, only a novel about a crazy sinologist who failed to keep his ivory tower in good repair...

Of all those stern, erudite, apocalyptic Europeans – to whose elevated company he has been admitted rather late in the day – Canetti impresses me as the most difficult to assess, even the hardest to describe. How genuine is his originality, how deeply is he indebted to Kraus and Broch? (Certainly not cripplingly.) There is no doubt about his seriousness, the depth of his thought; yet one might have hoped for a firmer incisiveness; we assent, or are ready to assent, to his statements, but we may be disappointed by his exposition and development of them, by the kind of rhetoric he employs. Fairly plainly, this is no grandiloquent or notably supple rhetoric, being blunt, assertive, four-square, and at times portentous, rather than exploratory as in Czeslaw Milosz, or nimble and witty as in Robert Musil, or protean and mischievous as in Thomas Mann. We want to be borne along, we have no misgivings about his sincerity, yet he is not wholly persuasive; his solemnity of tenor and his intensity promise – or threaten – more than they deliver. As we pass through his book, *The Human Province*, we feel we are being steamrollered even by aphorisms no more than a line and a half in length. 'God as a preparation for something more sinister that we do not yet know.'

Canetti explains that the 'jottings' which make up that book served as a safety-valve during the years spent on his *Crowds and Power* (1962) and well beyond its completion, in fact from 1942 to 1972. They saved him from paralysis, and from suffocation. Death and religion are recurrent themes, often found in conjunction. 'The fact that the gods die makes death more brazen'; 'No one should ever have had to die. The worst crime did not merit death; and without the *recognition* of death, there could never have been the worst crime.' Among lighter *aperçus* are 'A love letter from Sweden. Strindberg on the stamp', and 'He kept turning the other cheek until they stuck a medal on it.' And there is an entertaining list of eccentric societies, including one in which every man is painted and prays to his own picture, and another – so much for crowds – in which it is unthinkable for more than two people to stand together, and when a third party approaches, the two of them, 'shaken with disgust', quickly separate.

The majority of these jottings are considerably less playful. 'My greatest wish is to see a mouse devour a cat alive. But first she has to play with it long enough' and 'Oh, for a stethoscope to identify the generals in their wombs!' belong to the year 1942; and an anecdote about people living underground because the earth's surface is uninhabitable – 'War has moved into outer space, earth is heaving a sigh of relief before its end' – is dated 1945. Looking on the brighter side, however, 'as long as there are any people in the world who have *no power whatsoever*, I cannot lose all hope'.

Mann twists and turns, Musil ironizes in all directions, while Canetti looms. Canetti is not an entertainer; he is too stern and cold and unforgiving for that. Perhaps in the end he will be adjudged a major thinker rather than a major writer; or a thinker who has some difficulty in writing. Yet in his 1976 speech, 'The Writer's Profession', printed in *The Conscience of Words*, he speaks nobly on the true profession of the true writer, reproaching both those who use the solemn word *Dichter* (writer or poet) and those who scoff at it. A poet worthy the name would wince away from the name, but true poets do exist. 'If I were really a writer, I would have been able to prevent the war': when Canetti came across this anonymous sentence, dated 23 August 1939, his first inclination was to spurn it as an example of 'the blustering that has discredited the word *writer*'. But it haunted him, for there seemed to be more to it than that. Albeit an admission of complete failure (and in a sphere where few would expect anything other), it expressed, however irrationally, 'the admission of a *responsibility*'. After all, if words can lead to war, why can't words avert war? (As one might ask, if great literature can elevate, why can't pornography debase?) No condition is closer to events, more profoundly related, than feeling responsible for them, however 'fictively'. A kinship with Kraus displays itself here, as in Canetti's aphorism, 'Literature as a profession is destructive; one should *fear* words more.'

This responsibility is developed in his concept of the writer as the keeper and practitioner of 'metamorphosis', or the ability, explicit in myth, to become anybody and everybody, 'even the smallest, the most naïve, the most powerless person'. In this process, which embraces an acceptance of chaos and an effort to overcome it, the writer is spurred on by an inexplicable hunger – unlike the seeker after success, who always knows what, among his chances and choices, he should exploit and what he should throw overboard. The writer pursues nothingness only to find, and to mark for others, a way out of it. His pride is to fight against death and, using means other than theirs, against 'the envoys of nothingness, who are growing more and more numerous in literature'. True enough, the last days of mankind are always about to arrive; but we are not obliged to welcome them.

That Canetti has his own brand of humour, signally his own, is illustrated in the short, impassive character sketches, falling uncertainly between typology and fable, published under the title *Earwitness*. The Self-giver lives by taking back her presents; she gave them only in order to take them back; how painful it is if the present was edible and has been eaten up! Other subjects are more easily recognized as types, almost conventional 'characters', such as the God-swanker, 'a handsome man, with a voice and a mane', who can always find a passage in the Bible to endorse him, or if the first doesn't, he finds another that does; and the Blind Man, a traveller who, back home, looks at his photographs of places he has visited without seeing them at the time: the cameras never lies, it *proves*.

The more comical these sketches, the more pertinent they are. The Tear-warmer relies on sentimental movies since people won't always oblige by dying when you feel like a nice weep. The Paper Drunkard reads books that others haven't even heard of; he avoids speaking about his seven doctorates and mentions only three. And the Sultan-addict is a rare, or rarely heard from, species of feminist, yearning for harems because they offered women the chance to be truly feminine and outstrip men. 'The one thing that only a woman can do is to bear a prince, who kills all the other princes and eventually the sultan too when the sultan gets too old.' She feels sorry for Turkey, which has lost its former greatness and is now a modern country like any other.

The Damage-fresh Man needs no gloss; he thrives on the accidents of others, sniffing them out before they happen and looking them bravely in the face. So many bad things befall other people that there simply isn't time for any misfortune to happen to him. The Water-harbourer hoards water, even asking to fill bottles with it from his neighbours' taps. By revealing that there were no humans on the moon and also not a drop of water, the moon landings have confirmed what he always knew – that the people up there all died from wasting the precious liquid. Bizarre though the man is, he exhibits the knack we all have of conscripting logic to prop up our irrationalities, of fattening our fancies on selected facts. Then of course there is the Earwitness himself, who hears everything, forgets nothing, and in due course comes out with it all. On occasion, as if he were on holiday, he claps 'blinders' on his ears and is so friendly and trustworthy that people fail to realize they are speaking with 'the executioner himself'. One of Canetti's autobiographical volumes is called *The Torch in My Ear*, and he has related how Kraus, that constant listener and tireless executioner, opened new perspectives on language and its capacities for good and ill.

Good fun though these character sketches are, or intriguing, one feels that there must surely be something more momentous, larger of implication, hovering in the shadows, something about to be revealed, about to be. It is in his memoirs that Canetti's habit of observation and ruthless report operates at its peak. Compared with the portraits on display there, these miniatures are fleeting and insubstantial, as it were the playful (if chilly) products of a novelist's spare hours.

Therese, the housekeeper of *Auto da Fé*, is the creation of a major novelistic talent, comparable to (though more dreadful than) Frau Stöhr in Mann's *The Magic Mountain*; you can hear the starch crackle in her skirt, you can smell the starch. And yet the novel is essentially static, loaded, cut and dried from the start: in the course of a self-fulfilling prophecy a born hater of mankind is brought down by hateful men and women. There is an overbearing determinedness about it, a ferocity and contempt at which even Kraus, from whose sway Canetti had recently disengaged himself, might have flinched.

The novel, a final distillation of eight potential novels, was originally called *Kant Catches Fire*, but was published, in 1935, under the more austere title *Die Blendung* ('blinding' or 'bedazzlement'), and with the protagonist's name changed on Hermann Broch's insistence. Kant became Kien ('pine-wood'), thus retaining something of the man's combustibility, as Canetti has observed in a rare flash of everyday humour. When Broch read the manuscript, 'You're terrifying,' he told the author: 'Do you want to terrify people?... Is it the writer's function to bring more fear into the world? Is that a worthy intention?' At the time Canetti must have thought it so. Not that he was, or is, deficient in self-awareness, or awareness of other people's views of him and his work. In *The Play of the Eyes*, when he is doubting his ability to do full justice to Broch, and with his preparations for a life-work on the psychology of crowds also in mind, he writes:

> He could not help recognizing my tendency to include *everything* in my plans and ambitions as an authentic passion. What repelled him was my zealotic, dogmatic way of making the improvement of mankind dependent on chastisement and without hesitation appointing myself executor of this chastisement.

It may be that the 1981 Nobel Prize was awarded to Canetti more on account of his *Crowds and Power*, but *Auto da Fé* is to say the very least a unique work, and we would not be without it. 'It's good such a book exists,' the proprietor of a Strasbourg newspaper affirmed, adding that 'people who read it will wake up as from a nightmare and be thankful that reality is different'.

Canetti visited Strasbourg for a music festival in 1933, in the course of a refuse collectors' strike which brought out the city's medieval character. Suddenly, without warning, he found himself in the fourteenth century, a period that had always interested him because of its mass movements, the flagellants, the burning of Jews, the Plague. As he walked through the reeking streets he saw everywhere, both outside and inside behind closed doors, the dead and the despair of those still alive.

> What in Germany, beyond the Rhine, was felt to be a fresh start struck me here as the consequence of a war that had not yet begun. I do not foresee – how could I foresee? – what lay ten years ahead.

No, I looked six hundred years back, and what I saw was the Plague with its masses of dead, which had spread irresistibly and was once again threatening from across the Rhine.

Only when he climbed the Cathedral spire and took a deep breath did 'reality' reassert itself, and it appeared to him that the Plague had been thrust back into its proper century.

Canetti's eyes match the 'thirsty eyes' he attributed to Isaac Babel in the preceding volume of memoirs, *The Torch in My Ear*. They are hyperactive throughout *The Play of the Eyes*, although 'play' is not always the right word for what they are engaged in. While his idols generally have a toe or two of clay, his fools and *bêtes noires* are formed of something worse than mud. Franz Werfel had pop eyes and a mouth like a carp's:

> Since he took any number of important ideas from others, he often held forth as if he were a font of infinite wisdom. He overflowed with sentiment, his fat belly gurgled with love and feeling, one expected to find little puddles on the floor around him and was almost disappointed to find it dry.

It isn't hard to see why Canetti despised him and his "'O Man!" rubbish', but all the same the author of *The Forty Days of Musa Dagh* deserves better than this. Emil Ludwig, the once acclaimed biographer, 'wrote a whole book in three or four weeks and boasted about it' – perhaps he oughtn't to have boasted – while Richard Beer-Hofmann, the surviving leader of the Viennese *fin de siècle*, whom Canetti met on the same occasion, 'wrote no more than two lines a year'. (We wonder whether he boasted about that.) And grim and grotesque fun is made of those artistic relics, the widows of Gustav Mahler and Jakob Wassermann. Displaying her daughter by Walter Gropius, Alma Mahler (now married to Werfel) asked Canetti, 'Beautiful isn't she?... Like father, like daughter. Did you ever see Gropius? A big handsome man. The true Aryan type. The only man who was racially suited to me. All the others who fell in love with me were little Jews. Like Mahler. The fact is, I go for both kinds.'

Canetti met James Joyce once, in Zurich in 1935, and rudeness, on Joyce's part, ensued. The incident, of which he makes what seems rather too much, occurred during a reading of his play, *Komödie der Eitelkeit* ('Comedy of Vanity'), a reading which fell disastrously flat – except in the eyes of the author. Reporting an earlier reading of the same play, when Werfel shouted 'This is unbearable' and walked out, he comments, 'It is defeats of such catastrophic proportions that keep a writer alive.' He has always been a doughty fighter.

The larger and more intimate set pieces bear on the novelists Broch and Musil, the conductor Hermann Scherchen, and – unequivocally affectionate in tenor – the sculptor Fritz Wotruba (on whom he has published a monograph), the composer Alban Berg, and one other and mysterious person. Canetti speaks of the indelible impressions people leave on him, not surprisingly in view of his close and pitiless scrutiny of them. These portrayals are indisputably brilliant, the work of a novelist, a dramatist, as well as an unremitting watcher. That there is a trace of resentment in his hero-worship of Broch and Musil, and that elsewhere an incidental tinge of self-praise shows through, is understandable given the history of his reputation, its curiously sluggish growth. And the fact that for the greater part of this period nothing of his had been published, and he had only manuscripts to show for himself in the small, prolific world of Vienna, would have made him (in a phrase he applied to Musil) touchy in his self-esteem.

Just as their conversation had grown fascinating, Broch would announce, 'I must go to Dr Schaxl's now.' That the man who had written *The Sleepwalker* should break off to go and confide in a female analyst! 'I was filled with consternation. I felt ashamed for him.' Looking back, Canetti admits the possibility that Broch was running away from his avalanche of words, that he couldn't have endured a longer conversation and therefore arranged to meet him just before his appointment with the analyst.

Musil, who was 'a man of solids and avoided liquids and gases' and who possessed 'an unerring instinct for the inadequacy of the simple', he worshipped as greatly as he worshipped Broch. Musil was competitive, and 'his touchiness was merely a defence against murkiness and adulteration'. He wasn't in the least pleased to feature as one of the much trumpeted and (Canetti's words) 'odd triad', Musil, Joyce, and Broch. When he heard that someone had spoken highly of *The Man Without Qualities* he would at once ask, 'Whom else does he praise?' In 1931 Canetti sent the manuscript of *Auto da Fé*, in three heavy tomes, to Thomas Mann, who returned it with an apologetic note: he didn't have the strength to read it.[1] With what looks like convoluted humour, Canetti now acknowledges that Mann's letter declining to read the

---

1 It is never easy to be serious about important matters without sounding portentous or self-important. In an essay on Confucius, Canetti has talked of the sage's distaste for oratory and 'the weight of chosen words': he took death so seriously that he declined to answer questions about it. Incidentally, it was the shade of Confucius – 'To see the right and not to do it is to lack courage' – who inspired Kien to marry Therese. Weighty words, those.

manuscript was 'probably not unjust, for he had not read the book'. But after its publication, four years later, he received the letter he had hoped for, making amends. Musil had launched into his own and eagerly awaited praise of the book when, excited and befuddled, Canetti interrupted to say that he had had a long letter from Thomas Mann. Musil's face went grey. 'Did you?' he said, and turned on his heel. (A case of 'Who else has praised you?')It was the end of their friendship. 'He was a master of dismissal. He had ample practice. Once he had dismissed you, you stay dismissed.' This is saddening to read – a premonition of the kind of literary biography so popular today: by their frailties ye shall know them – and, aware of Canetti's own edginess, we can be forgiven for wondering whether it is true, the whole truth.

It is Scherchen, the conductor, a lesser person, who gets the roughest handling: a man of indestructible will, voluble in self-praise ('hymns of triumph, one might say, if it didn't sound so dull and colourless'), with never a commendatory word for others, stage-managing a circus of cowed protégés. For Canetti, he was 'a perfect specimen of something I was determined to understand and portray: a dictator'. Only when Scherchen fell in love with a Chinese girl whom he had seen conducting Mozart in Brussels, and cancelled all his engagements to rush off to Peking to marry her, did Canetti soften towards him. For once, instead of issuing orders, the man had voluntarily submitted to one.

The most glowing tribute is that paid to a man Canetti had watched in a café for a year and a half before being introduced to him. Dr Sonne, who lived in retirement, looked like Kraus but showed none of Kraus's anger, and spoke as Musil wrote but had none of Musil's purposiveness or urge to prevail. Sonne's was a spiritual influence, his charisma hardly to be conveyed in cold print; Canetti thought of him as 'the angel Gabriel', and served a four-year apprenticeship to him. He heard from somebody else that in his youth Sonne had written, under the name of Abraham ben Yitzhak, a few consummate poems in Hebrew, perhaps fewer than a dozen. They never discussed this, and for a time Canetti was faintly shocked to discover that his 'perfect sage', his peerless model, had *done* something; but then he admired him the more for turning his back on it and disparaging fame – whereas he, Canetti, was busy fighting for a reputation. According to T. Carmi's *Penguin Book of Hebrew Verse*, Avraham ben Yitshak printed only eleven poems during his lifetime (1883–1950), was rediscovered when his collected poems came out in 1952, and is considered by many to be the first truly modern Hebrew poet.

'She despised her sex. Her hero was not some woman, it was Coriolanus.' In the first of his autobiographical volumes, *The Tongue Set Free*, Canetti had much to say about his mother, the raging contradictions in her character, her intolerance and her magnanimity, possessiveness and scorn, wildness and implacability. At ten years old, he had equated her with Medea, encountered in a book about classical myths. Now, in her eyes, he had sold his soul to Vienna, he had even married, in secret, a Viennese woman, and she never wanted to see him again. *The Play of the Eyes* ends with the end of the long, tormented struggle between mother and son, or more accurately with her death, in Paris, in 1937. The account of her last days is totally unsentimental, as we would expect, and weirdly affecting. He brought her roses, from her childhood garden in Ruschuk, he told her, the Bulgarian town where he too was born. 'Her earliest memory was of lying under a rosebush, and then she was crying because she had been carried into the house and the fragrance was gone.' Coming straight from Vienna, he had actually bought the roses on the spot, in Paris. But she believed him. 'She accepted my story, she accepted me too – I was included in the fragrant cloud.'

(1986)

A Doomsday Book

Günter Grass

In a brief address delivered in Rome in late 1982, a sombre thank-you for receiving a prize, Günter Grass spoke of the superior staying-power of literature. However mighty the forces ranged against it and its makers, 'sure of its after-effect, it could count on time', even though this took time. Now, however, 'the book, formerly made to last for ever, is beginning to resemble a non-returnable bottle': we can no longer be sure we have a future. Grass closed by saying that the book he was nevertheless planning to write – writers persist in writing – would have to contain 'a farewell to the damaged world', to all its creatures, including us humans, who in our time have thought of everything, including the end.

The Rat, the book Grass was referring to, is a hectic meditation, darting and diverging in characteristic fashion, a gathering of old obsessions and newer pains, and a recall or roll-call of characters from his earlier works, a roll of honour and of dishonour, an elaborate Last Post for what he has created, and what he loves, for himself, and for all of us. Yet another apocalypse, another busy Last Days of Mankind.

It is Christmas, candles burning low, a festive dinner, the cracking of nuts, happy children… In a homely beginning the narrator finds under the Christmas tree the present he had surprisingly asked for: a rat, a She-rat. Pretty smartly, the She-rat is talking to him, seemingly in his dreams, arguing with him, and getting the better of the argument. When two by two the other animals entered the ark – she tells him – her people were turned away by Noah, in defiance of divine instructions. They were taken into God's hand, where they quickly procreated; and, finding hiding-places for themselves, stopped-up passages under the drowned earth, they were firmly established by the time the waters sank and the ark discharged its coddled cargo. As they survived that great flood, so they will survive the great fire next time. Indeed – for time is elastic here, running freely backwards and forwards – that is what they have done. For this, the She-rat insists, is the post-human era.

The rats have, or used to have, considerable admiration for mankind, 'so lovable, so spontaneous, by definition prone to error'. What most of all distinguished man was that he walked erect, albeit he walked in strange paths; and the She-rat divulges her wish that rats could blush, as man did, though usually for absurd reasons. (This is

Grassian whimsy: rats have nothing much to blush for.) How deeply the rats regret that man has finished himself off: for one thing, rats need human beings to tell stories (writers have a purpose!), many of the stories, like the affair of the Pied Piper, featuring rats. The She-rat oozes compassion; her people did their utmost to alert man to the peril he was in, by staging demonstrations in human fashion, scurrying in hordes through city streets, round and round Red Square, the White House, the Champs-Élysées, Trafalgar Square. But all in vain: men were united only in putting an end to themselves.

There was no Noah's ark this time, but one man is left alive, orbiting in an observation satellite. And he, perforce, is the narrator: 'you, full of stories and curly-headed lies, you, our friend, faithfully preserving the image of man for us.' And so the stories tumble desperately out, a little of this one and then a little of that one, as tenuously connected as events and circumstances in a hastily compiled obituary.

Nothing has been heard of Oskar Matzerath since he reached his thirtieth year, since *The Tin Drum*, but now he returns, on the brink of sixty, still small and humpbacked, suffering from prostate trouble, 'a common taxpayer', a prosperous business man with a large office, a villa, and a Mercedes. From making porn videos he has moved on to educational cassettes; he looks forward to the day when, thanks to the media, we shall be able to create reality in advance of its arrival. Covert allusions are made to Oskar's past, for instance his 'glass-oriented exploits'. And his grandmother, Anna Koljaiczek, she of the long and commodious skirts, is still alive. Invited to her 107th birthday party, he is driven by his chauffeur – Bruno, erstwhile his keeper in a mental hospital – to Gdańsk and on to Kashubia, and a family reunion, or a family farewell.

Then there is a largely pointless account of five females, to all of whom the narrator is attached by long threads and short, who are investigating jellyfish infestation in the western Baltic from *The New Ilsebill*, a ship named after the greedy wife of the fisherman who caught a talking flounder. The fish-hero of Grass's novel *The Flounder* rejected the Grimm version of events as misogynistic distortion, and rehabilitated Ilsebill. He surfaces again, but – understandably disinclined to compete with the garrulous rodent – only to inform the women that the end is nigh.

The story of Lothar Malskat, the honest forger of 'Gothic' paintings, is a parable about the currency reform of 1948 (the substitution of the Deutsche Mark for the old Reichsmark, devalued on exchange), prosperity founded on falsification, and the creation of two 'phoney' German states, each associated with one of the victorious camps, the Western or the Eastern. Where her kind were concerned, the She-rat notes, 'Germany was never split in two, it was one good feed.' Malskat is sent to prison, whereas, in that 'era of winking, of appearances, of whitewashing', Ulbricht and Adenauer, perpetrators of a double forgery, get off scot-free. So angry is Grass about this, a subject touched on lightly in *Headbirths* and *The Meeting at Telgte*, that he begins to bully the reader and to forfeit credibility. What's a bit of forgery compared with a holocaust?

The dislocated and tangled narratives make for arduous reading, more so than in Grass's greener days; and as soon as the narrator finishes an instalment of one of his ongoing stories, or simply stops to draw breath, the She-rat resumes her nagging, armed at times with chalk, blackboard, and pointer. 'You should have learned from your mistakes. You should have this, you should have that.' Mercifully, she seems not to have heard of AIDS. Taking refuge in his tales, or bolstering himself through self-cannibalization, the narrator continues to disbelieve her – 'It's all a pack of lies. There hasn't been any Big Bang' – and to claim that mankind can still save itself. He is under the impression that he is sitting at home in an armchair or perhaps strapped in a wheelchair.

The She-rat advances alternative accounts of how the Big Bang, technically the second one, came about. First: rat-droppings in the central computers of both the Protector Powers, the Western and the Eastern, triggered off the first strikes: a face-saving theory had it that this was contrived by a Third Power, conceivably the Jews. Second: each side trained laboratory mice to paralyse the other's command computer, but instead the mice started the countdown. Third: it was the rats, after all, who entered the computers through the sewage system and substituted their own countdown programme, later set off by the code word 'Noah'. Fourth: the technically benighted narrator, up there in his space capsule, initiated proceedings by inadvertently feeding footage from end-of-the-world science fiction movies into the Western and Eastern terminals. We can take our pick, though we may find ourselves tempted by a fifth interpretation and attribute the whole business to over-indulgence at Christmas.

As is commonly the case with Grass, there is plenty of what one takes to be bona fide documentation, even though it is the She-rat who states that during 'the last year of human history' breeders in Wilmington, Delaware, produced eighteen million laboratory rats for domestic and foreign markets, netting a profit of thirty million dollars. And the public issues are present, in profusion: Germany's post-war amnesia, garbage disposal, pensions, the butter mountain, immigration problems, Solidarity, food shortages in Poland, lead in gasoline, expense accounts, unemployment, over-population and undernourishment, pollution and deforestation.

This last distress generates the liveliest and most original of the four main narrative strands. Gathered in the Gingerbread House, characters from fairy tales are worrying over acid rain and dying trees: Little Red Ridinghood and her Grandmother, the Witch, Snow White, the Frog Prince, the Wicked Stepmother, Rapunzel, Briar Rose (who is forever having to be kissed awake by her young prince, described as 'a kind of male nurse')... They are joined by Hansel and Gretel, who make their first appearance as the runaway children of the German chancellor and then merge with the figures of Störtebeker and Tulla Pokriefke, once the wartime *enfants terribles* of *The Tin Drum*, *Cat and Mouse* and *Dog Years*, and now 'the unripe fruits of lasting peace'.

Hansel and Gretel have made their way through the dead forest with its garbage dumps, toxic-waste disposal sites, and off-limits military installations: no fit place for babes to be abandoned in. A delegation is sent to Bonn, in an old Ford, to meet Jacob and Wilhelm Grimm, respectively minister and under-secretary for forests, rivers, lakes, and fresh air. In a typical flash of sly humour, Rumpelstiltskin, chairman of the 'Save the Fairy Tales' committee, is careful to sign with three crosses, until Briar Rose reminds him that the gentlemen already know his name. The old Grandmother is presented with Volume I of the Grimms' *Deutsches Wörterbuch* of 1852, a monumental dictionary of beautiful words that are soon to be heard or seen no more. All of this will furnish Herr Matzerath with an excellent educational film, and perhaps, since morals among the dramatis personae are at a low ebb, a mildly naughty one, too.

Among much else we are treated to several fresh explications of the Hamelin legend. It can be read as (*a*) a political fable about people who follow their leaders like sheep; (*b*) a prefiguration of how the Jews were 'piped out of town and exterminated like rats'; and (*c*) a heavily euphemized chronicle pertaining to young Gothic punks (as we should label them nowadays) who carried pet rats around on their shoulders or inside their shirts, offended the aldermen sorely, and were enticed into a mountain cave and walled up there. As the narrator reflects, it is always easy to derive a moral from legends. Especially easy if you are Günter Grass, who was never one for passing up an opportunity to fantasize, to improvise and extrapolate in all directions, to turn traditions upside-down, to switch from one scenario to another.

The She-rat tells of quaint life-forms emerging after the Big Bang, flying snails (hardly the kind who keep a diary) and viviparous blue-bottles; later she asserts that she made them up just to amuse her human protégé; still later she resuscitates them as authentic phenomena. Either way they have little significance literally or allegorically. And to complicate matters further, blond, blue-eyed rat-people arrive in Gdańsk, aboard *The New Ilsebill*, with little curly tails yet walking erect. They are 'programmed to start from zero and burdened with no guilt', like our first parents. The female of the species is dominant; the offspring are obedient; they reproduce with gusto and they eat likewise; there is 'something gratifyingly Scandinavian about their behaviour, as if a certain Social Democratic quality were embedded in their genes'. These 'Watsoncricks' shall inherit the earth, or so we might think, but – in what resembles a replay of human history – they are wiped out by plague and hunger, and by the rats 'entrusted' to their care. The hominoids were a little too human.

Blind alleys and red herrings abound; nothing is allowed to stay put; subversion is itself subverted; nothing can be taken as certain. One of the poems scattered through the book raises the question,

> Could it be that both of us,
> the She-rat and I,
> are being dreamed, that we are the dreams
> of a third species?

Of God? The Almighty, less almighty than he claimed to be, according to the She-rat, seems to have given up the ghost after the affair of the flood. Grass's inventiveness, like his ability to squeeze the last drop out of whatever turns up, remains unsurpassed, but it can also strike us as an inability to leave well alone, to know when to stop. We gasp with astonishment and admiration, we groan with dismay, and on occasion, I fear, we yawn out of boredom. If we are to be frightened in time – 'in the end,' the She-rat declares, 'humans were too cowardly to be afraid' – this isn't the ideal way to go about it.

Inconsequence, we are aware, is a distinguishing mark of genuine folklore. And no one wants to be seen complaining of complexity in a literary work. And, yes, order and organization may be deemed trifling virtues when compared with a crowded and multifarious canvas. Yet if a book have not clarity, what does it profit us? Grass's teeming eschatological phantasmagoria, if it does not wholly appal, clouds the poor, overburdened mind. These warnings – if indeed they are warnings and not obsequies – tend to create confusion, cripple rational thought, and foster despondency. Like other prophets of calamity, Grass contributes his little shove downhill. If that's the game, the game is up; great fun for the author, and – let's admit – for the reader as well, so long as the reader doesn't take it too seriously. And, after all, I suppose by now we have learned not to take books too seriously.

Yet most of the time our leaders, whose duty it is to be serious, seem less reluctant than the rest of us to contemplate the Big Bang, the End, or at any rate those 'losses' which no doubt computers have already determined as being 'acceptable'. When Grass's narrator begs to be allowed to assume that, in spite of everything, some humans have survived, or will survive, and asks, 'this time let us live for one another and peacefully, do you hear, gently and lovingly, as nature made us', the She-rat replies, in the last words of the book: 'A beautiful dream'. If we are to be buried before we are dead, and while we can still in some degree enjoy the ceremony, then Grass is the man to undertake the job with acumen and gusto, wild and gritty humour, a mercifully numbing bitterness, traces of pathos, and more than a touch of ireful regret.

(1987)

Signs and Wonders

Robertson Davies

It helps if you are Jewish, but you don't have to be. Robertson Davies has for long been dealing in mysteries and magic, and always with clarity and – which is essential to any mystery worth its name – a solid, exciting story. However widely his branches spread, he is rooted in material reality, even in the provincial, often Canadian as it happens. Like Borges, he carries coolness and common sense into realms supposedly inimical to or irreconcilable with those qualities, and he sees what is called 'chance' as part of the intricate phenomenon of causality. Coincidence, says a supernatural commentator in his *What's Bred in the Bone*, is 'a useful, dismissive word for people who cannot bear the idea of pattern shaping their own lives'. And the Jungian analyst in *The Manticore*, the second novel in Davies's 'Deptford Trilogy', contends that mythic pattern is common in modern life, but few people still know the myths and fewer can detect the pattern under all the detail. More open, or more metaphorical, less theosophical or credal, than Isaac Bashevis Singer, yet Davies is at one with him in rejecting the word 'coincidence'.

Everything, things done or left undone, means something; what reveals itself in the flesh is what has been bred in the bone. This is nothing so simple as the doctrine of predestination, for a fair share is left to 'free will', the great gift of choice prized by Singer. The same card may be dealt out to various people, but how they play it or fail to play it depends on their individual attributes. A delicate balance of forces obtains, perceptible in its effects but barely analysable. Towards the end of *World of Wonders*, the third part of the trilogy, an authoritative character says this:

> God wants to intervene in the world, and how is he to do it except through man? I think the Devil is in the same predicament....It's the moment of decision – of will – when those Two nab us, and as they both speak so compellingly it's tricky work to know who's talking. Where there's a will, there are always two ways.

During *What's Bred in the Bone* we overhear at intervals a conversation between the 'Angel of Biography', a member of the Recording Angel's staff, known as the Lesser Zadkiel, and Maimas, the personal daemon of the central character, Francis Cornish. The Lesser Zadkiel is a compassionate soul and even, someone says, an angel of mercy, 'though a lot of biographers aren't',[1] whereas the Daemon Maimas states that as a tutelary spirit it is not his job to coddle softies; he is 'the grinder, the shaper, the refiner'. In one of their brief, pithy chats, and with the young Francis in mind, the milder angel deplores the breaking of hearts, but Maimas insists that what matters is to break the heart in such a way that when it mends it will be stronger than before. His job is to nudge Francis in the direction of the destiny he may have: he's not a guardian angel (sniff!) but a daemon, and his work is bound to seem rough at times. Like the Lesser Zadkiel, Maimas is a metaphor, he remarks towards the end of the book, a metaphor in the service of the greater metaphors that have shaped Francis's life: 'Saturn, the resolute, and Mercury, the maker, the humorist, the trickster'. His task was to see that these, the Great Ones, 'were bred in the bone, and came out in the flesh'.

But this makes the novel sound more, or more explicitly and exigently, philosophical or theological than it is. The author is that rare bird, an intellectual entertainer, and the story he tells is tightly organized, never drifting into inconsequence, its literal narrative and its figurative signals constantly in step, as with the best poetry. Or, a more germane parallel, the best painting.

The plot is complex, packed with incident and 'coincidence'; to attempt to summarize it would be foolish. 'I also was what was bred in his bone, right from the instant of his conception,' says the Daemon Maimas. And since nature and nurture are inextricable – 'only scientists and psychologists could think otherwise,' the Lesser Zadkiel mocks, 'and we know all about them, don't we?' – the reader follows Francis's life from his birth into a wealthy, patrician Canadian family, through schools and Oxford, his training as a restorer (and rather more) of old paintings, a shadowy career in the British secret service (not much myth left in the Great Game by now!), an unfortunate marriage and a happy though short-lived love affair, up to the moment of his death. If death is the right word: 'Where was this? Unknown, yet familiar, more the true abode of his spirit than he had ever known before; a place never visited, but from which intimations had come that were the most precious gifts of his life.' Perhaps the strange words of the angel in that *Marriage at Cana*, a painting by some Old Master (actually a creation of Francis's, undetected by the experts), were true. 'Thou hast kept the best wine till the last.'

Whoever is concerned with the ineffable must be liberal in

---

1 A sentiment prefigured in *The Rebel Angels*, with which this novel is lightly linked: 'We're not hyenas or biographers, to pee on the dead.'

adducing the effable, and firm and exact in portraying it. The way to the infinite, Goethe instructed, is by following the finite in as many directions as you possibly can. No excursion into mystery will be more than merely mystifying in the absence of clarity and cleanness of expression, and the authority they confer. In turn, these qualities rest on knowledge, simple knowledge it may be, but sound knowledge. In *Fifth Business*, the first volume of the 'Deptford Trilogy', there is much out-of-the-way (but material) history and hagiology, along with technical insights into stage magic and illusionism; in *The Manticore*, a sound grasp of Jungian theory and more than a passing acquaintance with the workings of the law; in *World of Wonders*, an informed and colourful chronicle of a travelling carnival, its freaks, contortionists, conjurors, its hypnotist, knife-thrower, sword-swallower, its Card-Playing Automaton.

> We have educated ourselves into a world from which wonder, and the fear and dread and splendour and freedom of wonder, have been banished. Of course wonder is costly. You couldn't incorporate it into a modern state, because it is the antithesis of the anxiously worshipped security which is what a modern state is asked to give. Wonder is marvellous but it is also cruel, cruel, cruel. It is undemocratic, discriminatory, and pitiless.

Merged with minor triumphs like the counterpointing of Catholics and Protestants in the Ottawa Valley town of Blairlogie, the dominant feature in *What's Bred in the Bone* is art, and the underworld of art, conjured up with what one would term expertise were it not that the experts make a sorry showing here. Francis is able to prove that a *Harrowing of Hell* purportedly executed by Hubertus van Eyck is a later forgery: the monkey hanging by its tail from the bars of hell is not the traditional *Macacus rhesus* but a *Cebus capucinus* from the New World, and monkeys with prehensile tails were unknown in Europe in van Eyck's day. If 'chance' had led Francis to the local zoo on the afternoon before the experts met in The Hague to sit in judgment, it was still his innate perceptiveness that made the connection.

Francis's early training consisted in drawing the corpses at the Blairlogie undertaker's establishment, which doubled as the local bootlegger's. Later he apprentices himself to the brilliant and shady Italian, Tancred Saraceni, a master restorer of old paintings, who is keeping the Renaissance 'in repair'. The two work in Germany, tarting up boring old canvases on Germanic themes, which are then sent to a London wine merchant, and subsequently acquired by high-ranking Nazis, patriotic connoisseurs, for the proposed national collection –

in exchange for Italian and other non-German works of far greater artistic value. When war breaks out, Francis's role in MI5, besides vaguely investigating questionable refugees, is to track the movements of looted works of art. Two of his own unsigned paintings will turn up in Goering's private collection.

A keen cinema-goer in his youth, Francis didn't care for Charlie Chaplin: 'he was a loser.' And Saraceni, like other unworldly figures in the novel, has a sharp eye for money; prudently he keeps it in numbered accounts in Switzerland. Once he had a wife, an Englishwoman, but she found his Roman apartment impossible to live in, cluttered with objects of art, and told him he must choose. 'My dearest one, the collection is timeless and you, alas that it should be so, are trapped in time.' She laughed, and removed to Florence, where she married again, more comfortably.

Saraceni becomes Francis's earthly daemon, or in homelier terms his guide, instructor in forgery (passages here amount to an art forger's handbook), and scurrilous oracle. The Daemon Maimas comments that a great man like Saraceni is necessarily rich in spiritual energy and not all the energy finds a benevolent outlet; an expert who has just crossed swords with him falls downstairs and breaks a hip. Though far less sinister, in his manner he recalls Leverkühn's visitant; Francis observes that when he is in Saraceni's presence, and particularly when the Italian is holding forth on art's heedlessness of conventional morality, he feels like Faust listening to Mephistopheles:

> The Kingdom of Christ, if it ever comes, will contain no art; Christ never showed the least concern with it. His church has inspired much but not because of anything the Master said. Who then was the inspirer? The much-maligned Devil, one supposes. It is he who understands and ministers to man's carnal and intellectual self, and art is carnal and intellectual.

Saraceni's views on modern art are shared by Francis, and by the author too, one surmises, for they point up the novel's 'tendency'. In earlier times the inner vision which is the business of all honest painters presented itself in a coherent language, the language of mythology or religion, but now both of these have lost their power to move the mind. And so

> the artist solicits and implores something from the realm of what the psychoanalysts, who are the great magicians of our day, call the Unconscious, though it is actually the Most Conscious. And what they fish up – what the Unconscious hangs on the end of the hook

the artists drop into the great well in which art has its being – may be very fine, but they express it in a language more or less private. It is not the language of mythology or religion. And the great danger is that such private language is perilously easy to fake. Much easier to fake than the well-understood language of the past.

Like Mann's, like Henry James's, Robertson Davies's people are both dismayingly and inspiringly intelligent; we may feel humble before them, but we don't resent them. It helps that they 'embrace the gamut between eschatology and scatology' – an attribute of the best fiction, Anthony Burgess opined in his review of *The Rebel Angels*. They have no need of streams of consciousness or other latter-day devices to impress their high seriousness upon the reader, or to make up for a poverty of story. Where the Unconscious is concerned, and other mysteries factitious or genuine, they are able to be perfectly and unselfconsciously conscious. Their author offers both pleasure and instruction. And of course that extra dimension in which the Anglo-Saxon arts have been deficient of late.

(1986)

More than Mere Biology

Josef Skvorecky

On its title-page Josef Skvorecky's novel, *The Engineer of Human Souls*, describes itself as 'an entertainment on the old themes of life, women, fate, dreams, the working class, secret agents, love and death'. All that in slightly under 600 pages. In the event we witness a miracle of narrowly achieved organization, helped by the gusto Skvorecky communicates and the reader's reluctance to lose his way for longer than a paragraph or two.

Like the author, the narrator is a Czech writer who emigrated in 1968 and is currently a professor of English in Toronto: at Edenvale College in his case, at Erindale College in the case of the author. His books are published by a small émigré press in Toronto, while the author's books, in their original language, are published by an émigré press run by Professor and Mrs Skvorecky. Danny Smiricky, the ficti-tious professor, specializes in American writers (plus Conrad), and the novel's scaffolding comes from the texts he is teaching. A modern story hangs by every ancient tale: in *Heart of Darkness* Kurtz prefigures Stalin, in Poe the Raven's 'Nevermore' applies to more lost things than one, and Lovecraft (H.P.), similarly of broad application, requires no gloss.

First of all, then, an entertainment, almost to excess, in humour ranging from slapstick to high wit, and in humankind from the utterly wicked to the virtually saintly. The novel also comprises a history of Czechoslovakia from the Nazi occupation through the subsequent sovietization with its various phases. And it also amounts to a Bible of exile. In each respect it accomplishes this by means not of gener-alizations but of particularities, as promised in an epigraph from Blake and confirmed towards the end by a line of Czech poetry: 'the poet's fleeting heart beats strongest in small stories.' Sir Philip Sidney's pref-erence was similar: the poet 'coupleth the general notion with the particular example'.

In his youth Danny Smiricky embarks on a hero's career by sabo-taging the Messerschmitt ammunition drums he is obliged to work on; in large part he is moved by desire for the girl Nadia, whose father has been killed by the Germans. His efforts are worse than futile, and his mates have to work overtime to restore the botched parts since they would never pass testing and because more important activities on another front would be jeopardized. In this, to Danny's astonishment, they are aided by the Oberkontrolleur, a former member of the German-American Bund who 'came home' in error. At the end of the war he is disposed of before Danny can testify on his behalf. Danny is soon cured of his taste for heroism, which can cost innocent lives, and at one stage thinks of entering a seminary in the hope of avoiding the gallows.

Other small stories crowd the generally hilarious account of the Czech community in Toronto. The exile's fate is a complex one, but Danny himself is happy enough. Although the Communist Party exists in Canada, it has no power 'as yet'; there is nothing to fear in the literary line since he writes in Czech and the professional critics leave him alone, indeed he goes unreviewed apart from occasional idle flatteries in the émigré press, 'sandwiched between harvest home announcements and ads for Bohemian tripe soup'. Moreover he is tolerant by nature, more amused than shocked by his students' ineptitudes – 'This novel is a novel. It is a great work, for it is written in the form of a book' – and likewise Canada's 'blessed ignorance'. This ignorance or innocence infuriates many of the émigrés: the feather-bedded rebels, the easy contempt for democracy (the grass is never very green on one's own side of the fence), the sight of male prostitutes skipping about in the streets: 'They deserve a dose of Bolshevism!' And how galling that Leni Riefenstahl's *Triumph of the Will* should suddenly erupt into fame and fashion as the first art film entirely made by a woman and hence of central significance to Women's Studies! Danny admits to himself that 'the real religion of life, the true idolatry of literature' cannot flourish in democracies, 'those vague boring kingdoms of the freedom not to read, not to suffer, not to desire, not to know, not to understand'. (Milan Kundera has commented, with pardonable exaggeration, that 'if all the reviews in France or England disappeared, no one would notice it, not even their editors'.) But one should take the smooth with the rough, and he notes that there is some progress – women's bottoms are now a third of the size they were in his parents' time.

Émigrés of an older generation wrangle over whether they should describe the projected National Liberation Army as *Incorporated* or *and Co.* or *Limited*: 'Of course it always makes a better impression in business circles if your company's incorporated.' One tenacious character plans to set up a radio transmitter in Ethiopia and by this means exhort the citizens of Czechoslovakia to buy ten boxes of matches each and break them to form a Churchillian V for Victory, an exercise that will both ruin the five-year plan and demoralize the Party bosses. In a version of art for art's sake, the State Security Police go on spying after all reason has long disappeared, and agents, professional or amateur, turn up in Canada with alleged messages from old friends and colleagues. One way of unmasking them is to get them drunk and enquire after certain supposedly well-known personalities who don't actually exist: they are bound to know them intimately.

Not all is sweetness and light – or drinking and love-making – in the Czech community; some of its members are sick of home, some sick for home, and some both. One of them denounces another to the Czechoslovak Association of Canada as a former Party member while someone else is rumoured to be a Fascist. Yet in these generations of immigrants, one layer set on another, Danny sees a close humanity: 'Pauperized, re-established, industrious, hungry for money, sentimental, hungry for freedom, limited, intellectual, mean, merciful. All kinds. Indestructible.' Veronika, the second-finest character in the book, wants Prague and freedom but knows she can't have both. She chooses Prague, and the last we hear of her is a cable to Danny: 'IM A FOOL STOP VERONIKA'. She would have done better – could she have brought herself – to marry the playboy admirer who has a vague idea that *Nineteen Eighty-Four* was a satire on America, probably on McCarthyism. Milan, unable to settle down in Toronto, buys a ticket home, sees a smiling 'comrade' at the embarkation gate, and turns tail – returning white-faced in time for the later stages of his own farewell party. As for Danny, he will – in Veronika's admonitory word – stop; he can return to his native Kostelec as easily in Canada, 'in the safety of a decadently anti-police democracy', as in Prague. He carries his homeland in his heart, just as it is carried within this novel.

The narrative shifts back and forth in time and place, and at one point, in the course of a few lines of print, we dart from present-day Canada to Danny's father's leg and how it was shattered at Zborov during the First World War and he died when it was amputated fifty years later, and then to 1948, when he was led off to prison by a Comrade Pytlik, exactly as the Gestapo had led him off five years earlier. The alternating of Danny's Czech past with Professor Smiricky's Canadian present has its purpose – everything is happening here and now – and the cost in extra attentiveness is not too high to be borne. We cannot expect hard living to make easy reading. That 'abominations tend to repeat themselves in variations that are embarrassingly similar' is a thought arising during an academic seminar, but its pertinence is far from academic. We hear how Nadia saved Danny and herself from having to sign a mass petition condemning the assassination of Reichsprotektor Heydrich: she fainted and he carried her off to the first-aid room. One of Danny's correspondents reports, ten

years later, that during the signing of a petition denouncing a trai-
torous gang of Titoist-Zionist-revisionists a young woman faints and
is helped to the first-aid room by a member of the Union of Youth.

Jazz, loved by both narrator and author, gives offence equally to
Nazis and Communists, as demonstrated in Skvorecky's novella, *The
Bass Saxophone*. There, a band got away with playing 'Tiger Rag' under
the Third Reich by calling it 'The Wild Bull'; here, the number appears
in the programme as 'Red Flag'. Danny's earnest friend Jan, who
strives to reconcile literature with the demands of socialism and is
eventually found hanged, mentions a picture in an exhibition of Soviet
art called 'The Defence of Sevastopol'; it shows a handful of idealized
Russian soldiers resisting a horde of villainous Germans. He
remembers that he has already seen a specimen of Nazi art in which
a scattering of noble German soldiers were dispatching a mob of
degenerate Russians; the title was 'The Conquest of Sevastopol'. *Plus
c'est la même chose* is heaped on *plus ça change*, and the last instance, at
least, may be thought both banal and inartistically neat: embarrassing,
you could say. Yet banality and inartistic neatness (and untidiness) are
part and parcel of the story. Such *exempla* contribute to the dense
texture of the novel, and it is hard to say what we would really rather
be without.

Personally I could dispense with some of the lavatory scenes and
smells – including an absurd and protracted episode in which a
smuggled manuscript is surreptitiously handed over in a Toronto
comfort station – and the tall horror-stories with which a youth regales
the Messerschmitt workers. Švejkian, all too Švejkian! And in addition
much of the what-abouting that passes between native Canadian intellectuals and Czech émigrés: what about Angela Davis? What about
the Rosenbergs? What about Sacco and Vanzetti? Once democracy
insists that people must be free to express opinions, then express
opinions they will.

Skvorecky's novel rivals *The Good Soldier Švejk*, another sprawling
canvas, in scatology but easily outdoes it in sexual zest. His slogan,
one thinks at times, could well be Sex Conquers All – or comes nearer
to doing so even than jazz. (In George Konrád's novel, *The Loser*, a
narrower Hungarian Calvary, the narrator jokes with Imre Nagy: 'You
will admit that a good fuck is worth more than ten revolutions' – while
the one may lead to an unwanted pregnancy, the other is bound to
end in rows of coffins.) But love is here as well: in the refusal to
despair, characteristic too of Milosz's poetry of Poland and its
memories of good things as well as of bad, and specifically in the figure
of Nadia, the book's finest character, truest love of the great lover

Danny, the factory girl who died young of tuberculosis.

> How she would lick her lips with her unfussy little tongue, how she
> was simple as a clarinet counterpoint in a village band and yet full
> of surprises…how she had displayed the wisdom of a beautiful
> mayfly who is crushed under foot before she can fulfil the one
> meaning her life has. But no. Nadia's life had a different meaning.
> It was more than mere biology.

'Every serious novel is *à thèse*,' the Professor tells his distrustful
students. 'But the thesis is always the same, except in novels *à thèse*.'
And the thesis is: *Homo sum; humani nil a me alienum puto.* All the same,
some things strike us as more alien than others. We may doubt that
Goethe was wholly sincere when he said, of his *Wilhelm Meister*, that a
rich manifold life brought close to our eyes ought to be sufficient
without any express tendency. Granted, it is the sort of challenge a
writer does well to toss at the feet of the thesis-hunter. And decent
writers will veer away from roles laid down for them; as, for example,
prescribed by Stalin: to build, like some engineer, the soul of the New
Man. However, one way of suggesting an implication, if not a thesis,
is to invoke another literary work whose tendency is itself not so very
express. *The Engineer of Human Souls* brings to mind an authorial intervention in *Middlemarch*: 'There is no general doctrine which is not
capable of eating out our morality if unchecked by the deep-seated
habit of direct fellow-feeling with individual fellow-men.' What better
check on general doctrine can there be than the poet's and the
novelist's 'small stories', told with verve and generosity?

(1984)

Last Words

On Anthony Burgess

By the time I had reached the last words of Anthony Burgess's *Earthly Powers* I had accumulated enough notes to make a modest book: a tribute, in part, to the sheer density of the writing, as well as the seriousness of its concerns. It would be unwise to skip during these six hundred and fifty pages. Only in retrospect can you identify for certain what could safely have been skipped as iterative or supererogatory. Since complaints will follow – grave matters incur grave complaint – let me venture at the outset that *Earthly Powers* carries greater intellectual substance, more force and grim humour, more knowledge, than ten average novels put together. It would make a film – 'Sooner or later you get all the books on the movies,' some deplorably innocent youth says: 'Just a matter of waiting' – or rather it would make a dozen films.

Kenneth Marchal Toomey, the narrator, is himself a novelist, born in 1890 and in his mid-eighties when we take leave of him. His lifetime sees momentous events – World War I, the Easter Rising, the aviators Alcock and Brown, Prohibition, Fascism, Nazism, World War II, the death camps, the history of modern literature, the history of cinema, a case of homosexual-style blasphemy (preceding the *Lady Chatterley* case, however), homosexual marriage blessed by autocephalic archbishops (not exactly from outer space, just autonomous), and much else, including in part the life of Toomey's creator. Here is, if not quite God's plenty, plenty of the Devil.

At the age of fourteen Toomey is seduced by George Russell (better known as AE) in a Dublin hotel, on the very day recorded in *Ulysses*. Meeting Joyce in Paris in 1924, Toomey tells him: 'Well, you gave George Russell an eternal and unbreakable alibi for that afternoon. But I know and he knows that he was not in the National Library.' Other celebrities among the great unfictitious dead receive similarly rough (and staggeringly high-handed) treatment; but let us leave that aside for the moment and ask – since Toomey is always with us through these many pages – why his creator has created him homosexual. It would be imprudent, perhaps even inaccurate, to suggest that this affects Toomey's 'representativeness', that it tilts the novel off centre. Beside the point, certainly, in that Toomey is chaste much of the time: for him war drives out sex. Burgess is hardly an author whom one would suspect of straining after new sensations or angles. It could be (I came close to thinking at one stage) that, heterosex being so awful, homosex has to be a little better. But no, Toomey doesn't 'glory in it': far from it, he dislikes his fellows in sex, 'hissing, camping, simpering', and the one man he truly loved – and lost through death, not through betrayal – he loved platonically. Indeed it would involve no serious distortion to say that there is only one good gay here, and lots of bad gays. Possibly homosexuality is an extra twist of the thumb-screw Burgess habitually applies to his central characters: they suffer, therefore they are. Most likely, I think, is that Toomey has to be a Catholic, and a lapsed one, and lapsed for some reason other than mere intellectual doubt or dissent from points of doctrine. God made him homosexual, and in so doing forced him to reject God.

And the Word was God. *Earthly Powers* is theological and linguistic in equal proportions, quite properly. Less properly, it is too heavily both: one can have too much of a good-and-evil thing. Burgess is, of course, an eminent wordsmith, and one of many metals. He knows that the plural of semen (it does sometimes need a plural) is 'semina'. And: '"Ice in the icebox," I said pleonastically.' (Yet the working classes might keep their coal in it.) When he gives Toomey's secretary-cum-catamite the name 'Enright', he spells it correctly, for he knows that in transliteration from one language to another it is foolish to introduce silent letters – like a 'w' for instance. (He may even know that the meaning of the name in Gaelic is 'unlawful attack'.) When – twice – Toomey meets an amiable stranger, 'a new planet swam into his, right, Ken it is, Ken'. When someone mentions that he has been sniffing round the town of Gorgonzola, we are nudged into noting the inadvertent aptness of the phrase.

During the Malayan episode, a return to the rich terrain of Burgess's early trilogy, now in a spirit of Maughamery, we are told – alas, jokes involving foreign tongues require explanation – that Mahalingam, the name of a Tamil character, means 'great ah generative organ'. In close proximity (for which state of affairs, among devout Malays, you could get into bad heterosexual trouble) is an account of that peculiar disorder known as *koro*, in which the sufferer believes that his penis is withdrawing into his abdomen and seeks to secure it with a pin or string. I have lived through one such outbreak in Singapore – Western-style doctors attributed it to an exceptionally cool spell of weather – during which the disorder spread to females, who complained of retracting nipples. Women won't be left out these days.

A candidate who lacks basic qualifications, and hence could not present himself in a white toga, is a 'nigrate'. The Maltese censors who finally allow Toomey his copy of Thomas Campion's poems confuse the poet with the martyr Edmund Campion. (A spot of autobiography there, I believe.) 'Richardtionary' is the homosexual euphemism for a useful book of reference: what, indeed, you might call an 'aide de *camp*'. (Less politely, 'shonnary': 'I always leave the dick out.') Burgess hammers in the fact that 'homo' in this connection is Greek and indicates 'same' and not, as some of his characters, imagine, Latin and signifying 'man'. And the Rilke joke – '"The last time I saw him was in a café in Trieste. He cried." "He often cried. But nobody heard him among the angelic orders"' – palls on the reprise. Far worse, much as one welcomes relief in that area, is the comical-Teutonic: 'Unfortunately have I in the *Hindenburg* not yet flown', *et* at some length *cetera*. The somewhat pop Pope, Gregory XVII, brother-in-law to Toomey, has pop songs sung about him – 'the new Gregorian chants'. Burgess never misses a trick: would he had missed a thousand. God may or may not be mocked, but words aren't to be. Play with them over-much, and they take umbrage, and revenge.

So Burgess is too clever for his own good? That is the sort of accusation made by people who really aren't all that bright themselves. And we had better remember Johnson (though he *was* bright) expressing the view that to Shakespeare a quibble was the fatal Cleopatra followed at all adventures and sure to engulf him in the mire, for which he lost the world – Shakespeare didn't lose the world. We have come near to objecting to what is most Burgessian in Burgess, what we read him *for*. Undeniably, there is a sickening, suffocating weight to this book. So, one is meant to be sickened and suffocated. At all events, it is egregiously difficult to say precisely where the author has stepped over the line, because it is hard to know where to draw the line. It has to be one's sense of artistic rightness that draws it, not squeamishness, gentility, frivolity or a semi-literate resentment of quibbles and puns. I believe that the author's obsessiveness (yes, authors ought to be obsessed) does fall foul of the dire law of diminishing returns – in respect of squalor and horrors as well as quibbles – and incurs a penalty, though I am not sure how grave the penalty is, how heavily it draws on his capital. Irritation on the reader's part, at the least, followed by lapses of attention; at the most a loss of credence. Oh for an occasional draught of Thomas Mann's coolness!

Toomey's real-life colleagues in the arts get an appallingly bad press. H.G. Wells is 'a satyromaniac', Ford Madox Ford has bad breath and a dirty mind, Norman Douglas is 'filthy' and 'boy-shagging', T.S. Eliot is wrong about the Tarot pack (as pointed out by Nabby Adams in *Time for a Tiger* long ago) and also (in which case, together with many others) about Seneca's act-division: 'there was a lot of the dilettante about Eliot', Bernard van Dieren is a 'dim thing with the grey face in napless velvet', Peter Warlock roars obscenities, Maynard Keynes ('trying to turn himself into a heterosexual with a ballet dancer') leers at Toomey, James Agate ('a well-known sodomite') makes a pass at the dreadful Heinz... In its much coarser way, this little world reminds us of the closing stages of Proust's novel, when one by one well nigh the whole cast show themselves inverts. Toomey might well condemn the fault, the condition that has deprived him of God, but it is the actors of it he detests most vigorously.

The disgust with sex is general and pervasive here. After watching a porn movie in which 'everybody was buggered by or buggered Socrates', Toomey whimpers, 'Sex, sex, sex, Christ, is there to be nothing in this world but bloody sex?' (A common cry of writers, including those who write about it.) True, as someone else has remarked, sex was the very first way of transmitting original sin. Yet it was also the way whereby the novel's few unequivocally admirable characters came into the world – notable among them, Toomey's saintly (and virtually sexless) brother Tom, a professional comedian given to comedy devoid of cruelty, that 'lost empire' (as Toomey calls it) which we all long for in our hearts, and long for the more keenly in the present circumstances.

It is saddening to see Burgess join in the wholesale reduction of old heroes to the ranks, or rank. After this, what kind of treatment can his fictitious persons expect? He has always been hard on them, the harder the more he feels for them, beginning with poor Malayan Victor Crabbe (a Crab-apple cuckolded by a Costard, stung by a crab-like scorpion, then wretchedly drowned), not excluding Shakespeare, and more recently including a whole country. His heroes are Christ-like, but like Christs to whom something lowering is bound to happen, such as falling off the Cross. When one of Toomey's boy-friends, a black, asks if he knows that big word 'humiliation', he replies: 'I practically invented it.' He could also have invented the sayings 'the good die young', 'whom the Lord loveth he chasteneth' and (above all) 'out of good still to find means of evil'.

Visiting Berlin for a film festival in the mid-1930s, sickened by Goebbels and an excess of Sekt, Toomey contrives to vomit on a swastika flag. During the première of a film about Horst Wessel, he pushes a genial short shy man out of the way of Concetta Campanati's pistol – Toomey's sister's mother-in-law, dying of cancer, is anxious to do a last good deed – and finds the man he has saved is Heinrich Himmler. Shortly before the outbreak of war he attempts to smuggle the (invented) Jewish novelist, Jakob Strehler, out of Austria. He fails in this, is caught, and buys his freedom by agreeing to broadcast to Britain. (The young official who conducts the interview apologizes for not liking his work: 'He had had Dr L.C. Knights as a tutor for a year at Cambridge and had been taught a rather rigorous approach to literature.') Back in London, Toomey points out to the court of inquiry that in his remarks he had inserted two acrostics highly offensive to the Nazi leadership – 'cunningly prepared', and all too well concealed.

But now we have to face the horrors, the other horrors. Early in the 1960s Toomey gives his nephew John Campanati, a young anthropologist interested in language structure, the money to go, together with his wife, to research in a new African state. (The money has been earned from writing 'sedative fiction' and film scripts.) By now the reader is likely to guess what will happen, more or less. John and his wife, two of the most likeable people in the book, are killed by terrorists. As if that isn't enough, it turns out later that actually they were murdered to provide the flesh and blood of the Eucharist for an 'African Mass' – *hoc est corpus meum* reconciled with hocus-pocus – a development for which the ecumenical Pope Gregory, uncle of the young anthropologist, brother-in-law of the munificent Toomey, has to be held responsible.

'Too much glamour altogether,' Toomey reflects at one point of the Campanati family. This may be a sign of nervousness on the author's part, yet it must be allowed that considerable enjoyment derives from this blown-up Italo-American version of the Forsyte Saga. Carlo Campanati, burly, gluttonous, forceful, heroic, extremely secular, extremely holy, dominates much of *Earthly Powers*. When (chronologically near its end) the novel begins, he has recently died, as Pope Gregory XVII, and is a candidate (certainly no nigrate) for canonization. Toomey has been asked to testify to Carlo's performance of a miracle, the cure of a child in the last stages of meningitis. ('It happened a long time ago,' he tells the Archbishop of Malta. 'And I don't know whether you, Your Grace, would understand this, but writers of fiction often have difficulty in deciding between what really happened and what they imagine as having happened… We lie for a living.') When, towards the close, we hear about a sinister evangelist called God (for Godfrey) Manning (God in Man), my prophetic soul began to get the shakes again. The police close in on the Children of God, Manning's community in California, and the faith healer conducts 1,700 members of his flock into eternity: in Jonestown fashion, except that by an extra turn of the screw the cyanide is administered in the Eucharist. Yes, God Manning was the child saved from meningitis. What is the theology, or the theodicy, of this sequence of events? Man is given free will by a loving God – who otherwise could scarcely *love* him – and hence man can will evil. But a miracle has nothing to do with man or his will, it is the direct intervention of God. And here an all-knowing God has intervened to procure future evil.

Concetta, Carlo's mother or adoptive mother, once remarked that according to Carlo good always won, in the long run: 'Well, that long run's just a little bit too long.' Where this novel is concerned, I think that such is indeed the case. 'What is the point of the dialectic of fiction or drama,' Toomey muses, 'unless the evil is as cogent as the good?' (He has no need to worry about that.) But we can also ask, do good and evil work in as schematic a fashion as a novelist may properly do? And are bad angels quite such sure shots at firing good ones out? At the very end, by a final tact or yielding, one small mercy is shown, shown the reader as well as Toomey and his much-loved sister Hortense. These two battered survivors will pass their remaining days together, waiting for death. For them, it seems, the end of the long run has been reached. 'I have always, all through my literary career, found endings excruciatingly hard. Thank God, or something, the last words were not for my pen…'

(1980)

Index of Names

Abdul Hamid, Sultan 86, 87
Adorno, Theodor 139, 145
Andersen, Hans Christian 47, 186
Arnold, Matthew 9n, 107, 113, 121
Auden, W.H. 8, 128, 137
Austen, Jane 166, 171

Babel, Isaac 244
Bach, Johann Sebastian 82
Balzac, Honoré de 69
Bamford, Mary E. 184
Beer-Hofmann, Richard 244
Bennett, E.K. 38, 39
Bentley, Eric 137
Berg, Alban 245
Berlau, Ruth 138
Bertram, Ernst 35, 36
Bierce, Ambrose 183
Birkett, Julian 217
Blake, William 150, 156. 157
Borges, Jorge Luis 254
Börne, Ludwig 110
Bouilhet, Louise 196, 199
Bray, Barbara 199
Braybrooke, Neville 161
Brazell, Karen 177, 178
Brecht, Bertolt 130–41
Broch, Hermann 239, 243, 245
Browning, Robert 220
Bruno, Giordano 148
Bryce, Viscount 88
Büchner, Georg 145
Burgess, Anthony 258, 264–9
Byron, George Gordon, Lord 29, 112

Canetti, Elias 6n, 7, 235–6, 239–47

Carlyle, Thomas 12n, 113
Carmi, T. 246
Cavafy, C. P. 125–9, 132
Celan, Paul 142–7
Chaplin, Charlie 84, 257
Chaucer, Geoffrey 229
Chesterton, G.K. 69
Coleridge, Samuel Taylor 40, 216
Colet, Louise 196, 197–9
Colleville, Maurice 45–6
Cook, Frederick A. 228
Cordier, Henri 180
Croce, Benedetto 25

Dalven, Rae 125
Davie, Donald 151, 152
Davies, Robertson 254–8
de la Mare, Walter 161
Dickens, Charles 39, 229
Dickinson, Emily 144
Dietrich, Marlene 32
Doyle, C.W. 183
Draper, Hal 111n, 112, 114–19, 121
Dryden, John 209
Du Camp, Maxime 196
Dunlop, Geoffrey 86n
Dürer, Albrecht 46

Eaton, Edith 183
Eckermann, Johann Peter 5, 12
Egerton, Clement 179
Ehrenberg, Paul 35
Eliot, George 9, 113, 119, 120, 121, 175
Eliot, T.S. 19, 157
Elliott, Alistair 111n, 119

Ellmann, Richard 105
Emerson, Ralph Waldo 69
Engels, Friedrich 107, 110, 118
Enzensberger, Hans Magnus 5n, 7n, 9n, 10, 71, 72
Esslin, Martin 139n, 140
Eyster, Nellie Blessing 183

Felstiner, John 142–5, 146
Field, Frank 230
Fielding, Henry 16, 20
Fischer, Samuel 35
Flaubert, Gustave 193–204
Frisé, Adolf 67
Freud, Sigmund 38

George, Stefan 36
Gladstone, William Ewart 87
Goethe, Johann Wolfgang von 3–10, 11–26, 27–30, 38, 40, 112, 116, 143, 144, 216, 223, 231, 236, 256, 263
Grass, Günter 6, 7, 110, 231, 248–53
Grimm, Jacob and Wilhelm 249, 251
Gropius, Walter 244
Grosz, George 137

Hamburger, Michael 9, 65, 130
Hamilton, Nigel 30, 33
Hanem, Kuchuk 196
Hanson, James 183
Hardy, Thomas 161, 209
Harte, Bret 183
Hays, H.R. 130, 137
Heald, David 57
Hegel, George Wilhelm Friedrich 5n
Heine, Heinrich 105–124
Heller, Erich 5, 31, 33, 53, 230, 235
Herbert, George 155
Herbert, Juliet 193–5, 196
Hesse, Hermann 71–8
Heym, Stefan 221–6

Hitler, Adolf 32
Hofmannsthal, Hugo von 9
Hölderlin, Friedrich 8, 72, 144
Hook, Sidney 139
Housman, A. E. 144
Husserl, Edmund 69
Huxley, Aldous 39

Isherwood, Christopher 137
Izumi Shikibu 176

James I, King 165
James, Henry 258
James, William 217
Jannings, Emil 32
Jené, Edgar 145
Johnson, Samuel 28, 70, 266
Johnson, Uwe 8
Jonson, Ben 217
Joyce, James 85, 244

Kafka, Franz 7
Kaiser, Ernst 63
Karloff, Boris 214
Keats, John 110, 191, 192
Keeley, Edmund 125n
Keene, Donald 169n
Kilmartin, Terence 171
Kingsley, Charles 113–4
Kingston, Maxine Hong 185, 186–92
Kirst, Hans Hellmut 8
Koch, Stephen 75
Konrád, George 262
Kraus, Karl 227–38, 239, 241, 242
Kundera, Milan 260

Lanchester, Elsa 140
Lang, Fritz 136
Laughton, Charles 138
Lawrence, D.H. vii, 24n, 70
Lear, Edward 161
Leatherdale, Clive 214, 215
Leavis, F.R. 229
Leavis, Q. D. 208n
Lee, Christopher 214, 215n

Le Fanu, Sheridan 215, 216
Lévy, Michel 202
Lewes, G.H. 4, 20
London, Jack 182
Lorre, Peter 138
Lowell, Robert 105
Ludwig, Emil 244
Lugosi, Bela 214
Luke, David 30, 207n
Luther, Martin 223
Lyon, James K. 134–41

McGonagall, William 154
MacIntyre, C.F. 8
McLuhan, Marshall 237
MacNeice, Louis 8
Maeterlinck, Maurice 69
Mahler, Alma 244
Mahler, Gustave 244
Mandelstam, Osip 144
Mann, Carla 35
Mann, Erika 30
Mann, Heinrich 30–3, 34
Mann, J. S. 31
Mann, Julia 31
Mann, Katia 30, 35, 130–1, 139, 140
Mann, Thomas 4, 5, 6, 7, 8, 10, 24, 27, 28, 30–6, 37–54, 71, 72, 73, 76, 91, 135, 139–40, 213, 240, 242, 246, 258, 266
Marlowe, Christopher 210, 223
Martens, Kurt 35
Marvell, Andrew 144
Marx, Karl 110, 112
Maupassant, Guy de 193
May, Derwent 156
Mayer, Elizabeth 9
Metternich, Klemens, Fürst von 110
Michaux, Henri 144
Middleton, Christopher 9, 130
Milosz, Czeslaw 148–52, 240, 262
Milton, John 181, 185, 211, 213, 221
Mirsky, Mark 68, 69, 70

Moncrieff, C.K. Scott 171
Morris, Ivan 165, 171n, 172–3, 174
Mott, Mary T. 182
Mozart, Wolfgang Amadeus 73, 246
Murasaki Shikibu 165–71, 172, 176
Murnau, F. W. 214
Musil, Robert 55–70, 240, 245, 246

Nadherny, Sidonie 232, 233
Nash, Ogden 161
Nestroy, Johann 231
Nietzsche, Friedrich 18, 35, 36, 38, 46, 48, 50, 69

Offenbach, Jacques 231
Oliver, Hermia 193–5
Owen, Wilfred 213

Parry, Idris 227
Pascal, Blaise 146
Pascal, Roy 10
Payne, Philip 67
Paz, Octavio 218
Picasso, Pablo 142
Polanksi, Roman 214
Polidori, John 214
Pope, Alexander 174
Prawer, S.S. 110
Prest, Thomas Peckett 219
Pringsheim, Katia 31, 35
Pritchett, V.S. 210
Proust, Marcel 56, 171, 267

Racine, Jean 153, 154
Rainer, Luise 136–7
Reed, T.J. 120n
Richardson, Samuel 20
Riefenstahl, Leni 260
Rilke, Rainer Maria 5, 8, 45, 135
Robinson, Ritchie 121
Roseveare, Edith 134
Russell, Jeffrey Burton 207, 208, 219
Rymer, James Malcolm 219

Sainte-Beuve, Charles Augustin 200
Salten, Felix 233
Sammons, Jeffrey L. 106–111
Sand, George 199–204
Sartre, Jean-Paul 44
Scherchen, Hermann 245, 246
Scherer, Edmond 9n
Scherer, Wilhelm 16, 22
Schlegel, A.W. 208
Schnitzler, Arthur 230
Schönberg, Arnold 45
Schopenhauer, Arthur 38
Schubert, Franz 71, 72
Schumann, Robert 46
Seidensticker, Edward G. 165, 169–71
Shakespeare, William 28, 124, 266, 267
Shelley, Mary 212, 213, 214, 216, 217
Shelley, Percy Bysshe vii, 212
Shepherd, Charles R. 183
Sherrard, Philip 125n
Shōnagon, Sei 165, 171–4, 175, 176
Sidney, Philip 259
Singer, Isaac Bashevis 254
Skvorecky, Josef 259–63
Smith, Mary 35
Smith, Stevie 153–62
Smollett, Tobias 16
Sommer, Piotr 149
Spence, Jonathan D. 188
Staël, Madame de 122
Stalin, Joseph 139, 140, 263
Steegmuller, Francis 195, 199
Steiner, George 220, 232
Stern, J.P. 65, 66, 67, 230
Sterne, Laurence 123
Stocker, Margarita 209
Stoker, Bram 214, 215, 218, 219
Svevo, Italo 69, 79–85
Suyin, Han 185
Swift, Jonathan 233

Swinnerton, Frank 83
Szasz, Thomas 230

Talaat Bey 94
Tchaikovsky, Peter Ilych 45
Theocritus 126
Timms, Edward 229–31, 235
Tiridates, King of Armenia 86
Tolstoy, Leo 39, 69
Toynbee, Arnold 87, 88, 91n
Tsiang, H.T. 183
Turgenev, Ivan 204

Ungaretti, Giuseppe 144

Valéry, Paul 144
Viertel, Hans 140

Wagner, Richard 32, 38, 210
Waidson, H. M. 7, 9
Waldrop, Rosmarie 145
Waley, Arthur 169–71, 173
Wasserman, Jakob 35, 244
Weigel, Helene 138–9
Werfel, Franz 8, 86–101, 244
Whitney, Atwell 181
Willett, John 130
Wilkins, Eithne 63
Wilkins, Sophie 63
Wilson, A.N. 218
Winston, Clara 33, 35
Winston, Richard 34
Woltor, Robert 181
Wordsworth, William 185
Wotruba, Fritz 245
Wu, William F. 181–5

Yitzhak, Abraham ben 246

Zaloscer, Hilde 46, 48n
Ziolkowski, Theodore 72–3, 74–5, 77, 78
Zohn, Harry 227, 228, 229, 230, 237
Zola, Emile 30, 31